More Worship Sketches

Sketches

2 Perform

Steven James

MERIWETHER PUBLISHING LTD.
Colorado Springs, Colorado

Meriwether Publishing Ltd., Publisher
PO Box 7710
Colorado Springs, CO 80933-7710

Editor: Rhonda Wray
Cover design: Janice Melvin

Library of Congress Cataloging-in-Publication Data

James Steven, 1969-
   More worship sketches 2 perform : scripts for two actors / by Steven James.
        p. cm.
Includes indexes.
   ISBN 1-56608-083-5
1. Drama in public worship. 2. Christian drama, American. I. Title:
More worship sketches two perform. II. Title: More worship sketches to perform. III. Title.
   BV289 .J34 2002
   246'.72–dc21
                                        2002153011

This book is dedicated to G.T.M.,
a man who has learned to wait. And trust.

Contents

Thanks and Acknowledgments

When I was working on "A Tale of Two Friends" for our Easter service, two of my friends from my church's drama ministry — Joel Van Eaton and Dr. Dan Earl — wrote drafts of their own that helped shape and develop the final form of this drama. My thanks goes out to them for their invaluable suggestions. It was a team effort.

In addition to Joel and Dan, special thanks also go out to the other members of our drama team: Dr. Eva Pickler, Jason Sharp, Dr. Ben Buckner, Dr. Alan McCartt, Sunday Feathers, and Stacy Marsh, for their ideas, insights, suggestions, friendship, and willingness to read through these sketches and give them life and poignancy.

Thanks to Richard Major and the members of his "Fundamentals of Directing Class" at Milligan College (Suzy Bomgardner, Hannah Carson, Chesa Gonzales, Anna Lee Johnson, Warren McCrickard, Christan McKay, Adam K. Meyers, and Jenny Trivett) for their time, thoughtful suggestions, and ideas.

Thanks to my wife (Liesl) and daughters (Trinity, an 8-year-old with a knack for writing dialog; Ariel, a 6-year-old who loves to listen to me read; and Eden, a 2-year-old who loves everything) for working through my ideas with me and offering suggestions; to Meredith Craig, for helping my dialog sound more like a girl; and to Aaron Wymer, for helping my dialog sound more like a guy.

Introduction

Drama is struggle. It's the tension that's created when things don't go as planned, or when the good guy doesn't win, or when life as you know it suddenly unravels before your eyes ...

"Hm. That fruit really does look pretty good ... Maybe I'll have a little bite after all."

"What? They want us to throw our babies in the Nile River? No! How could God let this happen?"

"Don't call me Naomi. Call me 'Mara' because God has made my life bitter" (Ruth 1:20, author's paraphrase).

"My God, my God, why have you forsaken me?" (Matthew 27:46).

Drama means questioning the way things are, exploring possibilities, and searching for answers that lie beneath the surface. Therefore, drama doesn't just reach the head, it also touches the heart. To scratch someone in the deep places of their soul is to touch them with the drama of the human story. The goal of using drama in ministry is to speak truth in a way that moves people to the place (spiritually, intellectually, emotionally, and imaginatively) where they can encounter God.

And so, as you use drama at your church, school, or conference center, remember that drama is not the same as preaching, and that exposing issues is not the same as explaining doctrine. Drama reaches into our souls and doesn't just hover around the safe places of our intellect where we can name and explain and rationalize our reactions. Drama unites the teachings of the church with the grittiness of everyday life in a world where pain and sadness and loss and suffering and wonder and glory and joy all swirl around us and in us and through us to shape and inform our lives.

And that's why our God is a dramatic God. That's why our God is a storytelling God. That's why he isn't satisfied with people comfortably sitting back and analyzing, categorizing, or theorizing about him. His Word engages us, body, mind, spirit, and heart. Because God isn't out to win an argument with humanity, he's out to win humanity. He isn't on a quest to win a debate with doubters, he's on a quest to win the hearts of seekers. All throughout Scripture he uses dramatic situations to communicate his love and to wake up those who fell fast asleep in a spiritual coma. To stir them (and us) to new life.

Using This Book

While similar to the first volume of *Worship Sketches 2 Perform*, this volume also includes:

- More interpretative sketches that may be used as Readers Theatre pieces. This allows actors to dramatically read the scripts on-stage and will make performances even easier to produce.
- A clearer organization of the dramas into age-specific categories to make it even easier for you to find the scripts that will work with your audience or congregation.
- Notes on technical needs, such as the number and type of microphones needed and suggestions for stage lighting.
- Minute markings to give you an idea of the flow and timing of the sketch. While not meant to be set in stone, these markers will serve as signposts to help you with the flow and pace of directing the sketches.

Finding the right drama for your group or event is a process of elimination. Start with what you know and work from there. Perhaps you know the topic or theme verse from your pastor's upcoming sermon. If so, start at the back of the book and look in the "Verse Index" or "Theme Index" to find dramas that will fit.

Or you may have two women who are available for a certain performance, and no men. If so, refer to the "Cast Index" in the back of the book. There you'll find a list of all the dramas in this book that are for men, women, either men or women, or for one man and one woman.

In the "Table of Contents," you'll see there are six sections to the book. Perhaps you know your drama will occur between two songs in your worship service, and you want something reflective and worshipful. Check out "Part 4 — Dramatic and Interpretive Readings." Or maybe it will be for elementary-aged children. If so, look in "Part 6 — Scripts for Children's Services or Puppet Plays." I've done everything I can think of to make it as easy as possible for you to quickly find the right drama for your group.

4

The dramas in this book tend to fall into six categories. After each category, you'll find a note telling where in the book that type of drama appears.

1. Dialogs — As two people discuss an issue, the tension grows from each one's unique situation or perspective. Dialogs are easier to learn than other types of creative dramatic presentations because they mirror natural conversation. Dialogs are the most common type of scripts found in this book. Most of the dramas in Parts 1, 2, and 5 include dialogs.

2. Tandem Monologs — Two actors alternate telling their stories. As the stories progress, the audience begins to realize the parallels between the stories or the true identities of the actors. Timing is important in this type of drama. Well-done tandem monologs have a powerful and lasting impact. Examples of these appear in Part 3 and Part 5 (see "Who Is My Neighbor?").

3. Monolog with a Scripture Reading — By alternating a monolog with a section of Scripture, the audience realizes the application or relevance of the verses to life in today's society. This technique is similar to tandem monologs, except that one person's part is a Scripture reading. "The Lord and the Lamb" and "Persevering" are examples of this technique.

4. Tandem Storytelling — Tandem storytelling simply means that two people tell the same story by alternating speaking parts. They may either narrate the entire story or take turns exchanging sections of dialog with each other. Since this is a popular technique with children, I've included several of these in the last section of the book. See Part 6.

5. Interpretive Readings — These thought-provoking pieces are intended to give people a new perspective by providing image-rich, reflective presentations of Scripture and doctrine. See Part 4.

6. Readers Theatre — In Readers Theatre, the actors dramatically read their scripts, alternating parts. Though they may hold a black folder containing the script, they maintain good eye contact with the audience. This is a non-threatening presentation technique because the actors don't need to memorize their parts. Some of the sketches in Parts 3, 4, and 6 could be used as Readers Theatre pieces.

Director's Tips

Here are four guiding principles to keep in mind as you direct the dramas in this book.

Principle #1 — Pour emotion into action.

Avoid the trap of letting your sketch dissolve into two "talking heads." Directors use the term "blocking" to refer to the movement and positioning of the actors during a drama. Very often movement and stage directions are difficult to translate into print, and because of this, many script collections don't include extensive stage directions or blocking ideas. As a result, some churches end up performing dramas that all look the same — like two people sitting in a restaurant having a conversation.

As you prepare your dramas, help your actors (1) move in ways that communicate what they're thinking or feeling, (2) interact with props that naturally appear in the scene, (3) walk to different places on-stage to deliver their lines for more impact, and (4) use posture and gestures to communicate emotions that the words of the scripts leave unspoken.

Don't act out a script word-for-word, but respond naturally to the words, emotions, and situations, just like you would in real life.

Principle #2 — Be prepared to find what you're not looking for.

Very often, the most poignant moments in a drama begin to appear only after the actors have learned their lines and have started rehearsing with movement, props, and the other elements of staging. Observe your actors and look for those moments that emerge during their dynamic relationship on-stage. As they do, let the script become the soil from which the drama grows. Let it bloom and blossom. Don't be afraid to let the drama become something a little different from what you originally had in mind.

A story naturally progresses through a struggle or problem, to a discovery, to a transformation in the life of the main character. Very often in the dramas in this book, the final transformation of the character is only hinted at. In other words, the drama tells the first part of the story, and then the message (or sermon) that follows the drama points the way to dramatic resolution.

Obviously, the language included in each drama is what I would suggest. It has been crafted and honed through numerous live performances or staged readings. Your actors and audiences might relate better to slightly different wording or phrases, however. The progression of images and scenes is more important than the precise arrangement of words. As your actors embody the scripts and the stories, let the language and phrasing develop with your specific audience in mind. Feel free to make minor adaptations to the wording of the sketches in this book as long as it does not alter the intended meaning of the piece.

Principle #3 — Pretend less, believe more.

For an audience to "see" the story, so must the actors. Even if the actor knows the story never happened in "real life," he must believe it's happening right now on-stage, and in the imagination of each of the listeners.

Watch the story happen around you. Try to see the story, not the words. Encourage your actors to respond to what happens on stage, accept it, and use it. It might be a cue, an unexpected response from the audience, or a forgotten line. Whatever it is, respond and press on, rather than trying to backtrack or cover up. Teach them to "listen with their eyes" and then respond with their bodies.

Everyone who comes on-stage in a drama must want something. Actors call this their "motivation." Why are they there? To whom are they speaking? What are they trying to achieve or accomplish? What goals or desires do they have? Often you'll find clues to each character's motivation in the cast description and director's notes included with each script. Look also at the dialog to learn what motivates each character, then encourage your actors to feel the tension that comes from their motivation.

Dramatic tension grows from desire. The more someone wants something, the more frustrated they'll become when they can't get it — and the harder they'll work to reach their objective. Look for this escalating tension in the dramas in this book.

As you practice, always try to be attentive. Instead of asking, "What should I be saying?" ask, "What is happening?" Focus on the events and images of the story rather than on remembering the "right" words. Don't remember and recite; instead, re-vision and re-experience the piece.

Principle #4 — Respond to the audience.

Audiences differ. The 8:00 a.m. Sunday crowd will laugh at different things than the 11:00 a.m. crowd. And they'll both respond differently than the group you have on Sunday evening or during the middle of the week.

We respond differently to each situation because the social setting varies and the goals and expectations differ. Every time you perform a drama, the audience is different, and their expectations are also unique. With this in mind, anticipate how your audience might respond to the different dramatic moments in your piece. Then prepare your drama with your specific audience in mind.

Really strive to connect with the people in your audience. Don't make them uncomfortable but, when appropriate, let the dramatic tension make them uneasy.

Part 1
Contemporary Dramas for Worship Services

Use the lighthearted dramas in this section for worship services, marriage conferences, outreach events, or Bible classes. They present contemporary characters facing contemporary problems and issues. While they're appropriate for audiences of all ages, adults will most readily identify with the issues brought up in these dramas.

Most of these scripts were written to precede the sermon and to help set the tone for the service by addressing the question or topic of the message.

You may also wish to use these sketches after, or in the middle of, a sermon. Work with your pastor or speaker to create a smooth transition from the drama to the message.

Seedlings

Summary: Nikki wants Carol to help her teach a Sunday school class, but Carol is hesitant to become involved.

Purpose: To encourage people to consider serving in children's ministry.

Time: 4–5 minutes

Tone: Humorous and heartwarming

Cast: Nikki — A woman looking for help in her Sunday school class (female)
Carol — Her friend who isn't so sure she wants to sign up (female)

Costumes: Casual and contemporary clothes. Carol is dressed for gardening or replanting her houseplants.

Props/Set: Potting soil, plants, packets of seeds, pots, gardening gloves, a small table

Themes: Children, choices, church issues, excuses, ministry, service

Text: "See that you do not look down on one of these little ones. For I tell you that their angels in heaven always see the face of my Father in heaven" (Matthew 18:10).

Notes: Keep the conversation between the two women lively and warm. Remember, they are good friends. There should also be a tenderness and vulnerability in Nikki's character that helps the audience identify with her. Carol continues working with her plants throughout the sketch. Use general stage lighting and two lapel microphones.

1   *SETTING*: Carol's porch, where she is transplanting some plants.
2   Potting soil and plants lay scattered across the table in front of
3   them. Both women are On-stage as the lights come up and the
4   scene begins.
5
6   **CAROL: Hey, Nikki, hand me that packet of seeds over there.**
7   **NIKKI: Here you go, Carol.**
8   **CAROL: Thanks.**
9   **NIKKI:** *(Looking around)* **Wow, I don't know how you do it. It**
10   **always looks like a greenhouse on your porch.**
11   **CAROL: Thanks.**
12   **NIKKI: Give me a houseplant and no matter how much I water it,**
13   **fertilize it, or sing it lullabies, it'll be dead within a month ...**
14   **I should hire myself out as a contract killer for geraniums.**
15   **CAROL: Oh, c'mon. It can't be that bad.**
16   **NIKKI: Oh, yeah? Last year, my sister gave me a cactus. I named**
17   **him Prickles.**
18   **CAROL: That's a nice name for a cactus.**
19   **NIKKI: Yeah. She said he was un-killable.**
20   **CAROL: Cacti are.**
21   **NIKKI: Well ... I killed him.**
22   **CAROL: You killed a cactus? How?!**
23   **NIKKI: Well, first I think I gave him too much to drink. Then I left**
24   **him on the porch and the water froze in his pot, so I tried to**
25   **revive him by putting him in the microwave ...** *(1 minute mark)*
26   **CAROL: You're not serious?**
27   **NIKKI: Yeah. Don't defrost a cactus any longer than four minutes.**
28   **It ain't pretty.**
29   **CAROL: Ooh.**
30   **NIKKI: Yeah ... First I drowned him. Then I froze him. Then I**
31   **burnt him to a crisp. I'm not exactly Martha Stewart.**
32   **CAROL: Well, the secret to taking care of plants is to start caring**
33   **for 'em while they're still small. When they're seedlings.**
34   **That's their most important time of growth.**
35   **NIKKI: Hmmm.**

1 CAROL: I need some more of that potting soil over there.
2 NIKKI: *(Handing it to her)* So anyway, like I was saying, before you
3   got me going about how I murdered Prickles, do you think
4   you might be interested? I really need someone else in the
5   classroom to help me out.
6 CAROL: *(Hesitantly)* I don't know. I don't think I'm really the
7   teacher type.
8 NIKKI: C'mon! You're great with kids!
9 CAROL: I do OK with my own kids, but watching a whole
10   classroom of other people's offspring sounds pretty scary to
11   me. And besides, you can handle that Sunday school class by
12   yourself — *(2 minute mark)*
13 NIKKI: It's always easier when you have someone there to give
14   you a hand.
15 CAROL: Maybe I just need to think about it.
16 NIKKI: *(After a pause)* So what's wrong with that plant, anyhow?
17 CAROL: Oh, I need to transplant it. Someone at the greenhouse
18   didn't take good care of it when it was small. It hasn't been
19   developing right. Timing is everything with plants. And
20   commitment. You gotta be there for 'em when they need you.
21 NIKKI: *(Thoughtfully)* And then just trust God to do the rest?
22 CAROL: Yeah.
23 NIKKI: *(Sighing)* I think it'd be a lot of fun working with you in the
24   classroom.
25 CAROL: I don't know. I've heard the horror stories. Kids running
26   wild, bouncing off the walls. Dirty diapers. Runny noses.
27   Craft projects to plan! I've seen those craft projects, Nikki.
28   They must buy glue in fifty-five-gallon drums —
29 NIKKI: C'mon, Carol. Don't you think you're getting a little
30   carried away?
31 CAROL: Nope. And once you're in, you're in. You sign up and the
32   next thing you know you're eighty-eight years old and you've
33   been teaching Sunday school for the last fifty-three years of
34   your life ... *(Ominously)* in the same room ... *(3 minute mark)*
35 NIKKI: Now you're being ridiculous. It's not like that, and you

1   know it. And there are lots of rewards.

2   CAROL: Oh, yeah? Like what?

3   NIKKI: Like … listening to the kids sing. They don't care if they're

4   off-key. All they care about is praising God from their fingers

5   to their toes … And hearing their laughter and seeing how big

6   their eyes get when you tell 'em about Jesus. And praying with

7   'em. Nobody prays like kids, Carol. Nobody.

8   CAROL: *(Thoughtfully)* Yeah … I know.

9   NIKKI: Holding hands. Wiping away their tears. Watching 'em

10   grow. Sometimes they burst into bloom right there in front of

11   you. And you get to be there when God first touches their lives.

12   To watch it. It's life-changing … But it's like you said, they

13   need someone to take care of 'em. Timing is everything. And

14   commitment …

15   CAROL: *(Remembering)* You gotta be there for 'em when they need

16   you.

17   NIKKI: And then just trust God —

18   CAROL: — to do the rest. *(4 minute mark)*

19   NIKKI: *(After a slight pause)* I'll tell you what — visit my class. See

20   what it's like. I'll show you the ropes. And maybe you can give

21   me a few pointers on raising plants along the way.

22   CAROL: I don't know. After what you did to that cactus —

23   NIKKI: I promise not to microwave any more houseplants. OK?

24   CAROL: OK … I'll see you Sunday.

25   NIKKI: In class?

26   CAROL: Yeah.

27   NIKKI: *(Gathering up the plants)* Great. Here, I'll help you carry

28   these back to the window. It's a big job.

29   CAROL: Thanks … It's always easier when you have someone

30   there to give you a hand. *(They exit. Fadeout.)*

31

32

33

34

35

May I Take Your Order, Please?

Summary: Carson just wants to order his food, but Tiffany is making everything harder than it should be.

Purpose: To show that the first step in witnessing is to really listen to the people to whom we're speaking.

Time: 3–4 minutes

Tone: Humorous

Cast: Carson — A guy who just wants to order his food (male) Tiffany — The lady working behind the counter who is trying to get him to buy more than he wants (female; with slight editorial changes, Tiffany's part could be played by a male actor)

Costumes: Tiffany is dressed in a typical fast food restaurant outfit. Carson is wearing casual clothes or business attire.

Props/Set: A countertop, a cookie, a piece of paper (that represents a survey form), a pen, a cash register or computer, a cowbell (optional), a microphone, plastic cows (to decorate the countertop), a wallet

Themes: Anger, assumptions, authenticity, church issues, communication, compassion, evangelism, frustrations, listening, modern life, witnessing

Text: "He who answers before listening — that is his folly and his shame" (Proverbs 18:13).

Notes: Carson is in a hurry and just wants to get his food. Tiffany is more concerned with getting through her lines than she is in really meeting Carson's needs.

The application of this sketch may not be evident to everyone at first. When people witness to others, they often just blurt their "lines" without really listening to the needs of the other person. Be sure that your pastor or speaker addresses the importance of meeting needs and listening when witnessing. (You may wish to remind him or her to mention how important it is to "listen to and love one an-udder!")

Have fun with the characters in this sketch. Let Tiffany be a little bit of an airhead, while Carson is more sophisticated. Carson's character is a likeable, typical guy. Use general stage lighting and two lapel microphones.

1   *SETTING*: Tiffany is working behind the counter at Burger World
2   when Carson walks in and places his order. The lights come up
3   and the scene opens just before Carson walks On-stage.
4
5   TIFFANY: *(CARSON enters and TIFFANY recites her lines, as if*
6   *reading from an imaginary script.)* **Hello, and welcome to**
7   **Burger World, land of the famous CowBurger.** *(After saying*
8   *the word "CowBurger," she either hits a cowbell dangling next to*
9   *the counter or, if none is available, she says, "Moo!" This same*
10   *routine is repeated throughout the drama.)* **May I take your**
11   **order, please?**
12 CARSON: **Yeah, I'd like a medium cheeseburger and a small fries.**
13   **To go.**
14 TIFFANY: **Will that be for here or to go?**
15 CARSON: **Uh, to go. And that's it. That's all I want.**
16 TIFFANY: **Will that be all, sir?**
17 CARSON: **Yes, that will be all.**
18 TIFFANY: **Would you like a drink with that?**
19 CARSON: **If I wanted a drink I wouldn't have said "That will be**
20   **all!"**
21 TIFFANY: **Perhaps you would like to try our famous CowBurger**
22   **today. It's on special this week for a limited time only. And it**
23   **comes with a glass of milk served with a decorative ceramic**
24   **udder.**
25 CARSON: **I don't want a CowBurger or a glass of milk, OK?**
26 TIFFANY: **OK, sir. Will that be all?**
27 CARSON: **That's all! That's it! Just the cheeseburger and fries!**
28 TIFFANY: **Would you like to mongo-size that for only a dollar**
29   **forty-nine extra?**
30 CARSON: **No.** *(1 minute mark)*
31 TIFFANY: **But then you'd get a free drink and end up saving**
32   **thirty-one cents.**
33 CARSON: **How could I get a** *free* **drink and** *save* **thirty-one cents**
34   **by** *spending* **a dollar forty-nine extra!?**
35 TIFFANY: *(She leans over and whispers.)* **They've got this all**

17

1   figured out. It's always a better deal if you buy a whole meal.

2   You could just walk over there and throw out your drink if

3   you decide you don't want it. Don't tell anyone I said that ...

4   And you'd still save money!

5   CARSON: I don't want to go and throw anything away! I don't

6   want to save money, I want to spend my money on a medium

7   cheeseburger and a small fries. That's it. That's all. That's

8   everything! That's all I want!

9   TIFFANY: *(Under her breath)* All right, it's your money. You can

10   throw it away if you want to ... *(To him)* So is that it?

11   CARSON: Yes, that's it.

12   TIFFANY: That'll be five dollars and fifty-five cents. *(She hands*

13   *him a sheet of paper, a pen, and a cookie as he reaches for his*

14   *wallet.)*

15   CARSON: What's this?

16   TIFFANY: We're giving away a free cookie to everyone who makes

17   a five dollar or greater purchase today. *(He hands her some*

18   *money, takes the cookie, nods, and takes a bite out of it.)* It's our

19   way of saying thanks for filling out our customer appreciation

20   survey. *(2 minute mark)*

21   CARSON: *(Talking with his mouth full of cookie)* Your what?

22   TIFFANY: *(Pointing to the sheet of paper)* Customer appreciation

23   survey. It'll only take you a few hours.

24   CARSON: *(Taking another bite of cookie)* I don't want to fill out a

25   survey.

26   TIFFANY: You have to. You already bit into your cookie. *(CARSON*

27   *spits out the rest of the cookie.)* It's OK. Once you've completed

28   the survey, your name will be added to our mailing list and

29   we'll send you promotional flyers for the next fifty-two years,

30   *and* you'll automatically be entered in a drawing to win a free

31   farm in Wisconsin, complete with fifty-two genuine dairy

32   cows!

33   CARSON: What would I want with a farm in Wisconsin and a

34   bunch of cows?

35   TIFFANY: *(Ignoring him)* You'll also be eligible for hundreds of

1   other prizes, including a free CowBurger *(Rings the bell or*

2   *shouts "Moo!")* and a glass of milk with a decorative ceramic

3   udder. Void where prohibited.

4   CARSON: Is it prohibited here?

5   TIFFANY: *(Looking at the survey)* Let's see ... Why, yes ... yes it is.

6   CARSON: It's prohibited here?

7   TIFFANY: Yes.

8   CARSON: The offer is void?

9   TIFFANY: Yes.

10   CARSON: Then why did you offer it to me?! *(3 minute mark)*

11   TIFFANY: I'm supposed to. It's part of my job. I have to say this

12   stuff to every one of our customers.

13   CARSON: Well, I wish part of your job was to listen to what I

14   really want and give it to me rather than just reciting things

15   off some script! You can keep your survey and your cookie

16   and your milk and your CowBurger — *(He reaches across the*

17   *counter and dings the cowbell, or she interrupts and says*

18   *"Moo!")* And your decorative udder! I'm leaving! *(He exits.)*

19   TIFFANY: Good-bye! Thank you for coming! *(Into a microphone)*

20   Cancel that cheeseburger and fries. *(To audience)* Hello, and

21   welcome to Burger World, land of the famous CowBurger.

22   *(Dings the cowbell or says, "Moo!")* May I take your order,

23   please? *(She freezes. Fadeout.)*

24

25

26

27

28

29

30

31

32

33

34

35

Unwrapping Your Gifts

Summary: Jolene and Sasha are discovering the role of giftedness in service. But are they really interested in discovering their true gifts?

Purpose: To highlight the importance of matching people's gifts up with their areas of service within the church.

Time: 4–5 minutes

Tone: Humorous and thought-provoking

Cast: Jolene — A woman who isn't happy when she discovers her spiritual gift (female)
Sasha — Her friend who doesn't want to know what her gift is (female)

Costumes: Casual, contemporary clothes

Props/Set: A table, two chairs, a few pens and papers, a calculator

Themes: Calling, church issues, evangelism, giftedness, ministry, missions, purpose, service, stewardship

Text: "Each one should use whatever gift he has received to serve others, faithfully administering God's grace in its various forms" (1 Peter 4:10).

Notes: This drama would work well at a pastor's conference or a training event for small group facilitators or other church leaders. It shows the importance of matching believers up with their unique gifts and interests. Some jobs may not seem as glamorous as others, but all callings are equally important in the kingdom of God. Use general stage lighting and two lapel microphones.

1   *SETTING*: The local coffee shop. Jolene is busily filling out her
2   spiritual gifts survey when the lights come up. Then Sasha enters
3   and the scene begins.
4
5   **SASHA: Hey, Jolene!**
6   **JOLENE:** *(Looking up for a moment)* **Oh, hey, Sasha!**
7   **SASHA: What are you doing?**
8   **JOLENE: Oh, I'm just finishing up this spiritual gifts survey they**
9   **gave us at church. I'm so excited!**
10 **SASHA: Why? What's it about?**
11 **JOLENE: Well, you fill in all these little boxes and then compare it**
12   **with the answer key, and it tells you what you're really good**
13   **at — you know ... so you can serve in different areas of**
14   **ministry, like evangelism or preaching or teaching or leading.**
15   **Things like that.**
16 **SASHA: So it's like a test?**
17 **JOLENE: Kind of.** *(Filling in the last blank)* **Um ... There!**
18 **SASHA: Done?**
19 **JOLENE: Yeah.**
20 **SASHA: So how did you do?**
21 **JOLENE: I don't know. Let's see ...** *(As she totals them up, she gets*
22   *excited.)* **What if I'm gifted to be a missionary to Africa or to**
23   **translate the Bible into some exotic language?! Maybe I'm**
24   **supposed to go to India and serve the poor, like Mother**
25   **Teresa! You just never know!** *(1 minute mark)*
26 **SASHA: Well, what does it say?**
27 **JOLENE: Um ... Let's see ...** *(Using the calculator)* **Let me just**
28   **total this up and check the reference sheet ... And! ...** *(Her*
29   *excitement suddenly abates.)* **Oh ... hmmm ... Huh ...**
30 **SASHA: Well? How did you do?**
31 **JOLENE: Um ... Hey, you know what? I just remembered I need**
32   **to stop by the pet store and pick up some bedding for Suzy's**
33   **hamster. I'd better get going.**
34 **SASHA: What are you talking about? How did you do on the**
35   **survey?**

1 JOLENE: *(Embarrassed)* **Oh, it doesn't matter.**

2 SASHA: **What do you mean it doesn't matter? You got me all**
3 **curious now. How did you do? What's your gift? I need to**
4 **know if you're gonna be moving to Africa!**

5 JOLENE: **Really, it's no big deal.**

6 SASHA: **Jolene! How did you do?**

7 JOLENE: *(Sighing)* **OK. It says, "Congratulations. You are**
8 **qualified to change diapers in the nursery!"**

9 SASHA: *(Still excited)* **And?**

10 JOLENE: **And nothing. That's it. That's my spiritual gift: diaper-**
11 **changing.**

12 SASHA: **That's your spiritual gift?** *(2 minute mark)*

13 JOLENE: **Yeah. Good-bye Mother Teresa; hello Mother Goose.**

14 SASHA: **Funny, I don't remember hearing about that one in**
15 **Sunday school. Just things like encouraging or showing mercy**
16 **or serving others and giving to the needs of the poor. But**
17 **diaper-changing?!**

18 JOLENE: **Maybe it appears in one of those newer translations.**

19 SASHA: **Hmmm.**

20 JOLENE: **Not the most glamorous gift, is it? Not like prophesying**
21 **or healing or anything.**

22 SASHA: **Oh, it's not that bad ... I mean, it could be worse.**

23 JOLENE: **How?**

24 SASHA: **You could be gifted at something like ... um ...**

25 JOLENE: **Yes?**

26 SASHA: **Something even less glamorous.**

27 JOLENE: **What's less glamorous than changing dirty diapers?!**

28 SASHA: **Preaching the sermon for Stewardship Sunday.** *(Or*
29 *another unpopular task at your local church)*

30 JOLENE: **Yeah. Good point.**

31 SASHA: *(After a pause)* **And anyway, diaper-changing is important,**
32 **and somebody's got to do it. Right?**

33 JOLENE: **I guess so.**

34 SASHA: **Besides, there's probably something wrong with your**
35 **survey. I mean, you're good at lots of stuff.** *(3 minute mark)*

1   JOLENE: Like what?

2   SASHA: Oh, I don't know, lots of stuff...

3   JOLENE: I'm waiting.

4   SASHA: Well, changing diapers, for one!

5   JOLENE: I've got that one covered.

6   SASHA: And ... filling out surveys! You're good at that!

7   JOLENE: Oh, great. I can fill out surveys and change diapers.

8   Every church in the country will be recruiting me.

9   SASHA: Oh, Jolene, don't feel bad ... At least your church has a

10   spiritual gifts survey.

11   JOLENE: What do you mean?

12   SASHA: Well, my church doesn't do anything like that. Instead,

13   it's like, if you have kids, you're expected to help in the

14   nursery. Whether you like it or not. Whether you're good at it

15   or not. And the staff is always trying to recruit more Sunday

16   school teachers. They'll take just about anybody!

17   JOLENE: Really?

18   SASHA: Yeah, it seems like it.

19   JOLENE: So why do people serve? Why do they volunteer?

20   SASHA: Because there's a need.

21   JOLENE: Not because they were called to it or gifted or anything?

22   *(4 minute mark)*

23   SASHA: Nope. We have a hard enough time just getting warm

24   bodies to fill up all the different committees and teaching

25   positions. I can't imagine what it'd be like if we actually tried

26   to match people up with their gifts and interests. We wouldn't

27   have anybody helping out!

28   JOLENE: Well, I'm still not too excited about being the queen of

29   diaper-changing. But I guess if that's my gift and everything —

30   SASHA: I wonder what my gift is?

31   JOLENE: I don't know. Wanna take the survey? *(Offering her a*

32   *packet of papers)* I have an extra copy of it here.

33   SASHA: I don't think so. If I knew what my gift was, I wouldn't

34   really have an excuse to keep saying "no" every time they ask

35   me to volunteer at church, would I?

1   **JOLENE: Nope. I guess not.**
2   **SASHA: Well, let me think about it. See you later!** *(She exits.)*
3   **JOLENE: Bye, Sasha.** *(To herself)* **Hmmm ... diaper-changing,**
4   **huh? Maybe if I change some of my answers, I can still make**
5   **it to Africa!** *(She turns her pencil over, looks both ways to make*
6   *sure no one is watching her, and begins to erase her responses. As*
7   *she is erasing, the lights fade.)*
8
9
10
11
12
13
14
15
16
17
18
19
20
21
22
23
24
25
26
27
28
29
30
31
32
33
34
35

Dad

Summary: During this sketch we see the progression of a father's relationship with his daughter throughout her life.

Purpose: To affirm family relationships and honor faithful fathers.

Time: 9–10 minutes

Tone: Humorous and heartwarming

Cast: Neil — A man watching his daughter grow up (male)
Karen/Brittany — (two roles) his wife in the first three scenes, and his daughter for the rest of the sketch (female)

Costumes: Casual, contemporary clothes

Props/Set: Two stools and a bundle of blankets on a stand between the two stools

Sound Effects: A clock ticking and a baby crying, if desired

Themes: Children, compassion, dating, family issues, Father's Day, grief and loss, life, love, married life, parenting, relationships, teenagers

Text: "Fathers, do not exasperate your children; instead, bring them up in the training and instruction of the Lord" (Ephesians 6:4).

Notes: During this sketch, we see scenes from the life of a father and his daughter as their relationship matures. As they go through their life, they struggle with the same things all fathers and daughters struggle with. The actors freeze while the clock is ticking.

Be sure that the actress playing Brittany shows a distinct difference in characterization between the mother and the daughter. She also needs to show the changes in the maturity of the daughter as the scenes progress. Use general stage lighting and two lapel microphones.

1   **SETTING**: The first scene begins with the actors On-stage, seated on
2   their stools. As the sound effects of a clock begin: "Tick, tock. Tick,
3   tock. Tick, tock ... " the lights come up and the scene begins.
4
5   **KAREN: Neil, I have something to tell you.**
6   **NEIL: What's that, honey?**
7   **KAREN: It's been two months.**
8   **NEIL:** *(Clueless)* **Since what?**
9   **KAREN: Since my last ...**
10   **NEIL: Your last?**
11   **KAREN: Uh-huh.**
12   **NEIL: You mean your last?**
13   **KAREN: Mm-hmmm.**
14   **NEIL: Oh ...**
15   **KAREN: Uh-huh.**
16   **NEIL: Ooooooh ... You mean?**
17   **KAREN: Mm-hmmm.**
18   **NEIL: You're not —**
19   **KAREN: I am.**
20   **NEIL: You are?!**
21   **KAREN: Oh, yeah.**
22   **NEIL: You're sure?**
23   **KAREN:** *(Smiling)* **Uh-huh.**
24   **NEIL: Oh ... Wow ...**
25   **KAREN:** *(Smiling)* **Yeah.** *(Sound effects of a clock: "Tick, tock. Tick,*
26   *tock. Tick, tock ... ")*
27   **NEIL: Breathe! Breathe! Breathe!**
28   **KAREN:** *(Breathing heavily)* **Whooh! Whooh! Whooh!**
29   **NEIL: Just like they taught us in that class, now! Breathe! Breathe!**
30   **Breathe!** *(1 minute mark)*
31   **KAREN: Leave me alone!**
32   **NEIL: Right.**
33   **KAREN:** *(Screaming)* **Ah!**
34   **NEIL: I'll just be right over here ...**
35   **KAREN: You did this to me! It's all your fault!**

1 **NEIL:** ... **On the other side of the room ...**
2 **KAREN:** *(Screaming)* **Ah!**
3 **NEIL:** ... **Where it's safe ...**
4 **KAREN:** *(Relaxing)* **Oh, oh ... Look, honey!** *(Sound effects of a baby*
5   *crying)* **Our baby!**
6 **NEIL: It's... It's ... a girl! I'm a daddy! I'm a real daddy!**
7 **KAREN:** *(Sweetly)* **Oh, Neil!**
8 **NEIL: Oh, Karen.** *(They both lean forward and pretend to give kisses*
9   *to each other.)* **What should we call her?**
10 **KAREN: Brittany! Isn't that what we decided?**
11 **NEIL: Brittany! It's perfect! My daughter, Brittany!** *(Sound effects*
12   *of a clock: "Tick, tock. Tick, tock. Tick, tock ... ")*
13 **KAREN:** *(Singing through this scene. Her singing should not be*
14   *sweet, but slightly distant-sounding and ominous)* **Rock-a-bye**
15   **baby, in the tree tops ...** *(2 minute mark)*
16 **NEIL:** *(Holding a bundle of blankets that represents a baby or miming*
17   *it)* **I can't believe I'm really a daddy.**
18 **KAREN: When the wind blows, the cradle will rock ...**
19 **NEIL: I'm gonna teach you to be just like your mommy.**
20 **KAREN: When the bough breaks, the cradle will fall ...**
21 **NEIL: I'm gonna be here for you, Brittany.**
22 **KAREN: And down will come baby ...**
23 **NEIL: No matter what happens, I'll always be here for you.**
24 **KAREN: Cradle and all ...** *(As KAREN finishes her lines, she turns*
25   *her back to the audience. Sound effects of a clock: "Tick, tock.*
26   *Tick, tock. Tick, tock ... ")*
27 **NEIL: Oh, Brittany, I'm so sorry. I don't know how to say this ...**
28   **I don't know how we're gonna make it without your momma.**
29   **I guess it's just gonna be the two of us from now on. Just the**
30   **two of us.** *(3 minute mark)*
31   *(Sound effects of a clock: "Tick, tock. Tick, tock. Tick, tock ... "*
32   *Then, the actress turns to face the audience again. This time she*
33   *is playing the part of the daughter, BRITTANY.)*
34 **BRITTANY: Daddy! Daddy! I drew you a picture!**
35 **NEIL: Oh, wow!**

1   **BRITTANY:** See?

2   **NEIL:** Yeah. What a nice ... um —

3   **BRITTANY:** You know what it is, don't you?

4   **NEIL:** Sure. It's a ... it's a cute little froggie!

5   **BRITTANY:** It's you, Daddy!

6   **NEIL:** Oh.

7   **BRITTANY:** See?

8   **NEIL:** Oh, yeah! Is that bump my head?

9   **BRITTANY:** That's your tummy.

10   **NEIL:** Oh. Thanks, Brittany.

11   **BRITTANY:** Because I love you, Daddy.

12   **NEIL:** I love you too, Sweetie. I'll just put it up here on the fridge

13   ... with all the others. *(Sound effects of a clock: "Tick, tock. Tick,*

14   *tock. Tick, tock ... ")*

15   **NEIL:** Pedal, Brittany! Pedal! You can make it!

16   **BRITTANY:** I'm scared, Daddy!

17   **NEIL:** I know! It's OK, I've got ya!

18   **BRITTANY:** Don't let me fall!

19   **NEIL:** I won't! I'll be right by your side. I promise!

20   **BRITTANY:** OK.

21   **NEIL:** You're doing great.

22   **BRITTANY:** Don't let go! *(4 minute mark)*

23   **NEIL:** Brittany, I just did ...

24   **BRITTANY:** Daddy?

25   **NEIL:** There!

26   **BRITTANY:** Daddy!

27   **NEIL:** See? I knew you could! I knew you could do it on your own!

28   **BRITTANY:** Look, Daddy! Look!

29   **NEIL:** You're making it all by yourself!

30   **BRITTANY:** Whee! ... Here I go, Daddy! Here I go! *(Sound effects*

31   *of a clock: "Tick, tock. Tick, tock. Tick, tock ... ")* **Daddy, Daddy!**

32   **I lost my first tooth! Look! Look!**

33   **NEIL:** Wow! You're getting so grown up.

34   **BRITTANY:** Should I put it under my pillow?

35   **NEIL:** Yeah, so the tooth fairy can find it.

1   BRITTANY: When does the tooth fairy come, Daddy?
2   NEIL: After you're asleep, sweetheart.
3   BRITTANY: Can you tell me a bedtime story?
4   NEIL: Sure. Climb into bed now.
5   BRITTANY: I hope the tooth fairy comes early so I can meet her.
6   NEIL: Shhh ... Now, listen ... Once upon a time, there was a
7   beautiful princess named ... Brittany —
8   BRITTANY: *(Excited)* Hey, that's my name! *(5 minute mark)*
9   NEIL: I know, sweetie ... I know ... now, be quiet so you can hear
10   the rest of the story ... *(Sound effects of a clock: "Tick, tock.*
11   *Tick, tock. Tick, tock ... ")* So this is your first big sleepover,
12   huh?
13 BRITTANY: Yeah.
14 NEIL: Do you have everything you need?
15 BRITTANY: I think so, Dad.
16 NEIL: Now, remember what I told you about being a good
17   listener —
18 BRITTANY: I remember.
19 NEIL: And don't stay up all night.
20 BRITTANY: I won't.
21 NEIL: OK. Do you have your teddy bear?
22 BRITTANY: Yeah.
23 NEIL: Good. He might have been lonely staying home all by
24   himself.
25 BRITTANY: *Her*self.
26 NEIL: Oh, yeah. Right.
27 BRITTANY: Good-bye, Daddy.
28 NEIL: Good-bye, princess. Have fun! *(Sound effects of a clock:*
29   *"Tick, tock. Tick, tock. Tick, tock ... ")*
30 BRITTANY: Dad, where do babies come from?
31 NEIL: Babies?
32 BRITTANY: Yeah.
33 NEIL: You wanna know where babies come from?
34 BRITTANY: Mm-hmmm.
35 NEIL: Uh, how about we go out for some ice cream?

1   BRITTANY: Ice cream! Oh boy! *(6 minute mark)*
2   NEIL: Yeah, oh boy ... *(Sound effects of a clock: "Tick, tock. Tick,*
3   *tock. Tick, tock ... " Pretending to hold a telephone)* **Hey**
4   **Brittany, it's for you. It's Mr. Buchanan, your science teacher.**
5   BRITTANY: Oh yeah, he said he'd call. He wants me to baby-sit.
6   NEIL: You're not old enough to baby-sit. Are you?
7   BRITTANY: Dad, I'm thirteen! I took that baby-sitting class last
8   fall, remember?
9   NEIL: Oh, yeah. You're thirteen?
10   BRITTANY: Of course, Dad!
11   NEIL: Oh. Yeah.
12   BRITTANY: So can I go? I'll be home by ten o'clock. I promise.
13   NEIL: Um. Yeah. Sure.
14   BRITTANY: OK. Can I have the phone ... Dad? The phone ...
15   *(Sound effects of a clock: "Tick, tock. Tick, tock. Tick, tock ... ")*
16   Dad, can I have the car keys?
17   NEIL: Where are you going?
18   BRITTANY: Blade asked me to pick him up for the dance.
19   NEIL: No. *(7 minute mark)*
20   BRITTANY: But Dad, I'm sixteen!
21   NEIL: I don't care how old you are, you're not going out with a boy
22   named Blade.
23   BRITTANY: But Dad! All my friends are dating!
24   NEIL: That's final!
25   BRITTANY: Daaad!
26   NEIL: And besides, you're not leaving the house dressed like that.
27   BRITTANY: Like what?
28   NEIL: In that skimpy little nightgown.
29   BRITTANY: Dad, this is the dress I bought last week! Everyone's
30   wearing stuff like this.
31   NEIL: If that's a dress, I'm the King of France. Now, go change.
32   BRITTANY: All right ... Your Majesty.
33   NEIL: Teenagers!
34   BRITTANY: Parents! *(Sound effects of a clock: "Tick, tock. Tick,*
35   *tock. Tick, tock ... ")*

1   NEIL: So Britt, how was your first semester at college?

2   BRITTANY: Great, Dad! But it's good to be home.

3   NEIL: I'll go get your stuff from the car.

4   BRITTANY: Thanks.

5   NEIL: By the way, that's a nice bracelet you've got there.

6   BRITTANY: Oh, yeah. It's from this guy — Brendan.

7   NEIL: Brendan, huh? Is he cute?

8   BRITTANY: He's kinda cute.

9   NEIL: So?

10   BRITTANY: Dad, we're just friends. *(8 minute mark)*

11   NEIL: Oh, just friends.

12   BRITTANY: Yeah.

13   NEIL: OK. Let me go get your stuff ... *(Sound effects of a clock: "Tick,*

14   *tock. Tick, tock. Tick, tock ... ")* Let's see that ring again, Britt.

15   BRITTANY: *(She shows it to him.)* See?

16   NEIL: Oh, lemme look at you ... Wow ... So this is your big day,

17   huh?

18   BRITTANY: Yeah, Dad. Do I look OK?

19   NEIL: You look like an angel.

20   BRITTANY: I don't look too fat in this dress?

21   NEIL: Are you kidding? You look amazing in that dress. Just like

22   your mom did.

23   BRITTANY: I love you, Dad.

24   NEIL: I love you too, princess. C'mon, we don't wanna be late ...

25   *(If desired, have them both stand, put their arms around each*

26   *other's waists, and turn their backs to the audience. Sound effects*

27   *of a clock: "Tick, tock. Tick, tock. Tick, tock ... " If possible,*

28   *replay this last scene from an audiotape, as the two actors stand*

29   *frozen On-stage. If that isn't possible, they can replay the scene.*

30   *Either way, as this last scene is played out, add some reverb and*

31   *slowly fade the volume.)*

32   NEIL: Pedal, Brittany! Pedal! You can make it!

33   BRITTANY: I'm scared, Daddy!

34   NEIL: I know! It's OK, I've got ya! *(9 minute mark)*

35   BRITTANY: Don't let me fall!

1   NEIL: I won't. I'll be right by your side. I promise!

2   BRITTANY: OK.

3   NEIL: You're doing great.

4   BRITTANY: Don't let go!

5   NEIL: Brittany, I just did …

6   BRITTANY: Daddy?

7   NEIL: There!

8   BRITTANY: Daddy!

9   NEIL: See? I knew you could! I knew you could do it on your own!

10   BRITTANY: Look, Daddy! Look!

11   NEIL: You're making it all by yourself!

12   BRITTANY: Whee!... Here I go, Daddy! Here I go! *(Sound effects of*

13   *a clock: "Tick, tock. Tick, tock. Tick, tock … " as the lights and*

14   *volume fadeout.)*

15

16

17

18

19

20

21

22

23

24

25

26

27

28

29

30

31

32

33

34

35

A Great Place to Go

Summary: Ronnie and Dan have found a place where they feel right at home. But is it really the community they need?

Purpose: To show the type of community a church should provide.

Time: 2–3 minutes

Tone: Humorous and thought-provoking

Cast: Ronnie — A man who has found a new community where he feels right at home (male)
Dan — His new friend who has just started attending (male)

Costumes: Casual, contemporary clothes

Props/Set: Two folding chairs and two Styrofoam cups with coffee in them

Themes: Assumptions, church issues, community, modern life, relationships, worship

Text: "All the believers were together and had everything in common. They broke bread in their homes and ate together with glad and sincere hearts, praising God and enjoying the favor of all the people. And the Lord added to their number daily those who were being saved" (Acts 2:44, 46b–47).

Notes: This sketch is quite brief, but the impact can be powerful when the last couple of lines are finally delivered. Don't let your actors give away the setting before the ending. This sketch will work great for a message on the types of needs people bring to church or the type of community believers should provide. Use general stage lighting and two lapel microphones.

1   *SETTING*: Ronnie is seated On-stage drinking coffee as the lights
2   come up and the scene begins. Then Dan enters and sees an empty
3   chair next to him. All throughout the sketch, they should be acting
4   as if they're in a church.
5
6   **DAN: Wow! It was really crowded out there. No place to park or**
7   **anything!**
8   **RONNIE: Yeah, it's been getting more and more popular here**
9   **lately.** *(Optional line — "Ever since 9/11")*
10 **DAN: Hey, is this seat taken?**
11 **RONNIE: No, go ahead.**
12 **DAN: Thanks.**
13 **RONNIE: Sure. No problem.**
14 **DAN: Ah, I just love coming here.**
15 **RONNIE: Yeah, me too … I'm Ronnie.**
16 **DAN: Oh, I'm Dan. Good to meet you.**
17 **RONNIE: Yeah, likewise.**
18 **DAN: So, you come here much?**
19 **RONNIE: Pretty much every Sunday since I was a kid. My mom**
20 **used to bring me — you know, when I was growing up — and**
21 **then I guess it just stuck because I started coming on my own**
22 **after high school. What about you?**
23 **DAN: Yeah, my parents never brought me. I just started coming a**
24 **couple months ago.** *(After a pause)* **I've been having some**
25 **trouble at home, you know, with my wife and kids. It's good to**
26 **have a place you can bring your problems.**
27 **RONNIE: Yeah. There's always someone here to listen, that much**
28 **is for sure.** *(1 minute mark)*
29 **DAN: I've noticed that.**
30 **RONNIE: Yeah.**
31 **DAN: It's a good atmosphere, too. And I really like the music.**
32 **RONNIE: They've been changing it around lately. Making things**
33 **more contemporary — sometimes they bring in a local band**
34 **or a soloist.**
35 **DAN: Yeah. That's cool. Good variety.**

1   RONNIE: *(Looking around)* This is a great place. It's kinda like
2   a family when you think about it. At least, it's been that way
3   for me.
4   DAN: Hmmm ...
5   RONNIE: *(Pointing)* Hey, you see her? Over there?
6   DAN: The one by the stage?
7   RONNIE: Yeah, she's been coming here ever since her husband left
8   her. She sometimes helps 'em out, you know, serving other
9   people when they get really busy. She doesn't get paid or
10   anything. Just volunteers. *(2 minute mark)*
11 DAN: Well, I believe it. When you find a place like this, you can't
12   help but get involved. *(After a pause)* This sure is a great place
13   to come when you reach a dead end in your life.
14 RONNIE: Or to look for answers.
15 DAN: And no one judges you here, you know? It doesn't matter
16   what you've done. Or where you've been.
17 RONNIE: You know, I just can't think of a better place to go when
18   you need someone to talk to than Joe's Bar and Grill.
19 DAN: Yeah, me neither. I wonder where people who don't have a
20   place like this go when they need a place to talk.
21 RONNIE: I don't know, Dan. I really don't know. *(As they drink*
22   *from their cups, the lights fade.)*
23
24
25
26
27
28
29
30
31
32
33
34
35

The Checklist

Summary: Jerry is busy marking things off his spiritual checklist. But Erin has a different perspective about what's most important in following God.

Purpose: To reveal that Christianity is a relationship, not a checklist.

Time: 4–5 minutes

Tone: Humorous and thought-provoking

Cast: Jerry — A guy who has made Christianity into a checklist (male)
Erin — His friend who helps him review his spiritual priorities (female)

Costumes: Casual, contemporary clothes

Props/Set: Clipboard, papers, a pen

Themes: Ambition, authenticity, Bible study, Christmas, conversion, distractions, faith, guilt, Jesus, misconceptions about Christianity, modern life, prayer, priorities, relationships, rest, spiritual health, stress, worship

Text: "Yet to all who received him, to those who believed in his name, he gave the right to become children of God — children born not of natural descent, nor of human decision or a husband's will, but born of God" (John 1:12–13).

Notes: Erin and Jerry are good friends who like hanging out together. Use two spotlights and two lapel microphones.

1 **SETTING**: The lobby of a church, right after the service. Jerry is
2 looking over the notes he took during the sermon when Erin
3 walks up and sees him. They're both On-stage as the lights come
4 up and the scene begins.
5
6 **ERIN: That sure was a great sermon, huh Jerry?**
7 **JERRY: Yeah. I took about sixteen pages of notes.**
8 **ERIN: Wow! Hey, you wanna go for a walk down by the park?**
9 **There's a great view of the river and the trees are just turning**
10 **colors —** *(Or another seasonal reason to go and enjoy a nature*
11 *walk)*
12 **JERRY: Not today, Erin! I've gotta get going and put that sermon**
13 **into action — you know, walk the talk!**
14 **ERIN: So how is your walk going, anyhow?**
15 **JERRY: Oh, awesome! Let's see,** *(He pulls out a clipboard with a*
16 *checklist)* **I just finished praying the Prayer of Jabez again —**
17 **I try to do it at least five times a day. You can't be too careful,**
18 **you know. And** *(Dramatically checking these things off as he*
19 *mentions them)* **I read a chapter of the Bible this morning —**
20 **check — memorized my Bible verse for the day — check — I**
21 **chose an easy one because I was pretty busy getting ready for**
22 **church — John 11:35: "Jesus wept."**
23 **ERIN: But that's only two words!**
24 **JERRY: Yeah. Only 750,498 to go and I'll have the whole Bible**
25 **under my belt.** *(1 minute mark)*
26 **ERIN: You're memorizing the whole Bible!?**
27 **JERRY: Sure, why not? If I learn fifty words a day, it'll only take**
28 **me forty-one years, one month, and three days. Wait a minute.**
29 **Now I'm forty-eight words behind. Hmmm ... Anyway, I've**
30 **witnessed to two people this morning — check — last night I**
31 **prayed for every one of the two hundred and eight people on**
32 **my prayer list by name — check — And I haven't missed a**
33 **church service in fourteen years — check. I feel great!**
34 **ERIN: Wow! You sure are busy!**
35 **JERRY: You gotta be! I mean, if I miss even one day, I feel really**

1 guilty and then I have to catch up. Anyway, how about you?
2 How's your walk?
3 ERIN: Oh, pretty good, I think.
4 JERRY: Are you participating in a structured Scripture memory
5 program?
6 ERIN: Not at the moment.
7 JERRY: Well, how many people are on your prayer list?
8 ERIN: I don't have a prayer list.
9 JERRY: What about witnessing? Have you shared the Gospel with
10 anyone this week?
11 ERIN: Not yet. Actually, I haven't done any of that stuff you listed.
12 JERRY: What! Are you backsliding? Falling away? Are you
13 engaged in spiritual warfare? Prayer alert! Prayer alert!
14 ERIN: Jerry! *(2 minute mark)*
15 JERRY: *(Not paying attention)* I'll pray for you, sister. I won't let
16 you just slip through the cracks! I won't let it happen! *(He*
17 *reaches out his hand and starts praying for her.)*
18 ERIN: Jerry! Jerry! I'm OK.
19 JERRY: Huh? What?
20 ERIN: I'm OK. I'm fine. I just don't have any of those checklists.
21 JERRY: But don't you take following God seriously?
22 ERIN: Of course I do. But I just don't think following God can
23 be reduced to a bunch of activities. Christianity is not a "to
24 do" list.
25 JERRY: *(Shocked)* It's not?
26 ERIN: Of course not. There's a lot more to honoring God than just
27 checking off little boxes on a sheet of paper. When was the last
28 time you put all your checklists and prayer lists away and just
29 thought about God and what he's done for you?
30 JERRY: You mean daydream?
31 ERIN: No, I mean meditate.
32 JERRY: Oh, like some kinda Buddhist monk or something? Ohm.
33 Ohm. Ohm —
34 ERIN: No! Reflect on it. Just think about him with no agenda or
35 outline or planned-out schedule. *(3 minute mark)*

1 JERRY: But if I don't have a checklist, how will I know when I'm
2 finished? How will I ever know if I've done enough? If I'm
3 caught up? What if I fall behind?
4 ERIN: Listen to me. We're friends, right?
5 JERRY: Sure.
6 ERIN: Are we ever finished being friends?
7 JERRY: No ...
8 ERIN: And when we get together for dinner, or to play tennis, or to
9 see a movie, or to go out for ice cream, or just to hang out, do
10 you bring a checklist along? Stuff like, "Say 'Hi'" — check —
11 "Shake her hand" — check — "Ask her how she's doing" —
12 check.
13 JERRY: Of course not.
14 ERIN: Why not?
15 JERRY: Because we're friends.
16 ERIN: And?
17 JERRY: And the goal of a friendship is to grow a deeper
18 relationship, not just check a bunch of things off a list.
19 ERIN: Uh-huh.
20 JERRY: *(Realizing what he said)* Oh ...
21 ERIN: Mm-hmmm.
22 JERRY: Maybe I have been kinda missing the point lately ...
23 *(Looking at his checklist)* But are you saying it's wrong to be
24 organized or to have prayer lists and stuff? *(4 minute mark)*
25 ERIN: No. Just don't let it get in the way of what really matters.
26 JERRY: My relationship with God.
27 ERIN: Right.
28 JERRY: Come to think of it, maybe I would like to go on that walk
29 after all.
30 ERIN: What about your checklist?
31 JERRY: I think I'll leave it here this time. After all, there's a lot
32 more to honoring God than just checking off little boxes on a
33 sheet of paper. *(He sets down the clipboard and they exit*
34 *together. Fadeout.)*
35

Get with the Program

Summary: Joel doesn't want to go to the evangelism committee meeting because he doesn't like the idea of "evangelism programs." Then Sue gives him something to think about.

Purpose: To motivate people to share their faith naturally and comfortably.

Time: 3–4 minutes

Tone: Humorous and thought-provoking

Cast: Joel — A man who is avoiding thinking about witnessing to others (male)
Sue — His wife who is frustrated with evangelism "programs" (female)

Costumes: Casual, contemporary clothes. Joel and Sue are at home on a Tuesday evening.

Props/Set: A cookie cutter, a countertop, cookie dough, a TV remote control, a recliner

Themes: Authenticity, church issues, communication, compassion, conversion, evangelism, frustrations, giftedness, guilt, honesty, integrity, listening, misconceptions about Christianity, witnessing

Text: "We are therefore Christ's ambassadors, as though God were making his appeal through us. We implore you on Christ's behalf: Be reconciled to God. God made him who had no sin to be sin for us, so that in him we might become the righteousness of God" (2 Corinthians 5:20–21; see also 1 Peter 3:15).

Notes: Let the dialog between Joel and Sue flow naturally and lightheartedly. We want to be on both of their sides. Use general stage lighting and two lapel microphones.

1 **SETTING**: Joel and Sue are at home. He's sitting on the recliner, and
2 she's finishing baking some cookies in the kitchen. Depending on
3 your staging capabilities, Joel is holding a remote control with the
4 TV on in the background. They're both On-stage as the lights
5 come up and the scene opens.
6
7 **SUE: Hey honey, are you going to that meeting at church tonight?**
8 **JOEL: Nah, they're just talking about some new evangelism**
9 **program. Those things always make me feel guilty. I think I'm**
10 **just gonna stay here and watch the game.**
11 **SUE: But dear, it's important for you to go.**
12 **JOEL: Why is that?**
13 **SUE: You're the pastor.**
14 **JOEL:** *(After a pause)* **Oh, yeah … So?**
15 **SUE: Joel!**
16 **JOEL: OK, OK, I guess you're right.** *(Sighing)* **But I just can't**
17 **stand these programs.**
18 **SUE: Well, I can understand why.**
19 **JOEL: What are you talking about?**
20 **SUE: Do they work?**
21 **JOEL: Um … no. Not really.**
22 **SUE: Well, I'm no great theologian or anything, but I think the**
23 **reason they don't work is because they're not honest.**
24 **JOEL: They're not honest? What do you mean they're not honest?**
25 **SUE: Well, remember the "Spiritual Survey" technique the church**
26 **did a few years ago?** *(1 minute mark)*
27 **JOEL: Sure. Where you go door to door and pretend you're**
28 **surveying people about spiritual things, but you're really just**
29 **using it as an excuse to give 'em a canned speech about God?**
30 **SUE: Right.**
31 **JOEL:** *(Clueless)* **So what's the problem with that?**
32 **SUE: Joel, it's not honest. They should've started by telling people,**
33 **"I'm gonna take the next twenty minutes of your time asking**
34 **you questions you don't want to answer so I can give you**
35 **answers you're not supposed to question."**

1   JOEL: Could you run that by me again?

2   SUE: The point is, it was deceitful. And then there's that "outreach

3   event" where you host a concert or something and don't

4   advertise that people are gonna have to sit through a sermon,

5   too.

6   JOEL: I thought you liked my sermons!

7   SUE: Well I, do. I just like to know when a sermon is coming so I

8   can prepare myself.

9   JOEL: Oh … How do you prepare yourself?

10   SUE: Earplugs. But that's not the point. The point is, you should

11   tell them a sermon is coming and not try to sneak it in once

12   you've got an audience.

13   JOEL: Earplugs?

14   SUE: Heavy-duty.

15   JOEL: I never knew. *(2 minute mark)*

16   SUE: Anyway, along with the tracts left in public restrooms, I'm as

17   fed up with all these evangelism programs as you are.

18   JOEL: Earplugs, huh?

19   SUE: Joel, are you listening to me?

20   JOEL: Yeah, and you're right again. Wouldn't it be great if there

21   were an evangelism program that didn't rely on guilt trips,

22   manipulation, canned speeches, or sleazy marketing

23   techniques?

24   SUE: That's why you need to go to that meeting.

25   JOEL: Maybe you oughta go …

26   SUE: I have to finish making these cookies.

27   JOEL: Oh … So what kind of evangelism technique would you

28   teach?

29   SUE: *(Holding up her cookie cutter)* Well, it wouldn't be a cookie

30   cutter approach, like the rest of 'em are. People are shaped

31   differently, and the way they share the Gospel should look

32   different, too.

33   JOEL: Hmmm.

34   SUE: *(Handing him a cookie cutter)* Here, take this to your meeting.

35   Give them something to think about tonight.

1   **JOEL:** *(After a thoughtful pause)* **You knew I wouldn't want to go**
2   **tonight, didn't you?**
3   **SUE: Uh-huh.**
4   **JOEL: And it's not just a coincidence you happened to have these**
5   **cookie cutters out, either — is it?** *(3 minute mark)*
6   **SUE: Nope.**
7   **JOEL:** *(After another pause)* **You're amazing, you know that?**
8   **SUE:** *(Blushing)* **Uh-huh. Now go to your meeting.**
9   **JOEL:** *(Getting up and taking her hand)* **C'mon. Let's both go. I**
10   **think they might need to hear from both of us tonight.** *(Freeze.*
11   *Fadeout.)*
12
13
14
15
16
17
18
19
20
21
22
23
24
25
26
27
28
29
30
31
32
33
34
35

The Christmas Letters

Summary: Trisha wants Nathan to help her finish labeling Christmas cards for all her friends, but he's sick of the frantic pace of the holidays.

Purpose: To help people focus on the true meaning of Christmas.

Time: 4–5 minutes

Tone: Humorous

Cast: Trisha — A woman who is very concerned with keeping up a good image (female)
Nathan — Her husband who wishes they could just get back to the basics of the Christmas season (male)

Costumes: Casual, contemporary clothes

Props/Set: Stacks of Christmas cards, snapshots, envelopes, pens, a laptop computer, a sofa

Themes: Appearances, authenticity, Christmas, grace, integrity, married life, modern life, priorities

Text: "But when the time had fully come, God sent his Son, born of a woman, born under law, to redeem those under law, that we might receive the full rights of sons" (Galatians 4:4–5).

Notes: Trisha is labeling the envelopes for this year's Christmas cards. She has convinced her husband to type up their family Christmas letter. He is doing his job grudgingly; she is doing hers just to impress people. Use general stage lighting and two lapel microphones.

1   *SETTING*: Nathan and Trisha's living room in the evening. Trisha is
2   seated on one end of the sofa with a pile of envelopes all around
3   her. She is copying names onto the envelopes from an address
4   book. Nathan is seated at the other end of the sofa with a laptop
5   computer. He's typing and she's writing as the lights come up and
6   the scene begins.
7
8   **TRISHA: What do you think? Should we send a Christmas card to**
9   **the Reagans?**
10   **NATHAN:** *(Busy typing)* **Huh?**
11   **TRISHA: The Reagans?**
12   **NATHAN: Sure, why not?**
13   **TRISHA: Well, they didn't send us one last year.**
14   **NATHAN: How do you know that?**
15   **TRISHA: Oh, I keep a list.**
16   **NATHAN: You keep a list of who sends us Christmas cards each**
17   **year?**
18   **TRISHA: Of course! How else could I make sure we keep up?**
19   **NATHAN: Keep up with what?**
20   **TRISHA: Everyone else who sends us their Christmas cards! We**
21   **can't fall behind. Now, we haven't seen Jessie and Brian since**
22   **we moved here from New Jersey, but they've sent us cards for**
23   **the last four years! Nathan, I'd say we owe them a card *and* a**
24   **picture. Hand me one of those snapshots over there.**
25   **NATHAN: We *owe* them a card?**
26   **TRISHA: Of course. So, have you finished typing up the Christmas**
27   **letter yet?**
28   **NATHAN: I'm almost done. I still don't get why we can't just send**
29   **a mass e-mail like everyone else.** *(1 minute mark)*
30   **TRISHA: It's too easy to send e-mails.**
31   **NATHAN: Too easy? But you want me to type up a letter anyhow!**
32   **TRISHA: Yeah, then we'll print it out on nice fancy paper and put**
33   **it in a card with a cordial and heartfelt hand-written note. It**
34   **doesn't mean as much to someone if you just send 'em an**
35   **e-mail — but taking the time to actually write a note! That**

1   means something!

2   NATHAN: It means you don't have an Internet account.

3   TRISHA: What?

4   NATHAN: Oh, nothing. Couldn't we just do this another day? I

5   wanna watch some basketball.

6   TRISHA: We have to get our letter finished before anyone else

7   sends us theirs.

8   NATHAN: Why?

9   TRISHA: So we're not catching up all season. I mean, if we get a

10   card from someone and we haven't sent them anything, we'll

11   need to quick send them a letter so it doesn't look like we

12   forgot about *them.*

13   NATHAN: But we did. I mean, we do forget about some people.

14   TRISHA: I know, but we can't let it *seem* like we did. And besides,

15   if we're late sending these out, people might think we're not

16   impeccably organized, orderly, efficient, and self-controlled.

17   *(2 minute mark)*

18   NATHAN: But we're not!

19   TRISHA: I know, but we can't let anyone else know that! So,

20   almost done?

21   NATHAN: I think so ... and ... *(Typing)* ... there! OK. I think it's

22   ready to print out. Let me just transfer this file to a disk so I

23   can print it from the other computer —

24   TRISHA: Let me hear it.

25   NATHAN: You wanna hear it print out?

26   TRISHA: No, I wanna hear the letter. What'd you write?

27   NATHAN: Oh, basic stuff. Here's what I wrote about me: "Nathan

28   drives his daughters around town a lot. He's in charge of the

29   laundry and mows the lawn on a weekly basis. He still has the

30   old same job, although he's making less money because of

31   corporate cutbacks. He's gotten one year older, he's starting to

32   lose his hair, and he's gained twelve pounds." How's that? It

33   goes on like that for another couple paragraphs. And then I

34   have some stuff on you and the girls.

35   TRISHA: Nathan!

1   NATHAN: Yeah, I mention your weight down here on page three —
2   TRISHA: You need to rewrite that!
3   NATHAN: Why?
4   TRISHA: You're not supposed to list stuff like that in your
5   Christmas letter!
6   NATHAN: Why not? *(3 minute mark)*
7   TRISHA: It sounds like our lives are too normal!
8   NATHAN: Yeah, and?
9   TRISHA: You're supposed to put a positive spin on everything so
10   that everyone who reads it will envy how perfect our family is!
11   NATHAN: How perfect our family is?
12   TRISHA: Uh-huh.
13   NATHAN: OK. So what would you write?
14   TRISHA: Let's see … "When he's not spending quality time with
15   his children, Nathan Alexander leads the charge against dirty
16   laundry and long grass. He has overcome financial obstacles
17   at work and become a more substantial individual over the
18   last year!"
19   NATHAN: A more substantial individual?
20   TRISHA: Yeah, that's the part about you gaining twelve pounds.
21   NATHAN: Oh.
22   TRISHA: What do you think?
23   NATHAN: It sounds like a press release, not a Christmas letter.
24   Look, Trisha, why do we go through this every year? The
25   cards, the letters, the parties, the appearances —
26   TRISHA: We need to keep up our image. *(4 minute mark)*
27   NATHAN: Because we want everyone to envy us and our perfect
28   little lives?
29   TRISHA: Uh-huh.
30   NATHAN: But our lives aren't perfect! That's the whole point of
31   Christmas!
32   TRISHA: It is?
33   NATHAN: Of course! Why else do you think we celebrate
34   Christmas?
35   TRISHA: To keep the Christmas card people in business?

1   NATHAN: *(Putting his computer down)* **Trisha, how about this year**
2   **we don't worry about the cards. Or about keeping up with**
3   **everyone. Or what people think of us. How about we just**
4   **spend time being thankful for what Christmas is really all**
5   **about.**
6   **TRISHA: The baby in the manger.**
7   **NATHAN: Yeah.**
8   **TRISHA: Maybe you're right. But I still don't think you should tell**
9   **people you gained twelve pounds.**
10   **NATHAN: Why not?**
11   **TRISHA: It was more like fifteen.**
12   **NATHAN: Really?**
13   **TRISHA: Yeah.**
14   **NATHAN: Oh … Oh well, that's life. Merry Christmas, Trisha.**
15   **TRISHA: Merry Christmas, Nathan.** *(Freeze. Fadeout.)*
16
17
18
19
20
21
22
23
24
25
26
27
28
29
30
31
32
33
34
35

The Shopping Trip

Summary: When Kevin decides to help Stacy choose a new pair of glasses, he has no idea what he's in for.

Purpose: To explore the consequences we face for the decisions, both big and small, that we make in life.

Time: 4–5 minutes

Tone: Humorous

Cast: Stacy — A lady who is having a hard time making decisions (female)
Kevin — Her husband, who just wants her to make up her mind (male)

Costumes: Casual, contemporary clothes

Props/Set: A countertop, a chair, some full shopping bags from the mall, and a display board with several dozen different glasses frames.

Themes: Choices, communication, consequences, dating, frustrations, God's sovereignty, married life, modern life, relationships

Text: "Elijah went before the people and said, 'How long will you waver between two opinions? If the Lord is God, follow him; but if Baal is God, follow him.' But the people said nothing" (1 Kings 18:21).

Notes: In a lighthearted way, this sketch brings up the question of how our choices affect our lives. Do all our choices matter? How do our choices mesh with God's choices? Don't let Kevin get too frustrated, keep it light. Stacy echoes the thoughts of most of us when she says the last line, "I just wanna make the right decisions, and I'm not always sure what they are … " Your speaker can address these questions in his or her message. Use general stage lighting and two lapel microphones.

1　*SETTING*: Stacy and Kevin are at an eye doctor's reception area at the
2　　　mall. She has just finished getting her eyes checked and is now
3　　　choosing some new frames for her glasses. Kevin has already seen
4　　　Stacy try on ten different frames when the scene begins. They
5　　　have shopping bags at their feet. Both are On-stage as the lights
6　　　come on and the scene begins.
7
8　STACY: *(Trying on a pair of glasses)* **So how 'bout these?**
9　KEVIN: **Wow. They look good.**
10　STACY: *(Taking off one pair and trying on another)* **What about**
11　　　**these?**
12　KEVIN: **Good.**
13　STACY: **You said that about the last pair.**
14　KEVIN: **That's because they were good.**
15　STACY: *(Taking off one pair and trying on another)* **OK, what about**
16　　　**these?**
17　KEVIN: **Oh, they look great.**
18　STACY: **So you like 'em better?**
19　KEVIN: **Sure.**
20　STACY: *(Excited)* **You do? Really?**
21　KEVIN: **Absolutely. Let's get 'em.**
22　STACY: **Are you sure?**
23　KEVIN: **Sure. I mean, I think so. I like 'em both. I don't know**
24　　　**which ones I like better.**
25　STACY: **You're not being very helpful.** *(During the following*
26　　　*exchange, STACY continues looking through the frames and*
27　　　*KEVIN responds with humorous exasperation, not bitter anger.)*
28　KEVIN: **I'm telling you, they all look good. And then if I say I like**
29　　　**'em, you don't buy them anyhow! Honey, it's been like this all**
30　　　**day!**
31　STACY: **Women like trying things on before making a decision. It's**
32　　　**part of the fun of shopping.** *(1 minute mark)*
33　KEVIN: **Part of the fun?**
34　STACY: **Yes.**
35　KEVIN: **Fun?**

1   STACY: Uh-huh.

2   KEVIN: This is fun?

3   STACY: Of course.

4   KEVIN: At the last store, you tried on like forty-two dresses!

5   STACY: I had to make sure I got the right one. *(Sweetly)* **By the**

6   **way, thanks for shopping with me today, honey. Most guys**

7   **would be home watching football on an afternoon like this.**

8   KEVIN: *(After a pause)* **How many more stores did you say we've**

9   **got left?**

10   STACY: Just three more stops.

11   KEVIN: *(He looks at the bags of clothes, then at his watch, and sighs*

12   *heavily.)* **Oh boy.**

13   STACY: What did you say?

14   KEVIN: Oh, I was just saying, *(Acting excited)* "Oh boy!"

15   STACY: *(Taking off one pair and trying on another)* **OK, what about**

16   **these?**

17   KEVIN: Stacy, you already tried those on. Like a half-hour ago.

18   STACY: I know, but I want to see how they look again.

19   KEVIN: This is not how guys shop.

20   STACY: What do you mean? *(2 minute mark)*

21   KEVIN: *(Acting this out)* **We walk into a store, pick something up,**

22   **look at it for four seconds, and then buy it or put it back for**

23   **good. We're like hunters. We see what we want, we go after it,**

24   **we get it, we tag it, we bag it, we bring it home to the family.**

25   **Oog!**

26   STACY: *(Accusingly, as if to say "You better say the right thing,*

27   *buster")* **So, if you're "The Hunter," what does that make me?**

28   KEVIN: *(Trying to rescue himself)* **Um... The Village Wise Woman.**

29   STACY: Good answer ... So what about these? Do you think they

30   bring out the highlights in my hair?

31   KEVIN: Look, do you want me to decide for you?

32   STACY: No.

33   KEVIN: Or tell you which ones to buy?

34   STACY: No. Yes.

35   KEVIN: What do you want?

1   STACY: Your opinion.
2   KEVIN: OK, I like these glasses.
3   STACY: Really?
4   KEVIN: Yes.
5   STACY: What about these?
6   KEVIN: Ah! I just told you I like those, and you grabbed another
7   pair! I like those, too. I like them all. *(3 minute mark)*
8   STACY: Oh, Kevin.
9   KEVIN: What do you want me to say? If you don't want me to
10   decide for you and you don't even listen to my opinion, what
11   am I doing here?
12   STACY: Helping me decide … Well?
13   KEVIN: *(Grabbing an armload of glasses off the table)* **Here. That**
14   **should do it.**
15   STACY: What are you doing?
16   KEVIN: Getting you some glasses.
17   STACY: Kevin, put those back!
18   KEVIN: *(He does.)* **OK, tell you what, why don't I go down to the**
19   food court and get us some coffee while you make your final
20   decision?
21   STACY: OK.
22   KEVIN: OK. What do you want? A latte, cappuccino, mocha,
23   decaf, flavor of the day, or espresso?
24   STACY: I don't know. What are you getting?
25   KEVIN: I'm getting a large espresso.
26   STACY: OK.
27   KEVIN: OK what?
28   STACY: OK, I'll have a large espresso, too.
29   KEVIN: Great. *(Beginning to leave)*
30   STACY: Wait. Um … make that a large mocha.
31   KEVIN: OK. *(Beginning to leave again)*
32   STACY: On second thought …
33   KEVIN: Would you please decide?!
34   STACY: Latte. *(4 minute mark)*
35   KEVIN: Are you sure?

1   **STACY:** Yes.

2   **KEVIN:** Positive?

3   **STACY:** Yes. No. I'm sorry, I just have trouble making decisions

4   sometimes.

5   **KEVIN:** Sometimes?!

6   **STACY:** I mean, what if I make the wrong choice?

7   **KEVIN:** It's a cup of coffee! How could it possibly matter?

8   **STACY:** But choices do matter. Everything matters.

9   **KEVIN:** Some things in life don't matter. You just decide and move

10   on! Look, I'm gonna go get you a cup of coffee. I'll be back in

11   a few minutes. *(He exits.)*

12   **STACY:** What kind are you gonna get me?

13   **KEVIN:** *(Good-naturedly, as he exits)* I haven't decided yet. But I

14   will when I get there. In four seconds. Oog!

15   **STACY:** *(She looks over all the glasses and says to herself.)* I wish life

16   were simpler. I just wanna make the right decisions, and I'm

17   not always sure what they are ... *(Freeze. Fadeout.)*

18

19

20

21

22

23

24

25

26

27

28

29

30

31

32

33

34

35

So What Do You Do?

Summary: When Roger and Kyle talk about what they do, Roger gets frustrated by Kyle's honest but unusual answers.

Purpose: To show that despite our outward differences, we're all the same on the inside; we all struggle with the same things in life.

Time: 4–5 minutes

Tone: Humorous

Cast: Kyle — A guy who likes to describe his life rather than just say the title of his job (male)
Roger — The man making friendly conversation who just wants to know what Kyle does (male)

Costumes: Casual, contemporary clothes

Props/Set: Suitcases, two airport-style chairs

Themes: Appearances, communication, honesty, life, questions, stereotypes

Text: "So I commend the enjoyment of life, because nothing is better for a man under the sun than to eat and drink and be glad. Then joy will accompany him in his work all the days of the life God has given him under the sun" (Ecclesiastes 8:15).

Notes: Roger and Kyle are strangers who meet in an airport on their way back home to Chicago and start talking about their jobs. But Kyle throws Roger for a loop when he chooses to describe all the things he does in life rather than just give a simple job title.

There is a voiceover at the beginning of the sketch that another actor could do Off-stage, or it could be taped and then played during the drama. Use general stage lighting and two lapel microphones (you will need an additional microphone if you choose to have an Off-stage actor read the voiceover part).

1   *SETTING*: Kyle and Roger are waiting in gate C-12 at an airport. As
2   the drama begins, they find out their plane has been delayed —
3   again. Both are On-stage as the lights come up and the scene
4   begins.
5
6   **VOICE: Maintenance has just informed us that flight nine-seven-**
7   **three-six to Chicago will be delayed. At this time we are**
8   **posting a seven-ten departure ... next Thursday. We're sorry**
9   **for any inconvenience this may have caused those of you who**
10 **have been waiting to fly home ... since yesterday. Please stay**
11 **in the gate area for updated information. Thank you.**
12 **ROGER:** *(Sighing and dramatically dropping his bags on the floor.)*
13 **You going to Chicago?**
14 **KYLE: Trying to. You?**
15 **ROGER: Yeah. I can't believe our flight got delayed again.**
16 *(Sighing again)* **I could have walked home by now.**
17 **KYLE: Yeah. I fly a lot. Finally you just learn that you're either**
18 **gonna get there or you're not. And if you do get there, you're**
19 **either gonna be a *little* late or *very* late. And there's not a**
20 **whole lot you can do about it either way.** *(1 minute mark)*
21 **ROGER: So what do you do?**
22 **KYLE: I tie my shoes.**
23 **ROGER: What?**
24 **KYLE: I tie my shoes.**
25 **ROGER: What are you talking about?**
26 **KYLE: Sometimes I tie my shoes. Right after I put 'em on.**
27 **ROGER: No, I mean, what do you *do*?**
28 **KYLE: Oh, I eat, I sleep, I breathe, sometimes I talk to people.**
29 **ROGER:** *(After a pause, as he lets that sink in)* **You eat, you sleep,**
30 **you breathe, and sometimes you talk to people?**
31 **KYLE: Yeah, yeah, yeah.**
32 **ROGER: Oh.** *(Pause)* **Listen, when I said "What do you do?" I**
33 **meant in your job.**
34 **KYLE: Oh, well, in my job I sit a lot. I order things sometimes. I**
35 **meet with people. We try to solve problems. Sometimes I fix**

1   **stuff. I fax. I e-mail. I drink coffee.** *(2 minute mark)*

2 **ROGER:** Are you a lawyer?

3 **KYLE:** No. Why do you ask?

4 **ROGER:** You gave me an answer that was perfectly correct but

5   totally useless.

6 **KYLE:** Oh.

7 **ROGER:** Look, maybe I'm missing something here, but I still don't

8   really understand what it is you do. I mean, usually when I ask

9   someone what they do, they tell me they're a teacher or a

10   doctor or a consultant or something. And you talk about

11   eating and sleeping and breathing and drinking coffee!

12 **KYLE:** Well, that's the stuff I do.

13 **ROGER:** But when someone asks you what you do, you're

14   supposed to tell me your job title!

15 **KYLE:** Says who?

16 **ROGER:** Says no one! It's just what everyone does.

17 **KYLE:** But what's more accurate?

18 **ROGER:** What do you mean?

19 **KYLE:** Well, a job title — which could mean just about anything

20   — or a list of what I actually do?

21 **ROGER:** Look. OK, I get it. What else do you do? *(3 minute mark)*

22 **KYLE:** I talk to strangers sometimes. I ride in planes. I drive my

23   car. I go places. I watch TV. I mow the lawn and buy groceries

24   and work out a couple times a week.

25 **ROGER:** You're not helping me here! I'm just curious what it is

26   you do!

27 **KYLE:** I help my kids with their homework.

28 **ROGER:** Stop it! I wanna know what you do!

29 **KYLE:** I do. I do help my kids with their homework.

30 **ROGER:** That's not what I meant.

31 **KYLE:** I read some and write some and teach some. I listen to

32   people explain things. I wait in lines and answer the phone and

33   get put on hold.

34 **ROGER:** Listen, buddy. All I wanna know is what you do for a

35   living!

1   **KYLE:** *(Reflectively)* **I pray. I trust some things I don't see, and I**
2   **see some things I don't trust. I get dressed and undressed. I**
3   **kiss my wife. I do things I enjoy, but not as often as I like; and**
4   **I do things I regret, more often than I'd care to admit. I feel**
5   **and love and care and cry, and wish and dream and hope. I**
6   **hurt sometimes and question things a lot and wonder what'll**
7   **happen to my children. So what about you? What do you do?**
8   *(4 minute mark)*
9   **ROGER: Uh, I'm a mechanic.**
10   **KYLE: Oh! What a coincidence. Me too!** *(ROGER looks at the*
11   *audience and shakes his head as the lights fade.)*
12
13
14
15
16
17
18
19
20
21
22
23
24
25
26
27
28
29
30
31
32
33
34
35

Part 2
Contemporary Sketches That Ask the Big Questions

Why doesn't God answer my prayers? Should I stay in this job or do that thing I feel God calling me to do? How can I balance fitting in with standing out? What is it that really makes for a successful life? How should I respond when people challenge my beliefs?

In this section, you'll find hard-hitting dramas that explore and challenge many of modern society's views about the meaning of life, success, and truth. These contemporary sketches will work well for adult or family worship services or conferences.

Fitting In

Summary: Since Bruce became a believer, he has struggled with finding the balance between living out his new faith and connecting with his old friends. Finally, Gary asks him to decide where he stands.

Purpose: To show that even our friends may not understand the changes in our lives when we become believers.

Time: 4–5 minutes

Tone: Serious

Cast: Bruce — A new Christian whose life and priorities are changing (male)
Gary — His friend who doesn't understand what's happening to him (male)

Costumes: Appropriate business attire (This scene happens at the office)

Themes: Assumptions, choices, evangelism, frustrations, integrity, listening, misconceptions about Christianity, new life, priorities, relationships, stereotypes, witnessing, work

Text: "Of course, your former friends are very surprised when you no longer join them in the wicked things they do, and they say evil things about you. But just remember that they will have to face God, who will judge everyone, both the living and the dead" (1 Peter 4:4–5, NLT).

Notes: Gary and Bruce are friends that have drifted apart ever since Bruce became a believer and shifted his priorities. Bruce isn't judging his old friends, he just doesn't really fit in anymore. Gary has some pent-up feelings that he lets out as their conversation gets more and more personal. Use general stage lighting and two lapel microphones. You may wish to use background sounds of an office setting.

1 **SETTING**: An office complex, late in the afternoon. Bruce is On-stage
2 and working at his laptop computer when the lights come up.
3 Then Gary enters and the scene begins.
4
5 GARY: Hey, Bruce!
6 BRUCE: *(Looking up from his computer)* Hey, Gary. Good to see
7 you.
8 GARY: You still working on that Bickman deal?
9 BRUCE: Yeah, it's been like three months now. But we're finally
10 making progress. I've got four other people assigned to this
11 project with me.
12 GARY: Yeah, I heard. Your team is doing good work.
13 BRUCE: Thanks.
14 GARY: *(After a pause)* Listen, I haven't seen much of you in the last
15 couple months.
16 BRUCE: Well, I've been up to my neck here at work, and then at
17 night ... well, I guess I've just been spending more time with
18 my kids.
19 GARY: That's nice ... I'll bet you could use a break. Hey, I've got
20 an idea — a bunch of us are getting together after work
21 tonight. You wanna join us?
22 BRUCE: Um, yeah. That'd be great. I'd like that.
23 GARY: Great. We're meeting at O'Callahan's *(Or another popular*
24 *sports bar)* at seven o'clock. Maybe play some pool, grab a
25 couple of drinks before the game comes on. They've got this
26 wide-screen TV — really state-of-the-art stuff. We always
27 hang out there on Thursdays. *(1 minute mark)*
28 BRUCE: *(Remembering)* Thursday? Is today Thursday? Oh, man.
29 I was thinking it was Wednesday. I've got this small group
30 Bible study tonight. I won't be able to make it after all.
31 GARY: You're kidding. Right?
32 BRUCE: Naw. I've been meeting with these people from my church
33 every Thursday night. It's like they say at my church,
34 *(Imitating an announcer)* "Small groups are big at Grace
35 Fellowship Church!" *(Or insert the name of your church. GARY*

1   *is silent.)* **Small groups are big** ... *(GARY is still silent.)* **It's**
2   **kind of a joke.**
3   **GARY: Uh-huh.**
4   **BRUCE: Some people laugh.**
5   **GARY: Yeah, well, I don't get it.**
6   **BRUCE: I can see.**
7   **GARY: No, I get your joke. I just don't get you.**
8   **BRUCE: What do you mean?**
9   **GARY: You'd rather hang out with a bunch of people you just met**
10   **at some church than the guys you've been friends with for**
11   **eight years!?**
12   **BRUCE: It's not that, it's just —**
13   **GARY: Hey, I got nothing against you and this whole religion**
14   **thing. I mean, whatever works for you.**
15   **BRUCE: It's not about religion, it's —** *(2 minute mark)*
16   **GARY: Your church then. Whatever. I don't care. I mean, you've**
17   **found God. Good for you. I'm glad and all that. But you've**
18   **changed and you're not the same guy anymore.**
19   **BRUCE: What do you mean?**
20   **GARY: We went to grad school together, Bruce. You and me!**
21   **You're the one who showed me around town. You're the one**
22   **who introduced me to Angie and took me to O'Callahan's the**
23   **first time. I mean, don't you even remember those days? We**
24   **had some good times.**
25   **BRUCE: Yeah, I remember.**
26   **GARY: Well, I'm not saying you gotta be wild or a party animal or**
27   **anything — but you're so into your new church and not doing**
28   **anything wrong or giving the wrong impression or whatever.**
29   *(Pause)* **People around here are sick of it.**
30   **BRUCE: What are you talking about?**
31   **GARY: You think you're better than us! It's like you look down on**
32   **people who aren't into church. Like you're judging everyone.**
33   **BRUCE: No, I'm not ... I —** *(3 minute mark)*
34   **GARY: Yes, you are. I mean, last spring — what was the deal with**
35   **refusing to help me move? At first you were all like, "No**

1   problem, man! I'll be there," and then you backed out on me
2   at the last minute!
3   BRUCE: You were moving in with your girlfriend! It just surprised
4   me, and I wasn't sure what to do, because I don't think it's
5   right for you two to be —
6   GARY: See? There you go again! Trying to prove you're better
7   than everyone. Trying to shove your religion down our
8   throats!
9   BRUCE: It's not like that! Maybe I should have helped you
10   move — I don't know. But I'm just trying to do what's right,
11   you know. Trying to honor God.
12   GARY: No, I don't know. But I do know what it's like to watch
13   your friend get brainwashed by a bunch of religious fanatics.
14   I do know what it's like to see someone you used to be friends
15   with turn into an intolerant bigot. That I know. 'Cause I've
16   seen that first hand.
17   BRUCE: That's not fair.
18   GARY: Listen, you've got your God and your church and your
19   small group Bible time. Good for you. I really don't care. But
20   you've changed, man, and it's not for the better. Good-bye ...
21   I guess your old friends just aren't good enough for you
22   anymore. *(4 minute mark)*
23   BRUCE: It's not like that, Gary —
24   GARY: *(Coldly, as he exits)* Really? It sure seems like it to me.
25   *(Frustrated at himself, BRUCE pounds his desk with his fist.*
26   *Fadeout.)*
27
28
29
30
31
32
33
34
35

Twilight

Summary: Dale and Jena are enjoying a relaxing evening watching the sunset. As they do, they begin to reflect on how quickly life passes by, and to rethink their views of success.

Purpose: To inspire people to think about life from an eternal perspective.

Time: 5–6 minutes

Tone: Humorous at first, then serious and thought-provoking

Cast: Dale — A guy who begins questioning the direction of his life (male)
Jena — His wife, who wants to enjoy the moment and not worry about deep philosophical issues (female)

Costumes: It's evening, and Dale and Jena are relaxing together on a romantic twilight walk. They could be returning from a fancy dinner, or they could be dressed casually, for a walk by the lake.

Props/Set: A park bench and an hourglass on a small stand or table

Themes: Ambition, appearances, choices, consumerism, dating, death, eternity, family issues, life, love, married life, meaning, priorities, purpose, questions, regrets, relationships, success

Text: "Yet when I surveyed all that my hands had done and what I had toiled to achieve, everything was meaningless, a chasing after the wind; nothing was gained under the sun" (Ecclesiastes 2:11).

Notes: At the beginning, have fun with the exchange in which Dale can't remember first meeting Jena. Jena needs to keep the scene lighthearted and not accusatory in her responses to him. Build their blocking and movement around the park bench. The "lake" is situated in the audience, so they're watching the sun set over the heads of those in attendance.

The characters in this drama have been married for seven to

ten years. They've had a good life. But as they think back on where they've been and what they've done, they wonder about the meaning and significance of it all.

Use general stage lighting and two lapel microphones. If available, place a tight spotlight on the stand with the hourglass. Consider having sound effects of crickets chirping, or waves slowly washing ashore. Dim the house lights to create the dusk-like mood.

1   *SETTING*: A local beach at sunset. Dale and Jena are enjoying a
2   romantic walk along the shore, reminiscing about their lives
3   together. They enter the stage together as the lights come up. Dale
4   takes the hourglass and turns it upside-down. Then, after a pause,
5   they begin their conversation.
6
7   **JENA: Oh, Dale, I love watching the sun set. I wish I could just**
8   **hold onto this moment forever ...** *(Snuggling close)* **Oh, honey,**
9   **remember when we first met?**
10   **DALE: Yeah. It was that beautiful moonlit night in the spring.**
11   **JENA: No, it wasn't. We met in the winter at that ski lodge.**
12   **Remember?**
13   **DALE: Oh yeah, yeah. I remember. It snowed so bad that weekend**
14   **we hardly made it out of the hot tub.**
15   **JENA: It didn't snow at all that weekend. It was clear and sunny**
16   **the whole time.**
17   **DALE: Oh yeah. Right. How could I forget?**
18   **JENA: Remember where we went to eat that Saturday night?**
19   **DALE: Sure.**
20   **JENA: Where?**
21   **DALE: Don't you remember?**
22   **JENA: Of course I remember. I'm just seeing if you do.**
23   **DALE: Oh.**
24   **JENA: So?** *(1 minute mark)*
25   **DALE:** *(Awkwardly)* **Well ... um, it was at that one place with the**
26   **... um ... well, you know ... the ... the great atmosphere, and**
27   **the food. They served good um ... look at that sunset! That is**
28   **an amazing —**
29   **JENA: You don't remember, do you?**
30   **DALE: Italian?**
31   **JENA: Mexican.**
32   **DALE: Fajitas?**
33   **JENA: Chicken quesadillas. I can't believe you don't remember!**
34   **DALE: I guess I just remember different stuff than you do.**
35   **JENA: Like what?**

1   DALE: Well, like the first time we went car shopping together and
2   we test drove that Porsche 911 Carrera with the all-leather
3   interior seats even though we knew we couldn't afford it ...
4   Remember that?
5   JENA: Was that the gray car with the ugly tires?
6   DALE: Ugly tires?! A sixty-thousand-dollar car does not have ugly
7   tires!
8   JENA: I'm sorry, they were ugly.
9   DALE: Sleek. Streamlined. Aerodynamic. State-of-the-art!
10   JENA: Ugly. *(2 minute mark)*
11   DALE: And I remember fixing our plumbing in the first house we
12   bought up there in Minnesota when it was like seventy degrees
13   below zero outside ...
14   JENA: I think I remember that.
15   DALE: ... Our wedding day.
16   JENA: *(Sweetly)* You remember our wedding day.
17   DALE: I remember our wedding night.
18   JENA: *(Rolling her eyes)* Oh, Dale, we've had a good life together.
19   DALE: Yeah, we have.
20   JENA: I'd say we've done pretty well, too.
21   DALE: What do you mean?
22   JENA: *(Slowly, thoughtfully)* Well, you, know. We have a nice house,
23   our kids are turning out all right. You have a good job, we've
24   done well financially ...
25   DALE: We're comfortable.
26   JENA: Yeah. *(They sit on the park bench.)*
27   DALE: It's funny what stuff you end up remembering. When I was
28   a kid, this was my favorite time of day.
29   JENA: Why is that?
30   DALE: Oh, we used to play this game in my neighborhood —
31   shadow tag. Where you had to run around and try to step on
32   someone else's shadow. That's how you tagged them.
33   JENA: What happened if you tagged them? *(3 minute mark)*
34   DALE: Then they chased you.
35   JENA: Oh.

1   DALE: *(Thoughtfully)* That's all it was. Just chasing someone or
2   being chased. Running around in circles as the sun set.
3   JENA: When I was a kid, I never thought I'd grow old. I had these
4   little doll houses and mama dolls and baby dolls and daddy
5   dolls.
6   DALE: — I haven't thought about that in a long time —
7   JENA: — I'd dress 'em all up and play pretend. It seemed like I'd
8   be young forever —
9   DALE: — I really miss those days —
10   JENA: — Like my childhood would never end —
11   DALE: — Chasing shadows in the twilight ...
12   JENA: It's too bad we can't hold onto the sunset. Or make this
13   moment last forever.
14   DALE: *(Lost in thought)* Always chasing shadows ...
15   JENA: Huh?
16   DALE: Oh, I was just thinking out loud. *(After a pause)* So, is that
17   what it means to be successful?
18   JENA: Is *what* what it means to be successful?
19   DALE: Being comfortable. Earning money. Is that what it's all
20   about?
21   JENA: Well, no.
22   DALE: Then what?
23   JENA: I don't know. *(4 minute mark)*
24   DALE: Isn't that what we've been living for all these years? What
25   we've worked toward?
26   JENA: Dale, you're getting all philosophical on me.
27   DALE: Chasing shadows ...
28   JENA: What are you talking about?
29   DALE: Just thinking. I mean, what is it that makes for a successful
30   life? A house, a job, kids?
31   JENA: Partly.
32   DALE: Good memories?
33   JENA: There's more to it than that.
34   DALE: Then what?
35   JENA: I don't know. Maybe being nice or something.

1   **DALE: Is that success? Being nice?**

2   **JENA: You're thinking about all this too much. Just enjoy the**

3   **moment before it passes.**

4   **DALE: Before the night comes?**

5   **JENA: Right.**

6   **DALE: Because you can't hold onto the sunset?**

7   **JENA: That's right.**

8   **DALE: Well, maybe that's part of the answer, but there's gotta be**

9   **more ...**

10   **JENA: Maybe. Quiet now. Just hold me. The night's almost here.**

11   *(5 minute mark. As they freeze and the scene ends, the lights on*

12   *the two actors fadeout, but a spotlight remains on the hourglass.*

13   *Then it, too, finally fades, until all that is heard is the water*

14   *washing ashore and the faint sound of crickets. Fadeout.)*

15

16

17

18

19

20

21

22

23

24

25

26

27

28

29

30

31

32

33

34

35

How Are You Today?

Summary: When Rusty and Matt start telling each other the truth, they begin to wonder how honesty would change their lives.

Purpose: To encourage people to be open and honest in their relationships.

Time: 5–6 minutes

Tone: Humorous

Cast: Rusty — A normal guy who realizes he's not being honest with people (male)
Matt — His friend who realizes he does the same thing (male)

Costumes: Rusty and Matt are in a locker room, getting dressed after working out. They're putting on their shoes, ties, watches, etc.

Props/Set: A long bench, gym bags, a cell phone

Themes: Appearances, authenticity, communication, complaints, hiding, honesty, life, truth

Text: "Do not lie to each other, since you have taken off your old self with its practices and have put on the new self, which is being renewed in knowledge in the image of its Creator" (Colossians 3:9–10); and "An honest answer is like a kiss on the lips" (Proverbs 24:26).

Notes: The characters in this drama are in their thirties. They're friends who haven't run into each other for a while. At the beginning, they're just going through the motions of life, but as the sketch goes on, they get more and more animated and personable. Use general stage lighting and two lapel microphones.

1 *SETTING*: The locker room at the local fitness center. Rusty and Matt
2   have just finished working out. They're both On-stage, putting on
3   their shoes, etc., when the lights come up and the scene begins.
4
5 RUSTY: So, Matt, 'til today I never knew you worked out here —
6 MATT: Oh, yeah, yeah, yeah, yeah. I try to come in a couple times
7   a week to keep the old spare tire *(Grabbing his stomach)* from
8   becoming a monster truck.
9 RUSTY: I hear ya. So, how are you doing these days?
10 MATT: Oh, good, good, good. How about you?
11 RUSTY: Good, good, good.
12 MATT: Good.
13 RUSTY: Good. *(After a pause)* You know, actually, I've been better.
14   I have a lot on my mind this week, a big project at work, and
15   I'm pretty tired from doing that treadmill.
16 MATT: Well, why did you say you're good?
17 RUSTY: I don't know. I always say I'm good.
18 MATT: Even when you're not good?
19 RUSTY: Yeah.
20 MATT: That's not good.
21 RUSTY: Nope. *(After a pause)* So are *you* good? *(1 minute mark)*
22 MATT: No, not really.
23 RUSTY: Why'd you say you're good?
24 MATT: I don't know. I always say I'm good.
25 RUSTY: Even when you're not good?
26 MATT: Yeah.
27 RUSTY: That's not good.
28 MATT: Nope. That's bad. I wonder why we never say we're doing
29   bad?
30 RUSTY: Maybe because sometimes when you say "bad," you mean
31   "really good," like when someone says, *(Saying it really cool)*
32   "that's bad!"
33 MATT: So bad is good?
34 RUSTY: Yeah.
35 MATT: And good is bad?

1   RUSTY: Right.
2   MATT: So when you say, *(Saying it really cool)* "I'm bad," that's
3   good.
4   RUSTY: Right.
5   MATT: But if you say, *(Saying it dull and unemotional)* "I'm good,"
6   that's not so good.
7   RUSTY: No.
8   MATT: In fact, it's bad.
9   RUSTY: Right.
10 MATT: But it's not as bad as if it were bad as it is when bad means
11   good?
12 RUSTY: Right.
13 MATT: *(Saying it really cool again)* That's *bad.*
14 RUSTY: You could say that again.
15 MATT: No, I don't think I could. *(After a pause)* The thing is,
16   though, no matter how I'm feeling — whether it's awesome or
17   lousy — I just say I'm good. It's weird. I never thought about
18   it before. *(2 minute mark)*
19 RUSTY: Hmmm. I wonder why that is.
20 MATT: I don't know. I guess it never came up.
21 RUSTY: No, I mean, I wonder why we don't tell each other the
22   truth about how we're doing.
23 MATT: Hmmm. I don't know.
24 RUSTY: I wonder what the world would be like if we were actually
25   honest with each other and told each other how we really feel.
26 MATT: I don't know. Let's find out. *(Backing up and approaching*
27   *RUSTY again)* Hey, Rusty, how are you doing?
28 RUSTY: Pretty rotten ... How about you?
29 MATT: Life stinks. I'm bald, overweight, overworked, and I wish
30   I had more money! Hey, this is fun!
31 RUSTY: Yeah, try me again!
32 MATT: OK. How are you doing, today?
33 RUSTY: My boss is breathing down my neck, my computer
34   crashes so much I have to wear a seatbelt just to surf the
35   Internet, and my truck is falling apart.

1   MATT: My car is falling apart.

2   RUSTY: My life is falling apart!

3   MATT: So is mine!

4   RUSTY: Me too!

5   MATT: All right!

6   RUSTY: Right on!

7   MATT: Awesome! *(They slap each other a high five.)* **Hey, do me**

8   **again! Do me again!** *(3 minute mark)*

9   RUSTY: OK, hey, Matt! How are you doing today?

10   MATT: I'm good except my wife is always complaining about the

11   toilet seat.

12   RUSTY: Oh, I hate that.

13   MATT: Yeah, why is it our job to put the seat down? Why isn't it

14   their job to put the seat up!

15   RUSTY: Good point!

16   MATT: And she asks me questions that are impossible to answer.

17   Like she comes up to me and asks me if she looks fat. What am

18   I supposed to say to that?!

19   RUSTY: Ask me again! Me! Me! Me!

20   MATT: OK. How are you doing, Rusty?

21   RUSTY: Stuff bugs me! Like when you walk up to a restaurant and

22   they have two doors and one of them is always locked, but

23   that's the one you try to open. Why don't they just unlock

24   both doors?!

25   MATT: That's a good one!

26   RUSTY: *(Getting into it, using his cell phone as a microphone and*

27   *acting like a stand-up comedian)* **And stupid signs annoy me. I**

28   **saw this highway sign; it said "Fine for littering," so I tossed**

29   **some garbage out the window.**

30   MATT: *(Pretending to do one of those drum beats sidekicks play for*

31   *comedians)* **Ba-da, bing!** *(4 minute mark)*

32   RUSTY: Yeah, and then I saw this sign; it said, "No parking.

33   Emergency Vehicles Only," so I'm thinking, I guess I can park

34   here then!

35   MATT: Ba-da, bing!

1   RUSTY: Then I saw this other sign by the highway with these
2   lights all around it. It said, "Construction workers present
3   when flashing." And I'm thinking, buddy, that's the last thing
4   I wanna see!
5   MATT: Ooh.
6   RUSTY: Yeah.
7   MATT: Not a pretty sight.
8   RUSTY: Nope ...
9   MATT: *(Laughing)* We are definitely in need of some counseling,
10   Rusty.
11 RUSTY: You could say that again.
12 MATT: How come we have so much trouble telling each other the
13   truth?
14 RUSTY: Who knows? Maybe we're afraid of what people will
15   think. Or scared to be vulnerable in front of 'em. It's a way of
16   hiding from each other.
17 MATT: Ooh, you're getting deep on me here.
18 RUSTY: You know what? I'm gonna be honest with people today.
19   I'm gonna tell them what I really think and how I'm really
20   doing — good or bad.
21 MATT: You know, I will too. I wonder what the world would be
22   like if we were actually honest with each other all the time. *(5*
23   *minute mark)*
24 RUSTY: Hey, look, here comes someone. *(Turning to the audience)*
25   Hey, you ... You there ... How are you doing today? *(They*
26   *freeze. Fadeout.)*
27
28
29
30
31
32
33
34
35

Saying Good-bye

Summary: When Scott drops his daughter off at college, they finally talk about some issues they've both been avoiding.

Purpose: To show that we have different ways of avoiding dealing with grief.

Time: 4–5 minutes

Tone: Serious and heartwarming

Cast: Scott — A caring yet workaholic father who has lost his wife and is now hesitant to say good-bye to his daughter (male)
Ariel — His once-wayward daughter who has been afraid to face the fact of her mother's death (female)

Costumes: Ariel is dressed like a typical college freshman. Scott is dressed like her father. They've been sitting in the car for a couple of hours.

Props/Set: Luggage, perhaps a bookshelf or a dresser to signify the inside of a dorm room.

Themes: Communication, death, family issues, forgiveness, grief and loss, hiding, honesty, life, love, parenting, relationships

Text: "Though he brings grief, he will show compassion, so great is his unfailing love. For he does not willingly bring affliction or grief to the children of men" (Lamentations 3:32–33) or "Cast all your anxiety on him because he cares for you" (1 Peter 5:7).

Notes: Grief is a real part of living in a fallen world. God is the God of all comfort, and he will be there to help us through the tough times, but we have to face our problems, rather than hide from them. This sketch has a delicate transition from saying good-bye on a college campus to talking about grief and loss. (Another way of saying good-bye.) Use general stage lighting and two lapel microphones.

1   *SETTING*: Ariel is in her new dorm room at college. Scott, her father,
2   is bringing in the last load of stuff from the car. There are
3   suitcases scattered around the room. She is On-stage as the lights
4   come up. Then Scott enters and the scene begins.
5

6   **SCOTT:** *(Grunting as he carries an armload of heavy luggage)*
7   **Where do you want these suitcases?**
8   **ARIEL: Um, over there is good —**
9   **SCOTT:** *(Setting the bags down)* **What do you have in these things,**
10   **bricks?**
11   **ARIEL: Just my books.** *(Rummaging through her bag)* **Oh, no! I**
12   **forgot my camera in the car.**
13   **SCOTT: Oh, I'll go back and get it.**
14   **ARIEL: No, don't worry, Dad. It's OK. I'll just pick it up when I**
15   **come home next month.**
16   **SCOTT: Are you sure?**
17   **ARIEL: Yeah. Positive. It's OK.**
18   **SCOTT:** *(After a pause)* **So, is that it then?**
19   **ARIEL: That's it. That's all my stuff.**
20   **SCOTT: You got all those financial aid forms?**
21   **ARIEL: Yeah.**
22   **SCOTT: And your schedule and everything?**
23   **ARIEL: I'm all set, Dad.**
24   **SCOTT:** *(Looking around)* **Boy, these dorms sure have changed a lot**
25   **since I went to school here.**
26   **ARIEL: They're not called dorms anymore, Dad. They're called**
27   **residence halls.**
28   **SCOTT: Oh. Residence halls, right …** *(1 minute mark)*
29   **ARIEL: Yeah.**
30   **SCOTT: Well, why don't they call 'em dorms anymore?**
31   **ARIEL: Well, "dorm" means sleeping — like a dormitory animal.**
32   **And we do more than sleep here. It's like the center of student**
33   **life.**
34   **SCOTT: Oh. I see. Where'd you hear all that from?**
35   **ARIEL:** *(Answering as she begins to unpack)* **My R.A. told me.**

1   SCOTT: R.A.?

2   ARIEL: Resident Assistant.

3   SCOTT: Oh. Right ... So some of these residence halls are coed

4   these days, aren't they? Like one floor for the guys and one for

5   the girls?

6   ARIEL: Dad, half the rooms are coed.

7   SCOTT: Oh, I get ya. Right. Wow. A lot has changed.

8   ARIEL: Yeah.

9   SCOTT: Your mother wouldn't have been very happy hearing

10   about that.

11   ARIEL: I know, Dad. Don't worry. I'll be fine.

12   SCOTT: Yeah.

13   ARIEL: Yeah. Look, I need to get unpacked and take a shower so

14   I can get ready for this opening banquet-thing tonight. *(2*

15   *minute mark)*

16   SCOTT: OK. I guess it's, um ... time to go, then.

17   ARIEL: Yeah, I'll be fine.

18   SCOTT: Yeah.

19   ARIEL: Thanks for driving me.

20   SCOTT: Sure... Are you sure you don't want me to take you out to

21   eat or anything?

22   ARIEL: Dad, we ate at McDonald's on the way up here.

23   SCOTT: I know, but it's almost dinner time.

24   ARIEL: It's three thirty in the afternoon.

25   SCOTT: Oh. I guess it just seems later.

26   ARIEL: Yeah.

27   SCOTT: *(Reaching for his wallet)* Got enough money?

28   ARIEL: I'm all set.

29   SCOTT: So this is it then?

30   ARIEL: Dad, I'm only going to college. It's not like I'm gonna be

31   gone forever.

32   SCOTT: Yeah. Time to make a fresh start.

33   ARIEL: I guess so.

34   SCOTT: I'm really proud of you, Ariel. You've worked hard for

35   this. It's too bad your mom couldn't be here to see you today.

1   ARIEL: Yeah.
2   ARIEL and SCOTT: *(They deliver these lines at the same time:*
3   *SCOTT says, "Ariel, I" and ARIEL says, "Dad, I.")*
4   ARIEL: You go first.
5   SCOTT: No, you. *(3 minute mark)*
6   ARIEL: OK. There's something I want to talk about.
7   SCOTT: What's that?
8   ARIEL: *(After a pause)* Well, we've never really talked about mom
9   dying.
10 SCOTT: I know.
11 ARIEL: I miss her.
12 SCOTT: Me too.
13 ARIEL: It was tough for you, wasn't it?
14 SCOTT: Yeah.
15 ARIEL: Is that why you worked so much the last two years?
16 SCOTT: Ariel, maybe this isn't the right time.
17 ARIEL: Dad, it's never been the right time.
18 SCOTT: Ariel —
19 ARIEL: Please, Dad.
20 SCOTT: OK, yeah. I guess that's why I worked so much.
21 ARIEL: And I didn't make it any easier, did I?
22 SCOTT: Oh, you were a good daughter.
23 ARIEL: No, I wasn't. We both know that. Not like I could've been.
24 SCOTT: People deal with grief in different ways.
25 ARIEL: I know I let you down. I know there were times ...
26   *(4 minute mark)*
27 SCOTT: *(Slowly)* Yeah. There were times.
28 ARIEL: I'm sorry, Dad. It just hurt so bad when Mom died.
29 SCOTT: I know.
30 ARIEL: It was like there was this huge hole in my life, and I didn't
31   know how to fill it, and I tried all kinds of things. I never got
32   to say good-bye. I didn't know what to do.
33 SCOTT: Me neither.
34 ARIEL: *(After a pause)* Um, Dad, maybe I could use some help
35   unpacking after all.

1   **SCOTT:**   Yeah.

2   **ARIEL:**   And that banquet's not really that big of a deal. We could

3   do dinner, later if you want …

4   **SCOTT:**   Yeah. That'd be nice. That'd be nice. *(He reaches out and*

5   *takes her hand as the lights fade.)*

6

7

8

9

10

11

12

13

14

15

16

17

18

19

20

21

22

23

24

25

26

27

28

29

30

31

32

33

34

35

The Answering Machine

Summary: When Mason asks Terry why God allows suffering, he realizes it's not as easy to answer him as he thought it would be.

Purpose: To encourage people to dig more deeply into the scriptural answers to the problem of pain.

Time: 6–7 minutes

Tone: Serious and thought-provoking

Cast: Terry — A Christian who thinks he knows all the answers (male)
Mason — The maintenance guy who has some serious questions (male)

Costumes: Mason is wearing custodian clothes, or a blue-collar-type outfit. Terry is dressed for work at the office.

Props/Set: A desk with a phone, an answering machine, a computer monitor, papers and other desk paraphernalia, a toolbox

Themes: Apologetics, assumptions, church issues, communication, evangelism, faith, God's existence, God's sovereignty, listening, questions, suffering, truth

Text: "Always be prepared to give an answer to everyone who asks you to give the reason for the hope that you have. But do this with gentleness and respect" (1 Peter 3:15b).

Notes: Mason is curious, rather than argumentative, about why there is so much suffering in the world. Terry is a little overconfident at the beginning of the sketch, as he just repeats arguments he has heard before. As Mason responds with reasonable objections, Terry gets more and more defensive. The pace of this drama is a little slow and reflective. Be sure your actors let the arguments and their implications sink in before continuing the dialog.

When dealing with the problem of pain, we need to honestly acknowledge the questions rather than dance around the issue with easy answers. Make sure your pastor or speaker addresses the questions brought up in this sketch so that the listeners don't leave feeling like God really is uncaring or evil. Use general stage lighting and two lapel microphones.

1   *SETTING*: Terry's office. Terry is On-stage, working at his desk when
2   the lights come up. Then Mason enters and the scene begins.
3
4   MASON: *(Pretending to push open or knock at TERRY's office door)*
5   Hello?
6   TERRY: Yeah?
7   MASON: Maintenance sent me up —
8   TERRY: Oh, great. Yeah. C'mon in.
9   MASON: OK.
10   TERRY: Thanks for coming. I don't know what's wrong with this
11   answering machine/voice mail thing, but it's always got a busy
12   signal. It's really frustrating. I'm trying to program a new
13   message in there, but it seems like it's stuck or something —
14   MASON: Well, let me take a look at that. *(He begins tinkering with*
15   *the machine.)*
16   TERRY: So, are you new on staff? I don't think I've seen you
17   around here before.
18   MASON: Oh, pretty new. A couple months, anyhow.
19   TERRY: New to the area?
20   MASON: Yeah.
21   TERRY: Getting settled in then?
22   MASON: Pretty much, yeah.
23   TERRY: *(After a pause)* Say, we have this class at my church to
24   welcome newcomers to the area. It might be helpful ... *(1*
25   *minute mark)*
26   MASON: Um, no thanks.
27   TERRY: Maybe, I mean, if you ever decide to. You'd be welcome
28   to join us sometime, just to check it out.
29   MASON: Really, thanks, but no thanks.
30   TERRY: OK ...
31   MASON: I'm not too into church.
32   TERRY: Why's that?
33   MASON: Well, I have a hard time believing in God, to tell you the
34   truth. Sometimes I wish I did, but I just don't.
35   TERRY: Really? Why not?

1 MASON: *(Stops working for a moment and looks up at TERRY.)* **I used**
2   **to. As a kid. But when I was in college, my sister was hit by a**
3   **drunk driver. Just a random thing. No sense to it. The guy**
4   **walked.**
5 TERRY: **Oh. I'm sorry.**
6 MASON: **Yeah, well, when she was in a coma, I prayed. I prayed a**
7   **lot. But it was like I just couldn't get through. And God never**
8   **got back to me. She died a week later. And since then, I've**
9   **never been able to understand how a good God could have let**
10   **that happen. That, or any of the suffering in the world.** *(Going*
11   *back to work. 2 minute mark)*
12 TERRY: **Oh, well, um. God lets us suffer because he lets us have**
13   **free will —**
14 MASON: **Look, no offense, but I've talked to people about this**
15   **stuff before. I'm not sure I wanna get into it —**
16 TERRY: **Just bear with me. You wouldn't want to be a robot,**
17   **would you?**
18 MASON: *(Sighing)* **'Course not.**
19 TERRY: **So God lets us make choices, and with free will comes the**
20   **possibility of suffering. The payoffs outweigh the benefits.**
21 MASON: **Maybe. But, in that case, it seems like God isn't as caring**
22   **as I am. I mean, if I had the power to stop that drunk driver,**
23   **I would have. Wouldn't you?**
24 TERRY: **Um, I don't know. I guess so …**
25 MASON: **Or if my daughter was gonna kill herself, I'd do anything**
26   **to stop her. But God lets people commit suicide every day.**
27   **Right?**
28 TERRY: **Um, yeah.**
29 MASON: **And I don't let my son take a bath by himself or run into**
30   **the street to get his ball. I put limits on his freedom. That's**
31   **what a loving parent does.** *(3 minute mark)*
32 TERRY: **Well, God *is* a loving parent. He's more loving than even**
33   **the best parent is.**
34 MASON: **Well, then what about the limits on freedom that love**
35   **demands? Why doesn't God set those?**

1   TERRY: What do you mean?

2   MASON: I mean, it seems like a loving God would do more to stop

3   suffering. Even if freedom is important, total freedom doesn't

4   show love. It shows you don't really care. If I didn't set any

5   limits for my children, I'd be arrested for neglect. Total

6   freedom isn't love, it's apathy.

7   TERRY: *(Stunned by the force of the argument)* Um. Well, suffering

8   provides people a chance to reflect on what's really important

9   in life. It's the way God gets our attention —

10   MASON: Well, if I want to get someone's attention, I can think of

11   better ways than killing 'em off by drunk drivers. Can't you?

12   TERRY: I guess so … Wait a minute. Your sister's death wasn't

13   God's fault. *(4 minute mark)*

14   MASON: But he allowed it, and he could have stopped it. What's

15   the difference? And besides, aren't there better ways to get

16   someone's attention than car accidents, crib death, or

17   Alzheimer's?

18   TERRY: I guess so.

19   MASON: What about rape or torture? Isn't there a better way to

20   wake people up than allowing that stuff?

21   TERRY: Well, God could stop the suffering —

22   MASON: Then, with all due respect, I wish he would.

23   TERRY: *(Getting frustrated)* God is able to turn bad things into

24   good ones. It's just that we don't see the whole plan yet. We

25   can't see the big picture, so we don't understand how it all

26   works together.

27   MASON: Yeah, I've heard that before, too. But if the only way God

28   can grow something good is from something bad, then he

29   really isn't very powerful, is he?

30   TERRY: *(Getting defensive)* Well, he can grow good things from

31   good things, too. It's just that sometimes he does it from bad

32   things.

33   MASON: OK, maybe. But if I had the power to either grow good

34   from good or good from bad, I'd always choose to grow good

35   from the good and just wipe out the bad altogether. I mean,

1   doesn't that seem like the more loving response? *(5 minute*
2   *mark)*
3   TERRY: Are you saying God's not loving?!
4   MASON: I'm not trying to argue. You're the one who brought all
5   this up. I'm just here to fix your phone.
6   TERRY: Um ... I'm sorry.
7   MASON: Haven't you ever really thought about this stuff for
8   yourself? Haven't you ever questioned it all?
9   TERRY: I guess not. I just sorta believed —
10   MASON: Well, I wish I could just believe it all like you. It sure
11   would make life easier. But when you've been hurt like I've
12   been hurt, you can't help but ask the questions. Don't you ask
13   the questions?
14   TERRY: I guess not.
15   MASON: I just can't get past all the suffering in the world. Why
16   would a loving God let it all happen?
17   TERRY: I thought I knew, but maybe I don't —
18   MASON: *(Finishing up on the machine)* Well, me either ... Well,
19   that should do it. I think your machine will stop repeating
20   itself and take in new information now. *(They shake hands.)*
21   TERRY: OK, thanks. Sorry I got upset, there. *(6 minute mark)*
22   MASON: Hey, it's all right. Let me know if you figure it all out
23   someday. I'd be glad to hear what you have to say.
24   TERRY: OK. See you later. *(MASON exits, TERRY sits down, stares*
25   *at the phone that MASON just fixed, rests his chin on his fist to*
26   *think, and freezes. Fadeout.)*
27
28
29
30
31
32
33
34
35

Deaccumulating

Summary: Becky and Randy decide to simplify their lives, but they soon find out that saying good-bye to their current lifestyle is harder than they thought.

Purpose: To motivate people to live a simpler and more satisfying life.

Time: 6–7 minutes

Tone: Humorous and thought-provoking

Cast: Becky — A lady who is trying to simplify her life (female)
Randy — Her husband who would rather keep things the way they are (male)

Costumes: They're both dressed casually. It's a Saturday afternoon, and Randy has just been to Tool-Mart. Becky is at home, lounging about the house and reading a book.

Props/Set: A large plastic bag, a large set of ratchets, a book, a recliner

Themes: Addictions, ambition, appearances, choices, Christmas, consumerism, distractions, married life, modern life, priorities, rest, simplicity

Text: "Keep your lives free from the love of money and be content with what you have, because God has said, 'Never will I leave you; never will I forsake you'" (Hebrews 13:5).

Notes: Becky is in the living room reading a book when Randy comes home from the hardware store. He has just bought a new set of ratchets and wants to show them off to her. She wants to talk with him about simplifying their lives, but he just wants to go and play with his new ratchets. Use general stage lighting and two lapel microphones.

1   *SETTING*: Becky and Randy's living room on a Saturday afternoon.

2   Becky is On-stage, seated in the chair reading when the lights come

3   up. Then Randy enters carrying the ratchets and the scene begins.

4

5   **RANDY: Hey, honey, look at this! I just got back from Tool-Mart.**

6   **Check it out — an entire set of one hundred forty-four**

7   **matching ratchets for only $179.95, plus tax.**

8   **BECKY: You just spent a hundred and eighty dollars on some**

9   **ratchets?**

10   **RANDY: Not just any ratchets. Matching ratchets. I'll never be**

11   **without the right-sized ratchet again! And besides, they come**

12   **with a lifetime warranty!**

13   **BECKY: Why do you need a lifetime warranty on ratchets?**

14   **RANDY: In case I ever break one for any reason, they'll replace**

15   **it — no questions asked!**

16   **BECKY: But dear, how could you break a ratchet when you never**

17   **use your tools? You never even go into your workshop!**

18   **RANDY:** *(Walking over to her and getting tender)* **That's because I**

19   **didn't have the right tools. And besides, I got these for you.** *(1*

20   *minute mark)*

21   **BECKY: Oh. Really. Just what I've always wanted — matching**

22   **ratchets.**

23   **RANDY: I mean, got 'em for *me* to use on stuff for *you*. Now I can**

24   **do all sorts of projects for you around the house. Because I**

25   **love you …**

26   **BECKY: But Randy, we don't have the money for you to spend one**

27   **hundred and eighty dollars on tools you don't know how to use.**

28   **RANDY: I know how to use a ratchet.**

29   **BECKY: Oh, yeah? How?**

30   **RANDY: Well, you take it and you, you know … you like … you**

31   **ratchet it. You know … like … ratcheting.**

32   **BECKY: Mm-hmmm.**

33   **RANDY: I'll learn.**

34   **BECKY: The point is, we didn't *need* those ratchets. I've been**

35   **thinking a lot about our lifestyle lately — our needs and our**

1   wants. *(Holding up her book)* **It's all in this new book I've been**
2   **reading.**

3 **RANDY: Uh-oh.**

4 **BECKY: Why do you say that?**

5 **RANDY:** *(Keep this exchange lighthearted)* **Anytime you start out by**
6   **saying you've been reading a new book, I know I'm in trouble.**
7   *(2 minute mark)*

8 **BECKY: Why?**

9 **RANDY:** *(Joking around)* **It usually means I'm gonna have to**
10   **attend a seminar somewhere.**

11 **BECKY: Oh, don't be silly.**

12 **RANDY: Either that, or I'm gonna have to do all that touchy-feely-**
13   **chick-flick stuff and get in touch with my emotional side —**

14 **BECKY: Not this time.**

15 **RANDY: Why not?**

16 **BECKY: This book is all about living a simpler and more satisfying**
17   **life.**

18 **RANDY: A simpler life, huh?**

19 **BECKY: Yeah, and more peaceful. Think about it, Randy — less**
20   **clutter, fewer hassles, less stress.**

21 **RANDY: Sounds nice.**

22 **BECKY: And there are all kinds of practical ways we can de-junk**
23   **our life. We just need to deaccumulate.**

24 **RANDY: What?**

25 **BECKY: Deaccumulate.**

26 **RANDY: What's that?**

27 **BECKY: Well, you know what it means to accumulate, right?**

28 **RANDY: Sure. To get more stuff.**

29 **BECKY: Well, deaccumulating is just the opposite. It's getting rid**
30   **of the things you don't need.**

31 **RANDY: That's not really a word.**

32 **BECKY: Now, to deaccumulate, we need to get rid of everything in**
33   **our lives that's not essential or beautiful. If it's just taking up**
34   **space, it needs to go.** *(3 minute mark)*

35 **RANDY: OK, let's start in the kitchen. How about we get rid of**

1   that bread machine?
2 BECKY: Well, I use that sometimes.
3 RANDY: How often?
4 BECKY: I used it for Christmas.
5 RANDY: You set out hors d'oeuvres on it! That doesn't count!
6 BECKY: Fresh bread is nice.
7 RANDY: So are matching ratchets.
8 BECKY: We keep the bread machine.
9 RANDY: OK, then, how about we lose the juicer, the food
10   dehydrator, the self-grinding wheat mill, and your cappuccino
11   maker?
12 BECKY: I have a better idea.
13 RANDY: What's that?
14 BECKY: Let's start in the workshop.
15 RANDY: *(Hugging his ratchets to his chest)* Now hold on a minute
16   there, lady!
17 BECKY: But you have so many tools, Randy!
18 RANDY: Tools are a man's best friend.
19 BECKY: I thought dogs were a man's best friend.
20 RANDY: That was before they invented tools. And besides, I need
21   every one of those tools.
22 BECKY: Why?
23 RANDY: *(Hesitantly)* To make things. To build stuff.
24 BECKY: What was the last thing you built?
25 RANDY: That shelf down in the basement. *(4 minute mark)*
26 BECKY: You made that when we first moved in eight years ago!
27   And it's all crooked!
28 RANDY: It's got ... personality.
29 BECKY: All right, tell you what. Let's just move on to the next
30   area. *(Looking in her book)* We need to cut back on our
31   obligations.
32 RANDY: What obligations?
33 BECKY: You know, things that drain time and energy from our
34   schedules. Like PTA meetings and softball games and soccer
35   practices for the girls and things like that.

1   RANDY: I'm not giving up my softball games. That's my release —
2   BECKY: I can't stop helping at the PTA. I told them I'd serve as
3   treasurer next year.
4   RANDY: And the girls really love soccer. If we took 'em out, they'd
5   be behind when they got to high school.
6   BECKY: OK, let's just skip that one. Next: Limit our relationships.
7   RANDY: What do you mean?
8   BECKY: How many letters did you write before you had e-mail?
9   RANDY: I don't remember. Almost none.
10 BECKY: And now?
11 RANDY: Well, I don't know, a couple dozen e-mails every week. I
12   need to write back to everyone who writes me. *(5 minute mark)*
13 BECKY: Right, and you have to deal with all those junks e-mails,
14   too. And all that drains time away from the relationships that
15   matter most. *(Pointing to her book)* It says so right here.
16 RANDY: Are you saying get rid of our computer?!
17 BECKY: Hmmm. I don't know.
18 RANDY: But how would I balance the checkbook and find out the
19   show times for movies without a computer?
20 BECKY: OK, I guess we better keep the computer. What about our
21   cell phones? Do we really need one for everyone in the family?
22 RANDY: What would we do without cell phones?
23 BECKY: I don't know. I can't remember life before cell phones.
24   OK, cable TV. What about that?
25 RANDY: Sports.
26 BECKY: Documentaries.
27 RANDY: Movies.
28 BECKY: Martha Stewart.
29 BOTH: *(They look at each other and then say this in unison.)* Oprah.
30 BECKY: OK, what about two cars? One just sits in our driveway
31   most of the time.
32 RANDY: OK, good point. Let's get rid of your car.
33 BECKY: I was thinking of yours.
34 RANDY: My car is newer.
35 BECKY: But we need the extra space in my car to get the kids

1   **around.** *(6 minute mark)*

2   **RANDY: OK, let's not worry about the car for right now. Besides,**

3   **if we didn't have two cars, we wouldn't be able to run errands**

4   **on the spur of the moment whenever we want to, day or night,**

5   **any day of the year —**

6   **BECKY: Good point … Well, that about sums it up! Deaccumulating**

7   **wasn't that much work after all!**

8   **RANDY: Great! Well, I'll see you at dinner! I'm gonna be**

9   **downstairs unpacking my ratchets.**

10   **BECKY: OK, I'll be in the kitchen making some cappuccino. Gosh,**

11   **I'm really glad we went through all this. Our life is gonna be**

12   **a lot simpler now.**

13   **RANDY: Yeah, I feel more at peace already.** *(Fadeout as they exit to*

14   *different sides of the stage.)*

15

16

17

18

19

20

21

22

23

24

25

26

27

28

29

30

31

32

33

34

35

The Magic Formula

Summary: Cheryl is helping her younger sister, Renee, plan her wedding. But when Renee offers to pray for a future husband for Cheryl, they realize they have different views about prayer.

Purpose: To explore the issues related to unanswered prayer.

Time: 5–6 minutes

Tone: Humorous and thought-provoking

Cast: Cheryl — A woman who has given up praying for a husband (female)
Renee — Her naïve sister who is trying to encourage her (female)

Costumes: Casual, contemporary "hang out" clothes, perhaps sweatshirts or sweatpants — something you might wear around the house

Props/Set: A sofa, a coffee table, two coffee cups, bridal magazines, assorted pamphlets, flyers and promotional brochures about brides or weddings

Themes: Choices, faith, frustrations, God's sovereignty, misconceptions about Christianity, modern life, prayer, questions, resentment, single life

Text: "If any of you lacks wisdom, he should ask God, who gives generously to all without finding fault, and it will be given to him. But when he asks, he must believe and not doubt, because he who doubts is like a wave of the sea, blown and tossed by the wind. That man should not think he will receive anything from the Lord" (James 1:5–7).

Notes: Cheryl and Renee are sisters, hanging out at Renee's apartment. Renee, who is in her mid-twenties, is engaged and giddy. Cheryl will be thirty-five years old next month and is more laid back. Be sure the first part of this drama (the whole marriage sequence) is quick, friendly, and lively.

Both Cheryl and Renee are partially right about prayer. Renee is right that God listens and answers, Cheryl is also right that sometimes he doesn't give us what we ask for. This would be a great drama for a singles conference or Bible study group, or a message on unanswered prayer. Use general stage lighting and two lapel microphones.

1   *SETTING*: Renee's studio apartment. Cheryl is helping her plan her
2   wedding. They're seated on the sofa looking over bridal
3   magazines as the lights come up and the scene begins.
4
5   **CHERYL: OK, let's see ... So far, we've decided you're gonna**
6   **have a small, private ceremony and a chocolate cake.**
7   **RENEE: Can you believe I'm getting married? I can't believe I'm**
8   **getting married. It's so exciting, isn't it?**
9   **CHERYL: It's exciting, Renee.**
10 **RENEE: Oh, Cheryl, thanks for taking the time to help me plan! I**
11   **could never do it on my own!**
12 **CHERYL: Of course. That's what big sisters are for.**
13 **RENEE: I'm so excited I can't even think straight!** *(Serious, yet*
14   *clueless)* **And to think we only have eleven months left to finish**
15   **planning. We better get going.**
16 **CHERYL: Calm down, Renee. Breathe. Relax. OK?**
17 **RENEE: OK.**
18 **CHERYL: Now, let me see those dresses you liked.** *(RENEE hands*
19   *CHERYL a bridal magazine.)* **Hmmm ...**
20 **RENEE: If I lose that weight, I can fit into this strapless one. I'll**
21   **look just like that girl modeling it!**
22 **CHERYL: She looks like she's fourteen.**
23 **RENEE: Yeah. Great, huh?**
24 **CHERYL: Well, are you gonna lose the weight?** *(1 minute mark)*
25 **RENEE: Maybe! All I have to do is work out every day for the next**
26   **eleven months and eat raw vegetables for dinner every night.**
27 **CHERYL: Well?**
28 **RENEE: Nope. Not a chance.**
29 **CHERYL: Didn't think so.** *(Pointing to another dress)* **OK, so we go**
30   **with this one. Great! We're moving right along now.** *(A little*
31   *exasperated)* **We've been at this for two weeks and we've**
32   **already made three whole decisions.**
33 **RENEE:** *(Clueless)* **Great, huh?**
34 **CHERYL: Yeah, at this rate we'll have your wedding planned just**
35   **in time for your tenth anniversary. Now, how about the**

1   flowers?

2   RENEE: I've been thinking about this one a lot. I've always liked

3   roses, 'cause they're so romantic and fragrant ... On the other

4   hand, carnations are really peaceful and delicate ... On the

5   other hand, tulips give everything such a nice springy feel ...

6   On the other hand —

7   CHERYL: How many hands are there? Look, let's put the flowers

8   away for a minute. How about the color of your bridesmaids'

9   dresses?

10   RENEE: Don't we have to decide on the flowers first so they

11   match?

12   CHERYL: Couldn't we just decide on the dresses and then pick the

13   flowers? *(2 minute mark)*

14   RENEE: Oh, I don't know. I'm just so excited to finally be

15   marrying Frankie!

16   CHERYL: *(A little resentfully)* The man of your dreams.

17   RENEE: The man of my dreams! Oh, there's just so much to do!

18   *(Speaking really fast)* We still need to find a preacher and

19   decide on the songs and whether or not we're gonna let

20   Frankie's little brother sing that solo!

21   CHERYL: I don't think you better.

22   RENEE: Why not?

23   CHERYL: His voice is still changing.

24   RENEE: Oh, yeah. *(Sighing, then talking faster and faster until she is*

25   *squealing)* And we need to decide about the reception and the

26   dance and the invitations! It's just so exciting and thrilling

27   and can you believe I'm really getting married!?

28   CHERYL: It really is exciting, Renee. I'm really glad for you.

29   RENEE: So ... what about you, sis? You still seeing that guy from

30   work I introduced you to — Alan?

31   CHERYL: Um, that didn't really work out.

32   RENEE: But he's so nice!

33   CHERYL: He looked like those pictures of Bigfoot!

34   RENEE: I thought you liked outdoorsy guys.

35   CHERYL: Renee, he had hair on the palms of his hands!

1 RENEE: Oh. What about that other guy you were seeing?
2 CHERYL: Lennon? *(3 minute mark)*
3 RENEE: Yeah. What about him?
4 CHERYL: He moved to New Zealand ...
5 RENEE: Huh —
6 CHERYL: ... to live with this girl he met on the Internet.
7 RENEE: Oh.
8 CHERYL: Maybe I'm just destined to fly solo.
9 RENEE: Oh, c'mon, sis. I know God's got someone perfect lined
10   up for you. I just know he does! You're gonna find the right
11   guy. I promise!
12 CHERYL: Thanks.
13 RENEE: Tell you what. I'm gonna pray that God sends you a
14   totally gorgeous guy by this time next month!
15 CHERYL: I appreciate the gesture, Renee, but I'd really rather
16   you didn't.
17 RENEE: Why not? You afraid God just might answer the prayer
18   of your little sister?
19 CHERYL: No, Renee, I'm afraid he won't.
20 RENEE: Huh?
21 CHERYL: I said, I'm afraid maybe God won't answer your prayer.
22 RENEE: Oh. Like that you'd get your hopes up and then he
23   wouldn't answer it the way you want?
24 CHERYL: Something like that. *(4 minute mark)*
25 RENEE: But doesn't the Bible say we can ask for anything in
26   Jesus' name and he'll give it to us? (See John 14:13–14.) So I'm
27   gonna pray for a husband for my big sister!
28 CHERYL: Renee, I've tried. I prayed. For years. I prayed and
29   waited. And at the beginning, I really believed he would
30   answer me. But he hasn't, OK? So don't pray for me, because
31   I've seen people who believed, and when their prayers weren't
32   answered, it was devastating to 'em. It shattered their faith.
33 RENEE: But God does answer prayer. He promises to.
34 CHERYL: Sometimes God doesn't answer our prayers. No one
35   talks about it much, but it's true.

1   RENEE: So you've stopped praying?

2   CHERYL: God is in control, right? Sovereign? So he's gonna do

3   what he wants, and neither your prayers, nor mine, nor

4   anyone else's are gonna change that. Maybe he just wants me

5   to be single.

6   RENEE: I don't know. I've always believed God answers prayers.

7   He's answered mine. *(5 minute mark)*

8   CHERYL: Renee, I'm gonna be thirty-five next month. My time

9   is running out. I'm not telling you to doubt God, I'm just

10   saying — prayer isn't a magic formula. We don't always get

11   what we ask for. So how much should we believe and how

12   much should we just be realistic? ... Look, I'd better go. I'll

13   come over later this week and help you plan some more. I

14   gotta get going. G'bye. *(She stands to exit.)*

15 RENEE: *(Calling to her as she leaves)* I'm gonna pray for you,

16   Cheryl. You'll see. It'll all work out! God's listening, I just

17   know he is ... *(To herself)* Isn't he? *(Freeze. Fadeout.)*

18

19

20

21

22

23

24

25

26

27

28

29

30

31

32

33

34

35

The Gift

Summary: When Kendra's daughter is almost hit by a car in the parking lot, she reprioritizes her life.

Purpose: To help people think about the brevity of life and to be thankful for each day.

Time: 3–4 minutes

Tone: Humorous and thought-provoking

Cast: Kendra — A woman who has been thinking about the important things in life (female)
Angie — Her friend who realizes her problems aren't really that big after all (female)

Costumes: Angie is wearing maternity clothes (the scene takes place at her baby shower); Kendra is dressed in casual, contemporary clothes

Props/Set: Gift boxes, wrapping paper, two cups of coffee, a sofa, and a coffee table

Themes: Ambition, death, family issues, grace, hope, life, meaning, parenting, priorities, second chances, thanksgiving

Text: "Man is like a breath; his days are like a fleeting shadow" (Psalm 144:4).

Notes: Angie is focused on externals at the beginning of the sketch. Kendra has recently been reevaluating her life and her problems and is more at peace. Use general stage lighting and two lapel microphones.

1   ***SETTING***: Angie's living room. Kendra and her friends have thrown a
2   baby shower for Angie. The party is finished and everyone else
3   has just left. Kendra is staying to help Angie clean up. Coffee cups
4   and a tray of snacks lay on the coffee table. Wrapping paper is
5   strewn across the room. Angie and Kendra are both On-stage
6   when the lights come up and the scene begins.
7
8   **ANGIE:** *(Calling out the door as the last guest leaves)* **OK! Good-**
9   **bye, Liz! Yeah, thanks for coming!** *(Miming closing the door;*
10 *then collapsing on the coach and sighing)* **Oh, what a day.**
11 **KENDRA: Rough, huh?**
12 **ANGIE: You said it. Don't get me wrong, I love that you guys threw**
13 **me this baby shower. I'm just worn out.**
14 **KENDRA: Lots going on?**
15 **ANGIE:** *(Deliver these lines very fast)* **Well, the water heater broke**
16 **yesterday and there wasn't any warm water for showers today**
17 **so my hair is still a mess and the plumber can't come until**
18 **Monday and I'm supposed to cook this casserole for a potluck**
19 **meal at church tomorrow night and I couldn't find the recipe**
20 **so I tried calling Jennifer 'cause last year I got it from her but**
21 **I lost her cell phone number —**
22 **KENDRA: Wow. You sure have a lot going on.**
23 **ANGIE: I'll say. That, and I've been working two jobs ever since**
24 **Ray got laid off. And my mom is gonna visit next week so I**
25 **gotta get the house all cleaned up and this sweater I bought**
26 **the other day doesn't even fit so now I have to return that to**
27 **Target** *(Or another local department store)* **plus — of course —**
28 **we've got this baby on the way.** *(Big sigh)* **So anyway, how are**
29 **you?** *(1 minute mark)*
30 **KENDRA: Well, I guess the best way to say it is — I'm thankful.**
31 **ANGIE: You're thankful?**
32 **KENDRA: Yeah.**
33 **ANGIE: Thankful?**
34 **KENDRA: Uh-huh.**
35 **ANGIE: Most people say, "Oh, pretty good," or "I'm fine," or "I've**

1   been really busy lately," but you say you're thankful?

2   KENDRA: Mm-hmmm.

3   ANGIE: What are you so thankful about?

4   KENDRA: Well, I was at the fitness center yesterday — you know,

5   I do aerobics on Mondays.

6   ANGIE: Yeah?

7   KENDRA: So I picked Christine up from the child care, and as we

8   were walking across the parking lot, her diaper fell down

9   around her ankles.

10   ANGIE: You're thankful she had a droopy diaper?

11   KENDRA: No, I'm thankful because when I bent down to help her,

12   this guy in a Jeep was backing up. He couldn't see either of us

13   — and for some reason I looked up just in time and saw him

14   when he was about two feet away. Just as I grabbed for

15   Christine, he backed into me. *(2 minute mark)*

16   ANGIE: Are you OK?

17   KENDRA: Yeah, I spun to the side and he just bumped me. But if

18   I hadn't looked up that instant, she would have rolled under

19   the Jeep, Angie ... Who knows what would have happened.

20   ANGIE: Oh, my gosh!

21   KENDRA: Anyway, I'm thankful because, I don't know if it was

22   God or an angel or what, but for some reason I looked up and

23   saw that Jeep just in time. If I hadn't, I might not be over here

24   tonight at your baby shower, but at home planning my two-

25   year-old's funeral ...

26   ANGIE: Ooh. You just gave me chills.

27   KENDRA: Kinda makes you think, huh?

28   ANGIE: It's scary.

29   KENDRA: Puts things in perspective.

30   ANGIE: Yeah. No kidding.

31   KENDRA: And the thing was, Angie, she didn't even know what

32   was going on. She just kept giggling and saying "Diaper down!

33   Diaper down!" Like it was the funniest thing in the world.

34   ANGIE: So she had no idea what almost happened? *(3 minute*

35   *mark)*

1   **KENDRA: No. She was just a few inches from being hit by that**
2   **Jeep, just a fraction of a second from being killed, and she**
3   **didn't even realize it.**
4   **ANGIE: Wow. I wonder how many close calls like that we have in**
5   **our lives that we never even find out about.**
6   **KENDRA: I don't know. But that's why I'm thankful.**
7   **ANGIE:** *(Thoughtfully)* **It's easy to forget how fragile life is.**
8   **KENDRA: And how precious.**
9   **ANGIE:** *(As she picks up one of the boxes and a piece of wrapping*
10   *paper)* **Every day, every moment is a gift, isn't it?**
11   **KENDRA: Yeah, you're right. It's easy to forget, but every**
12   **moment is a gift.**
13   **ANGIE: Hmmm. Maybe the water heater and that recipe and that**
14   **sweater aren't such a big deal after all.** *(As they clean up,*
15   *fadeout.)*
16
17
18
19
20
21
22
23
24
25
26
27
28
29
30
31
32
33
34
35

Signs of the Times

Summary: Drew's idea for the new church sign doesn't seem to fly with his friend Alex. But what should the new sign really say?

Purpose: To encourage believers to be more open and accepting of visitors and unbelievers who might attend their churches.

Time: 5–6 minutes

Tone: Humorous and thought-provoking

Cast: Drew — A guy who wants his church to be more open to people who are different (male)
Alex — His friend who has a more limited view of who should attend their church (male)

Costumes: Drew is wearing painting clothes; Alex is dressed in casual contemporary clothes

Props/Set: Table with a large sign, paints, paintbrushes, and other sign-making paraphernalia (or a computer and a large screen on which to present each proposed sign)

Themes: Assumptions, church issues, compassion, evangelism, missions, prejudice, stereotypes, witnessing

Text: "But if you show favoritism, you sin and are convicted by the law as lawbreakers" (James 2:9).

Notes: Keep this drama lighthearted. You want your audience to see how true Drew's ideas are, even if they don't seem very "practical." If you have the technological capabilities, consider having Drew work at a computer and flash his wording changes on your screen through Microsoft PowerPoint or another similar presentation program. Use general stage lighting and two lapel microphones.

1   **SETTING**: The church fellowship hall, where Drew is finishing
2   painting the new church sign. The lights come up on Drew. Then
3   Alex enters and the scene begins.
4
5   **ALEX: Hey, Drew, how's that new sign comin'?**
6   **DREW: Great, Alex! I'm almost done.**
7   **ALEX: Good. The elders** *(Or another governing body in your church)*
8   **have been waiting a long time for this new welcome sign.**
9   **DREW:** *(Still working on the sign)* **Yeah.**
10   **ALEX: They wanted something eye-catching and thought-**
11   **provoking that gives people a clear message explaining what**
12   **our church is all about.**
13   **DREW: Well, I think I've got just the sign.**
14   **ALEX: Let's see it. What does it say?**
15   **DREW:** *(Holding up his sign and reading it. You may wish to have him*
16   *show the sign to the audience)* **"Prostitutes, drunks, strippers,**
17   **drug addicts, racists, gays, and ex-cons all welcome. Please**
18   **come in!"**
19   **ALEX: What?! What kind of a sign is that?**
20   **DREW: A welcome sign, just like the elders** *(Or the other governing*
21   *church body)* **wanted.**
22   **ALEX: You can't put that sign on the front of our church!**
23   **DREW: Why not?**
24   **ALEX: Because it talks about —**
25   **DREW: What?**
26   **ALEX: Different groups of ... of ...** *(1 minute mark)*
27   **DREW: People?**
28   **ALEX: Well, yeah. And —**
29   **DREW: Sinners?**
30   **ALEX: Right! And we wouldn't want our visitors to think that**
31   **we're all like that or anything.**
32   **DREW: That we're all sinners?**
33   **ALEX: Yeah.**
34   **DREW: We are.**
35   **ALEX: Well, yeah. I mean, it's just that, this is supposed to be a**

1   welcome sign.

2   DREW: Well drunks and strippers are welcome, aren't they?

3   ALEX: *(Hesitantly)* Well, of ... of course.

4   DREW: Then let's tell 'em! Let's invite 'em in!

5   ALEX: But what would our members think about a sign like that?

6   DREW: Who is this sign for, our visitors or our members?

7   ALEX: Well, um ... I think you need to work on the wording a

8   little bit.

9   DREW: Hmmm. Maybe you're right. OK, what if I changed it to

10   this: "Atheists, Buddhists, Muslims, Hindus, Jehovah's

11   Witnesses, and Mormons are all welcome here."

12   ALEX: Hmmm ... Too religious-sounding.

13   DREW: *(Thinking for a moment, then responding)* "Republicans,

14   Democrats, and Independents, please join us!" *(2 minute mark)*

15   ALEX: Too political.

16   DREW: *(Thinking, then responding)* "We welcome people from all

17   backgrounds, religions, ethnic descent, and economic levels."

18   ALEX: Too politically correct. It sounds like we're running for

19   office.

20   DREW: What about this? "Hillbillies, rednecks, bikers, bankers,

21   plumbers, doctors, and lawyers are all welcome."

22   ALEX: Hmmm. Do you really wanna include lawyers in there?

23   *(They pause, look at each other, and then both nod and say*

24   *something like, "Yeah, yeah, I guess we should.")* I don't know,

25   though ...

26   DREW: OK, how about this? "Homeless people, orphans, widows,

27   pregnant teenagers, AIDS patients, and starving children

28   from war-torn countries come on in."

29   ALEX: Hmmm ... Too depressing.

30   DREW: How 'bout, "Come to me, all you who are weary and

31   burdened, and I will give you rest. Take my yoke upon you

32   and learn from me, for I am gentle and humble in heart, and

33   you will find rest for your souls"? (Matthew 11:28–29).

34   *(3 minute mark)*

35   ALEX: Hmmm ... Not bad ... It's the right idea. A little too wordy,

1   **though.**

2   **DREW: OK, how about this? "Give me your tired, your poor, your**

3   **huddled masses yearning to breathe free."**

4   **ALEX: Hmmm ... Nice! Kinda poetic. I like it! That's it! Did you**

5   **just write that?**

6   **DREW: It's on the Statue of Liberty!**

7   **ALEX: Oh ... I wonder if it's copyrighted ...**

8   **DREW: Look, this is getting us nowhere. What do *you* think the**

9   **sign on the front of our church should say? "No shirt, no**

10   **shoes, no service"?**

11   **ALEX: No, how about, "Welcome to God's house. No drinking,**

12   **smoking, pets, or hats allowed"?**

13   **DREW: No pets?**

14   **ALEX: It's God's house. We don't want a bunch of animals**

15   **roaming around. It'd look like a barn in here!**

16   **DREW: Jesus was born in a barn! There were animals everywhere!**

17   **And what about no hats? Why can't we wear hats?**

18   **ALEX: It's rude.**

19   **DREW: Says who?** *(4 minute mark)*

20   **ALEX: I don't know. I think it's in the Bible somewhere. "Thou**

21   **shalt not wear-eth hats upon thy head-eth when thou walk-est**

22   **into the house-eth of the Lord-eth."**

23   **DREW: You made that up! Look, what's the purpose of this sign**

24   **anyway? To welcome people into our church, or to keep 'em**

25   **out?**

26   **ALEX: To welcome 'em in. To make 'em feel right at home.**

27   **DREW: OK, then how about this? "Hypocrites of all kinds**

28   **welcome. You'll fit right in."**

29   **ALEX: Hey, that's not fair!**

30   **DREW: Well, you're right. But I think maybe you'd better find**

31   **someone else to finish up this sign. I'm afraid I'd put**

32   **something on there that would offend too many of our**

33   **members.** *(DREW exits.)*

34   **ALEX: Wait! Come back! Where are you going?** *(Picking up the*

35   *original sign and sighing:)* **Hmmm. "Prostitutes, drunks,**

1	strippers, drug addicts, racists, gays, and ex-cons all welcome.
2	Please come in!" No, that would never work here. I mean,
3	what would people think of a church like that? *(5 minute mark.*
4	*ALEX props up the sign so that the audience can read it, then he*
5	*exits. Fadeout.)*
6	
7	
8	
9	
10	
11	
12	
13	
14	
15	
16	
17	
18	
19	
20	
21	
22	
23	
24	
25	
26	
27	
28	
29	
30	
31	
32	
33	
34	
35	

The Calling

Summary: When Eric decides he wants to start a new job, both he and his friend Tim end up with a lot to think about.

Purpose: To help people understand the difference between a job and a calling.

Time: 5–7 minutes (depending on how much time the actors spend working on the bookcase)

Tone: Thought-provoking

Cast: Eric — A man who is thinking about a career change (male)
Tim — His pastor who regrets never stepping out in faith and pursuing his true calling as a carpenter (male)

Costumes: Eric and Tim are working in Eric's basement workshop. They're wearing appropriate work clothes.

Props/Set: Boards, tools, hammer, nails, pencil, tape measure, two sawhorses

Themes: Ambition, calling, choices, consumerism, distractions, excuses, faith, frustrations, integrity, modern life, prayer, priorities, questions, second chances, service, success, work, worship

Text: "Moreover, when God gives any man wealth and possessions, and enables him to enjoy them, to accept his lot and be happy in his work — this is a gift of God" (Ecclesiastes 5:19).

Notes: Eric has invited his pastor, Tim, over to help him build a bookshelf. As they begin talking about Eric's possible career change, Tim has all the right answers until he is forced to admit that he, too, has not pursued his true calling.

God calls some people to be evangelists, others teachers, others plumbers and doctors. The secret to finding satisfaction in our jobs isn't in finding a position "in ministry," but rather "ministering in" whatever job God has called and gifted you to do.

At the beginning, Tim tells Eric what we might expect. But when he realizes what he's saying, it finally hits home. Eric is younger, maybe in his mid-twenties or early thirties. Tim is a few years older and has been in "full-time ministry" most of his adult life. Even though Tim has always known the difference between a job and a calling, he has not yet acted on his convictions. Use general stage lighting and two lapel microphones.

1   *SETTING*: The basement workshop at Eric's house. Both men are On-
2   stage (surrounded by boards, tools, and sawhorses) as the lights
3   come up and the scene begins.
4
5   ERIC: So Pastor —
6   TIM: Call me "Tim."
7   ERIC: So Tim, thanks for coming over to help me with this
8   bookcase.
9   TIM: Oh, I love this stuff. I've always liked carpentry. Wanna hand
10   me that tape measure over there?
11   ERIC: Sure ... *(He hands it to him)* and I gotta say ... I did have an
12   ulterior motive in inviting you over today.
13   TIM: What's that?
14   ERIC: Well, I got something I wanted to bounce off you.
15   TIM: Shoot.
16   ERIC: I've been thinking about maybe switching jobs ... you
17   know, looking for my true calling.
18   TIM: Hmmm. So what kind of job you looking for?
19   ERIC: I don't know. Maybe something with a little more security.
20   TIM: *(Looking up from his work and laughing slightly)* Listen, there's
21   no security out there, Eric. Anyone who's been around for a
22   while can tell you that. It's all up for grabs.
23   ERIC: But they've been laying people off at my factory left and
24   right — *(1 minute mark)*
25   TIM: No job is secure. I'm telling you, it doesn't work like that.
26   You go somewhere else, you get a new boss, you don't get
27   along, and six months later you're looking for another
28   position.
29   ERIC: Well, then ... to provide for my family.
30   TIM: Wait a minute. Who provides for your family?
31   ERIC: I do.
32   TIM: Who does?
33   ERIC: I — All right, what am I supposed to say — God?
34   TIM: Well, what do you think?
35   ERIC: All right, but what about my salary? I mean, Lacey and I,

1   we're living on the edge.

2   TIM: You don't want a big salary.

3   ERIC: Why not? Of course I do! We've got a baby on the way!

4   TIM: Eric, people with loads of money in the bank don't have to

5   rely on God as much. They end up trusting their money.

6   You're better off with less. Believe me.

7   ERIC: Well, if I'm not supposed to get a job based on the salary or

8   the security, what am I supposed to do?

9   TIM: There's only one question you should be asking yourself. And

10   it has nothing to do with money or benefits or anything like

11   that.

12   ERIC: Well, what's the question, then? *(2 minute mark)*

13   TIM: *(Looking up from his work)* Where does God want me to serve

14   him right now? *(He goes back to work.)*

15   ERIC: You're kidding. That's it?

16   TIM: That's it.

17   ERIC: No way. Life couldn't be that easy. What about my family?

18   What about the bottom line?

19   TIM: That is the bottom line.

20   ERIC: But that doesn't seem very smart. Basing your whole life on

21   what you think God wants you to do? What if you're wrong?

22   TIM: *(The words are beginning to sink in.)* Well, you gotta choose.

23   Either trust him with your future, or trust in yourself and

24   your retirement plan and your pension program and your

25   investments. It boils down to, um … faith.

26   ERIC: But what about the money?

27   TIM: Let's say you work a job that doesn't give you much money,

28   but you're convinced God wants you there. Don't you think

29   he'll provide for you?

30   ERIC: I guess so …

31   TIM: *(As he says this, he gets a faraway look in his eyes because he*

32   *realizes he is talking about himself)* Most people know the

33   question, they just never take the time to answer it — or act

34   on it. A job is something you do to pay the bills. Your calling

35   is something you do because you're convinced it's God's will.

1   Most people don't have the courage to pursue their calling, so
2   they just settle for a job instead. *(3 minute mark)*
3   ERIC: Hmmm. Yeah, maybe you're right.
4   TIM: *(Regretfully)* But don't put it off. Tomorrow's not guaranteed,
5   Eric. You either give God today ... or you end up giving him
6   nothing at all.
7   ERIC: But what you're telling me is pretty radical. I mean, you're
8   basically saying forget everything I've ever been told about
9   making it in the workplace and just look for where God wants
10   me to be.
11   TIM: Exactly.
12   ERIC: That's it?
13   TIM: That's it. That's the difference between getting a job and
14   finding your calling.
15   ERIC: *(After a pause)* Hey, maybe God's calling me into the
16   ministry, huh? Just like you.
17   TIM: Yeah ... yeah, just like me.
18   ERIC: So when did you know God was calling you to be a pastor?
19   TIM: Um, wanna hand me that pencil there?
20   ERIC: Sure. *(He hands it to him.)* So when did you realize you were
21   supposed to serve God like this from the pulpit?
22   TIM: Lemme ask you a question, Eric. Would you have called me
23   over here today if I were just your pastor and didn't know
24   anything about carpentry? *(4 minute mark)*
25   ERIC: Huh? Um ... Probably not. But I know you're a good
26   carpenter. Isn't that what you used to do before you became
27   a pastor?
28   TIM: Yeah, it is.
29   ERIC: But now you spend your life making a real difference in the
30   lives of others — now that you've found your true calling.
31   TIM: Eric, let me tell you something. When I was a carpenter, I was
32   happy. I loved it. And then I started thinking the same stuff
33   you are — that maybe God was calling me to the ministry and
34   everything. So I started telling people about it, and they were
35   all excited for me.

1   **ERIC:** Yeah, and?

2   **TIM:** And I went to seminary, I got my degree, and I became a

3   pastor.

4   **ERIC:** *(Thoughtfully)* Somehow I think there's more to this story. Is

5   that what you're trying to tell me?

6   **TIM:** I was so sure that God wanted me to do something

7   "important" that I stopped doing the one thing I was good at

8   — the one thing I was called to do.

9   **ERIC:** You mean being a carpenter?!

10   **TIM:** Yeah. *(5 minute mark)*

11   **ERIC:** But what about everything you just told me?!

12   **TIM:** Everything I just told you is true.

13   **ERIC:** But —

14   **TIM:** I haven't had the guts. OK? To go back. To do it again. I've

15   gotten too ...

16   **ERIC:** Comfortable?

17   **TIM:** Yeah.

18   **ERIC:** But you're a good pastor.

19   **TIM:** Just because you're good at something doesn't mean God

20   has called you to do it. I've been working in churches for the

21   last eighteen years now, and all that time, I've known God had

22   something else in store for me. Don't make the same mistake

23   I did, Eric. It's not too late for you.

24   **ERIC:** It's not too late for either of us, Tim. *(Freeze. Fadeout.)*

25

26

27

28

29

30

31

32

33

34

35

Part 3
Creative Scripture Presentations

In this section you'll hear from biblical characters such as Cain, Abraham, Sarah, Ruth, Naomi, Job, Lot, King David, Judas, and Peter. You'll also discover the real significance of the Lord's Supper and how it relates to the Jewish Passover meal. You'll explore what it would be like if talking to God were like talking to your boss, your mom, or a radio talk show hostess.

In these creative tandem monologs and interpretive presentations, you'll see Scripture (and its many-faceted characters) in a new light. You'll also discover the relevance of the Bible to the issues, questions, and struggles we face today.

(The sketches in this section were written for adult or family worship. See the dramas in Parts 5 and 6 for creative retellings of Scripture for teenagers and elementary-aged children, respectively.)

A Tale of Two Friends

Summary: Peter and Judas come to the same conclusion that they have let their friend down and contributed to the death of Jesus.

Purpose: To reveal how our sin sent Jesus, our best friend, to the cross.

Time: 5 minutes

Tone: Serious

Cast: Peter — a man who realizes he has failed his Lord (male)
Judas — a man who realizes he has just betrayed his friend (male)

Costumes: Something simple and stylistic, such as blue jeans and a neutral oxford or turtleneck

Props/Set: Sound effects of crickets chirping, or other gentle night sounds

Themes: Easter, forgiveness, Good Friday, grace, grief and loss, guilt, Jesus, regrets, repentance, second chances, sin

Text: Various; "When Judas, who had betrayed him, saw that Jesus was condemned, he was seized with remorse and returned the thirty silver coins to the chief priests and the elders. 'I have sinned,' he said, 'for I have betrayed innocent blood.' 'What is that to us?' they replied. 'That's your responsibility'" (Matthew 27:3–4). "Immediately the rooster crowed the second time. Then Peter remembered the word Jesus had spoken to him: 'Before the rooster crows twice you will disown me three times.' And he broke down and wept" (Mark 14:72).

Notes: Timing is essential in this dual monolog. There shouldn't be too much of a pause between the two actors' lines. Especially at the end, they should almost be interrupting each other. Use some blocking and movement, but keep it simple. The actors each freeze while the other person is delivering his lines. Use two spotlights and two lapel microphones.

1   *SETTING*: The stage is bare. Peter and Judas enter simultaneously.
2   Judas stands Stage Right, Peter Stage Left. There is a spotlight on
3   each actor. The rest of the stage is black.
4
5   **JUDAS: He was my friend. He had been for, oh, a couple years. He**
6   **chose me.**
7   **PETER: He confused me. I never really understood what he was**
8   **talking about. I didn't get it. It just didn't make any sense.**
9   **JUDAS: I was really honored that morning when he announced my**
10   **name along with the other eleven. Not everyone was chosen. I**
11   **was. And he trusted me. That's why he let me handle the**
12   **money for our group. And I was gonna make him proud. It**
13   **was my chance to be part of something big!**
14   **PETER: Everything's been so different since that day I left my nets**
15   **to follow him ... I was a part of something big! I was in on the**
16   **ground floor! And then came the night in the Garden.** *(Gentle*
17   *sound of crickets chirping in the background. 1 minute mark)*
18   **JUDAS: Things didn't go quite as planned. Jesus wasn't taking**
19   **control like he should have. He kept talking about power and**
20   **kingdoms and stuff, but all that time he didn't do anything ...**
21   **Just talked. He wouldn't let the people crown him king. He**
22   **just withdrew by himself instead ... I guess I got antsy and**
23   **frustrated. I don't remember when the thought first occurred**
24   **to me. But after it did, I couldn't get it out of my mind. Yeah,**
25   **maybe I could help move things along.**
26   **PETER: It was cold that night. And it'd already been a long day. I**
27   **was tired and confused. We couldn't believe he'd been arrested.**
28   **I didn't know what to do. Nothing made sense anymore.**
29   **JUDAS: So I talked to Caiaphas. And the way he explained it, well,**
30   **it started to make sense to me. I mean, Caiaphas was only**
31   **interested in preventing bloodshed ... Finally I knew my time**
32   **had come. I knew what I had to do.**
33   **PETER: A few men had started a campfire. Everyone was talking**
34   **in whispers when all of a sudden this little girl says it, loud**
35   **enough for everyone to hear. "Hey! Look at him! He was with**

1   **them!"** *(2 minute mark)*

2   **JUDAS: I led them through the garden, a trail of lights behind me.**

3   **I was their guide. I was the one they were following.**

4   **PETER: Everyone looked at me. I didn't know what to say. "Me?**

5   **Huh. No. I don't know him." I slipped away from the fire into**

6   **the cold, where I hoped no one would bother me. But I stayed**

7   **close enough to hear them talk.**

8   **JUDAS: I knew right where he'd be. I knew the plans. And there!**

9   **I could see him, up ahead, in the shadows. He was with his**

10   **favorites. The inner circle. I could tell. I knew them all. I**

11   **pushed the branches aside and stepped toward them.**

12   **PETER: I hoped they'd forget about me, standing there in the**

13   **shadows. But they didn't. They muttered under their breath**

14   **and pointed their fingers at me. Finally one of the men who'd**

15   **started the fire called over to me, "Hey, you over there! You**

16   **were with him. Come here." I didn't know what to do.**

17   **JUDAS: I knew exactly what to do. It'd all been arranged. I'd greet**

18   **him with a kiss on the cheek, the way a friend greets a friend.**

19   **"Rabbi!" I smiled. I held him. I kissed him. And he whispered**

20   **into my ear, "Judas, do you betray me with a kiss?" I stepped**

21   **back.** *(3 minute mark)*

22   **PETER: I waited a moment and then stepped forward. "See? I**

23   **recognize your face," he said, "You were there in the garden."**

24   **But again I denied it. And as I said the words, they began to**

25   **feel natural. I almost started to believe them myself.**

26   **JUDAS: They grabbed him. And he didn't put up a fight. He just**

27   **turned to us and said, "Am I leading a rebellion, that you have**

28   **come with swords and clubs? Every day I was with you in the**

29   **temple courts, and you didn't lay a hand on me. But this is**

30   **your hour — the hour when darkness reigns." That's when all**

31   **the other disciples turned and ran** (Matthew 26:55–56, author's

32   paraphrase).

33   **PETER:** *(Starting slow, building in energy)* **For nearly an hour I**

34   **stood there, until I thought they'd forgotten about me. Some**

35   **people left the fire, others arrived with fresh news. But as the**

1   sun began to rise, they pointed at me again. This time they all

2   did. They recognized me. "You were in the olive grove!" They

3   knew. And that's when I lost it. I swore up and down I'd never

4   heard of him. I cursed his name. I hadn't used words like

5   those in years — in fact, not since that day when I first left my

6   nets ... *(4 minute mark)*

7   JUDAS: It didn't hit me right away.

8   PETER: And before I could close my mouth, a group of soldiers

9   crowded into the courtyard. They were leading a prisoner.

10   JUDAS: I didn't realize what I'd done.

11   PETER: It was Jesus.

12   JUDAS: He was my friend.

13   PETER: *(Pause for a beat)* Our eyes met just as the rooster's cry cut

14   through the dawn. And I remembered our conversation:

15   "Before the rooster cries, you will deny me ... " No, Jesus, I

16   will never deny you ...

17   JUDAS: He chose me!

18   PETER: I will never deny you!

19   JUDAS: He loved me!

20   PETER: Oh! What have I done?

21   JUDAS: What have I done? He was an innocent man!

22   PETER: I've betrayed my friend.

23   JUDAS: *(Close, begin line as Peter says "betrayed.")* I've betrayed

24   my friend.

25   PETER: And it's my fault ...

26   JUDAS: *(Dropping to his knees)* It's all my fault ...

27   PETER: ...That he's dead ...

28   JUDAS: ...He's dead ...

29   PETER: ...He's dead. *(They freeze. Fadeout. They exit in the dark.*

30   *Empty stage.)*

31

32

33

34

35

The Journey

Summary: When God doesn't seem like he's keeping his promises, Abraham and Sarah are forced to live lives of real faith.

Purpose: To show that God's promises are trustworthy.

Time: 5–6 minutes

Tone: Serious

Cast: Abraham — A man who has struggled to trust God (male)
Sarah — His wife who stuck with him and waited for God's promises to come true (female)

Costumes: Something simple and stylistic, such as blue jeans and a neutral oxford or turtleneck

Props/Set: Two musician's stools (optional)

Themes: Calling, children, distractions, faith, following God, God's power, God's sovereignty, grace, hope, life, married life, Mother's Day, prophecy fulfillment, suffering

Text: "And Sarah declared, 'God has brought me laughter! All who hear about this will laugh with me. For who would have dreamed that I would ever have a baby? Yet I have given Abraham a son in his old age!'" (Genesis 21:6–7 NLT; see also Genesis 12–25, Hebrews 11:8–19, Romans 4:20–21).

Notes: Since Abraham and Sarah are telling this story from the perspective of the end of their trip, you may wish to have older actors in this sketch. Use some movement, but keep it simple. The actors each freeze while the other person is delivering his/her lines. Build your blocking around the stools. Use two spotlights and two lapel microphones. You may wish to have light, airy instrumental music in the background.

1 ***SETTING***: The stage is bare except for two musician's stools. One
2   spotlight comes up on Abraham as the drama begins. When he
3   finishes his first lines, another light comes up on Sarah. Abraham
4   is on Stage Left, Sarah is on Stage Right.
5
6 **ABRAHAM:** When I first moved to the area, everyone would
7   listen to the way I talked and then shake their heads and
8   say, "You aren't from around here, are ya?" And you know,
9   they were right.
10 **SARAH:** I liked our old place. We were doing good, you know?
11 Lots of money saved up. Ready to retire. I never expected us
12 to move. I never expected any of this to happen. We'd already
13 decided it was time to slow down and kinda pull back
14 from life.
15 **ABRAHAM:** I was seventy-five years old when I started this trip.
16 When I started it! And what a trip it's been.
17 **SARAH:** And then Abe starts talking about how God told him it
18 was time to leave. I couldn't believe it. "Why?" I asked,
19 "Where are we going?" He smiled and said, "I don't know.
20 God just told me to start the journey. He didn't tell me where
21 it's gonna end." *(1 minute mark)*
22 **ABRAHAM:** Sometimes you hear a voice, and you think maybe it's
23 God telling you to do something. But you're not sure, you
24 know? You wonder. And then you doubt.
25 **SARAH:** We left our friends, our country, our home. Just because
26 of a voice. Just because of a promise that Abe said he heard. I
27 didn't hear it. The voice never spoke to me.
28 **ABRAHAM:** But there are other times when you know. You know
29 what God wants. Despite what everyone tells you. Despite how
30 stupid it might appear. Despite all the practical advice and
31 good council in the world. You know somewhere deep inside
32 that it's God talking. So, even though it may not seem to make
33 sense, you do it. You obey.
34 **SARAH:** But I went. And I didn't complain. I believed him. Or at
35 least, I believed that *he believed* it was God talking to him. So

1   we left our home and we started on this journey.

2   ABRAHAM: There were times when I doubted. When I just didn't

3   know. When I took things into my own hands. But every time

4   I did ... well ... let's just say things didn't work out like I

5   thought they would. *(2 minute mark)*

6   SARAH: He told me to pretend I was his sister. Down in Egypt. It

7   almost ended in disaster.

8   ABRAHAM: It was a hard trip. But then, God gave me the best

9   promise of all.

10   SARAH: So one day, Abe starts telling me we're gonna have a

11   baby. A baby! Can you imagine?!

12   ABRAHAM: We'd never been able to have kids, Sarah and I. We'd

13   tried. For years, we'd tried. It was really hard on her.

14   SARAH: I'd given up any hope of having a baby of my own years

15   ago. It just wasn't a possibility anymore. I didn't even dare to

16   dream that dream again.

17   ABRAHAM: It was a promise almost too good to be true. But once

18   again, things didn't quite go as planned.

19   SARAH: The baby didn't come. We moved from country to

20   country. And we waited. I didn't complain. I didn't say a

21   word. But the baby didn't come. *(3 minute mark)*

22   ABRAHAM: I started questioning it. Wondering if maybe God

23   had meant something other than what he'd said. Second-

24   guessing. Because time was ticking by and it didn't seem like

25   he was keeping his promise.

26   SARAH: So we made ... an arrangement, with a lady named

27   Hagar.

28   ABRAHAM: I never had any idea it would turn out so bad.

29   SARAH: Hagar had a son. My husband's son.

30   ABRAHAM: The whole thing was a mistake. I know that now. But

31   at the time, I didn't know what to do. It seemed like the only

32   option.

33   SARAH: We just couldn't believe God had really meant what he'd

34   said. That I would have a baby of my own.

35   ABRAHAM: And then one day, these three men showed up at

123

1   our door.

2   SARAH: "Before this year is up," that's what they said, "you'll

3   have a baby boy." Messengers from God! And I laughed. I

4   couldn't help it. There was no way it was gonna happen.

5   *(4 minute mark)*

6   ABRAHAM: It was like, once we started the journey, God kept

7   making us live by faith rather than figure things out by

8   ourselves. We kept looking toward the final destination, but

9   God was more interested in the way we made the trip.

10   SARAH: But then, just like God promised, before the year was up,

11   I had my baby! My own son! I was old enough to be a great-

12   grandmother. I'd waited a lifetime ...

13   ABRAHAM: Nothing is too tough for God. Nothing.

14   SARAH: But I had a baby of my own! So we named him

15   "Laughter." Because the joke was on us!

16   ABRAHAM: We've been through a lot over the years.

17   SARAH: We waited.

18   ABRAHAM: Sometimes God seemed slow in keeping his promises.

19   SARAH: Sometimes there was nothing but a promise to hold onto.

20   ABRAHAM: Sometimes we doubted.

21   SARAH: Sometimes we second-guessed everything and took things

22   into our own hands.

23   ABRAHAM: But through it all, I guess we learned to wait.

24   SARAH: And wait.

25   ABRAHAM: And trust. *(5 minute mark)*

26   SARAH: Because there's one thing we learned for certain ...

27   ABRAHAM: If you stick with him through the journey,

28   SARAH: He's got laughter waiting for you —

29   ABRAHAM: When you finally reach the end of the trip. *(Freeze.*

30   *Fadeout.)*

31

32

33

34

35

When God Doesn't Make Sense

Summary: Naomi learns an important lesson about God's faithfulness through the example of her daughter-in-law, Ruth.

Purpose: To show that God is faithful, even when circumstances are stacked against us.

Time: 6–7 minutes

Tone: Thought-provoking

Cast: Naomi — A woman who has faced many difficulties and is struggling with trusting God's faithfulness (female)
Ruth — Her obedient and faithful daughter-in-law (female)

Costumes: Something simple and stylistic, such as neutral-colored or matching dresses

Props/Set: Two musician's stools (optional)

Themes: Anger, children, faith, family issues, God's sovereignty, grief and loss, love, Mother's Day, parenting, purpose, questions, relationships, resentment, suffering

Text: "'For your daughter-in-law, who loves you and who is better to you than seven sons, has given him birth.' Then Naomi took the child, laid him in her lap and cared for him" (Ruth 4:15b–16).

Notes: In this sketch, both Ruth and Naomi share their version of the same story. Naomi is older; Ruth is a young woman. Use some blocking and movement, but keep it simple. Use musician's stools if desired. One actress freezes while the other actress is delivering her lines.

This sketch could be delivered in two parts; for ideas, see the notes provided in the script. Scene 1 lasts 3.5 minutes; Scene 2 lasts about 3 minutes. At the points in the drama where the actresses address each other, they don't actually make eye contact, they just turn aside a bit from directly addressing the audience. Use two spotlights and two lapel microphones.

1   ***SETTING***: Ruth and Naomi are On-stage and seated on stools when
2   the lights go up. There is a spotlight on each actress. The rest of
3   the stage is bare.
4
5   **SCENE 1**
6
7   NAOMI: I know what it's like to lose someone you love. You get
8   angry at God. You blame him. You get bitter.
9   RUTH: It was the drought that brought 'em here. No food in Israel.
10   So they moved here, to Moab. And I'm glad they did. 'Cause
11   Naomi and Elimelech had a couple cute sons. One of them was
12   really cute ...
13 NAOMI: Each of my boys found a wife in that land. Nice girls —
14   Orpah and Ruth. After my husband died, I stayed there with
15   my sons and their wives. I was hoping there'd be some
16   grandchildren on the way. But none came. Not one.
17 RUTH: You have to understand, in our land it was shameful not to
18   have kids. Some people even thought it was a curse not to bear
19   children. *(1 minute mark)*
20 NAOMI: Those two women became like daughters to me. And then
21   the unthinkable happened.
22 RUTH: My husband and his brother — they both died. In the same
23   year. And when it happened, it was like a storm crossed over
24   Naomi's face.
25 NAOMI: First, moving away from my home. Then my husband.
26   Then my two sons. It was like God was out to get me.
27 RUTH: And the storm never left. It changed her, deep inside. She
28   hardly seemed like the same person.
29 NAOMI: Finally, when I found out the drought was over, I decided
30   to go back home. Far away from that place and all those
31   memories.
32 RUTH: She tried to run. But running doesn't work.
33 NAOMI: I'd grown close to Ruth and Orpah, and they offered to
34   come with me. But I refused. "Stay here. Get married. Settle
35   down," I told them. But Ruth wouldn't listen. *(2 minute mark)*

1   RUTH: *(As if addressing NAOMI)* **Wherever you go, I'll go. And**
2   **wherever you live, I'll live. Your people will be my people. And**
3   **your God will be my God** (Ruth 1:16, author's paraphrase).
4   NAOMI: **No, Ruth wouldn't leave my side. She chose my people**
5   **over hers. And my God — the God of Israel — over the gods**
6   **of her people. Even though it meant leaving behind everything**
7   **she'd ever known. Together we returned to Bethlehem.**
8   RUTH: **It wasn't an easy choice. I was young. I knew I could've**
9   **found another guy in my own country and started over. I**
10   **knew all that. But Naomi had taught me about her God, and**
11   **it seemed like a good chance to choose who to follow. Where**
12   **to stand.**
13   NAOMI: **Coming home was tough. My old friends recognized me.**
14   **Everyone was thrilled to see me. But I told them to just leave**
15   **me alone. The memories had followed me.** *(3 minute mark)*
16   RUTH: **The truth is, Naomi, she blamed God. She never stopped**
17   **believing in him, but I think she did stop loving him. "I'm not**
18   **the Naomi you remember," she told 'em. "Don't call me that**
19   **name anymore. Call me Mara, which means bitter. Because**
20   **God has made my life bitter and sad. God Almighty has**
21   **brought all this pain into my life"** (Ruth 1:20, author's
22   paraphrase). **That's what she said.**
23   NAOMI: **We were poor, but we finally found a place to stay, just as**
24   **the barley season was beginning.** *(If desired, you could stop*
25   *here for music or a word from the speaker. Then, continue the*
26   *drama after the message or worship time. We begin to see a*
27   *change in NAOMI's character in this scene. She is intrigued with*
28   *the idea of setting her daughter up with this man, BOAZ.)*
29
30
31   **SCENE 2**
32
33   RUTH: **One day I asked Naomi if I could go pick up leftover grain.**
34   **It was all I could do to help. We didn't have any other way of**
35   **getting food. And in that land, without a husband or a father**

1   to help provide for you … it was easy to get overlooked.

2 NAOMI: So I told her to go. And when she returned with nearly a

3   bushel full of grain, I knew she'd gotten *someone's* attention.

4 RUTH: I could tell by the way she asked me about the grain that

5   she had something in mind. "May God bless the man who took

6   notice of you," she said.

7 NAOMI: When a man gives a woman that much barley, he's got

8   more on his mind than just the harvest season. Let me tell you

9   that. "Go back to his fields," I told her. "And stay close to this

10   man." And she did. *(1 minute mark for Scene 2)*

11 RUTH: Well, one day Naomi pulled me aside before I headed to the

12   fields. She had this glint in her eye. "Ruth," she said, "Put on

13   your best clothes. Get out your makeup and perfume. Take a

14   bath. Tonight I want you to go and let Boaz know how you feel

15   about him."

16 NAOMI: *(Slyly)* I knew he'd be alone. It was the perfect chance for

17   Ruth to … well … I didn't tell her to do anything I wouldn't

18   have done if I were young. And single. And a man had shown

19   me that kind of attention … And given her that much barley

20   … What can I say? She was a woman. He was a man. She

21   knew what to do.

22 RUTH: The next day, when I walked in the door, she just smiled at

23   me and asked, "How did it go last night, Ruth?" and I told her

24   everything he said. And about the barley he gave me before he

25   let me come back home — *(2 minute mark for Scene 2)*

26 NAOMI: *(To audience)* A whole skirt full of barley. Things were

27   moving along even faster than I expected. *(Addressing RUTH)*

28   "You just wait, honey. Boaz is gonna call. Trust me."

29 RUTH: He did. He took care of arranging for the marriage and

30   everything, just like Naomi said he would.

31 NAOMI: It was no coincidence that we returned to town at just

32   that time of year …

33 RUTH: And then, we were married …

34 NAOMI: … And that Ruth went to just that field …

35 RUTH: … And it wasn't long and we had our first baby. A boy …

1 NAOMI: ... On just that day ...

2 RUTH: ... But we didn't name him. We left that honor up to
3   Naomi and her friends.

4 NAOMI: ... And met just that man.

5 RUTH: ... The storm had finally left her face.

6 NAOMI: We named him Obed. And that day, my friends stopped
7   calling me Mara.

8 RUTH: Nothing is a coincidence. Not with the God of Israel ...
9   Naomi's God, my God, had brought joy back into her life.

10 NAOMI: They handed me that baby and, as I held my grandson
11   for the first time, they called me Grandma Naomi. They called
12   me Naomi again. And at that moment, it felt just right. For the
13   first time in years, everything felt just right. *(Freeze. Fadeout.)*

14

15

16

17

18

19

20

21

22

23

24

25

26

27

28

29

30

31

32

33

34

35

The Lord and the Lamb

Summary: Camille didn't understand the Lord's Supper until she realized the context of the Passover meal.

Purpose: To clarify the purpose and significance of the Lord's Supper.

Time: 4 minutes

Tone: Worshipful

Cast: Camille — A person who grew up with misconceptions about the Lord's Supper (male or female; note that Camille's part could be performed by two people rather than one. Notes are included in the script)

Reader — A dramatic reader of the text concerning the Lord's Supper (male or female)

Costumes: Consider having the Reader play the role of Paul and dress in period garb. Camille is dressed in casual, contemporary clothes.

Props/Set: A chair for Camille (or two chairs, if you use an extra person); you could also have the Reader hold up the elements of the Lord's Supper at appropriate times during the drama

Themes: Church issues, death, Easter, faith, forgiveness, grace, guilt, hope, Jesus, Lord's Supper, misconceptions about Christianity, Passover, prophecy fulfillment, worship

Text: 1 Corinthians 11:23–28 (New Living Translation text is included in the script)

Notes: You'll notice that Camille's speaking part has been divided into small sections. If you use one actress, just have her say each section together. Her part has been subdivided for you in case you wish to add a third actor to this drama. The part of the Reader could be done as a voiceover, or he or she could be On-stage with Camille. Use general stage lighting and two (or three) lapel microphones.

1 *SETTING*: A chair (or chairs) for Camille is at Stage Left. The Reader
2   is standing at Stage Right, with a small table on which the bread
3   and cup have been set. The rest of the stage is bare.
4
5 CAMILLE A: I never really understood the whole thing.
6 CAMILLE B: They used to call it "Communion" at the church I
7   went to as a kid. But I've heard it called "The Lord's Supper"
8   or the "Eucharist" or "Mass." Even "The Breaking of the
9   Bread."
10 CAMILLE A: I just never really understood what it was all about.
11 READER: "For this is what the Lord himself said, and I pass it on
12   to you just as I received it" (1 Corinthians 11:23a).
13 CAMILLE B: I mean, it *is* kind of mysterious.
14 CAMILLE A: But the problem comes when people make it out to
15   be more than it is, or less than it is.
16 CAMILLE B: Like when they turn it into some kind of sacred and
17   magical ceremony, or when they make it *less* than it is by not
18   taking God seriously or by just going through the motions. *(1
19   minute mark)*
20 READER: "On the night when he was betrayed, the Lord Jesus
21   took a loaf of bread, and when he had given thanks, he broke
22   it and said, 'This is my body, which is given for you'"
23   (1 Corinthians 11:23b–24).
24 CAMILLE A: Yeah, Jesus actually said the bread was his body.
25 CAMILLE B: But remember, he was sharing a Jewish Passover
26   meal with his friends. They were remembering the lamb that
27   was slain so that God's anger would pass over the slaves in
28   Egypt.
29 CAMILLE A: The meal was all about hope. And freedom. And
30   grace. And deliverance.
31 READER: "Do this in remembrance of me" (1 Corinthians 11:24).
32 CAMILLE B: They must have been thinking,
33 CAMILLE A: "But Jesus, what do you mean do it in remembrance
34   of you? We do it to remember the lamb that was slain!"
35 READER: "In the same way, he took the cup of wine after supper,

1	saying, 'This cup is the new covenant between God and you,
2	sealed by the shedding of my blood'" (1 Corinthians 11:25).
3	CAMILLE B: A new covenant ...
4	CAMILLE A: During Passover ... *(2 minute mark)*
5	CAMILLE B: And they remembered the lamb that was sacrificed.
6	That was the old covenant. Jesus was telling them that he was
7	the main course, and they didn't even realize it.
8	CAMILLE A: He was saying he was going to be slain as the final
9	sacrifice. As the lamb. That takes away the sin of the world.
10	READER: "Do this in remembrance of me as often as you drink it"
11	(1 Corinthians 11:25b).
12	CAMILLE B: And the disciples watched the whole thing, thinking,
13	CAMILLE A: "That blood represents the lamb's blood! What do
14	you mean by saying it's your blood? Do it in remembrance of
15	you? What are you talking about? You're not the lamb ... Are
16	you?"
17	READER: "For every time you eat this bread and drink this cup,
18	you are announcing the Lord's death until he comes again"
19	(1 Corinthians 11:26).
20	CAMILLE B: Not the lamb's death from the old covenant; the
21	Lord's death in the new covenant.
22	CAMILLE A: Not slavery from Egypt, but a much more common
23	kind. Slavery to yourself. And your choices. And your past.
24	*(3 minute mark)*
25	CAMILLE B: The lamb and the Lord. One and the same. For you.
26	READER: "So if anyone eats this bread or drinks this cup of the
27	Lord unworthily, that person is guilty of sinning against the
28	body and the blood of the Lord" (1 Corinthians 11:27).
29	CAMILLE A: And that's what has happened ever since. He's still
30	the main course. He's still the lamb that takes away our sin.
31	CAMILLE B: Yours and mine. The sin of the world. But some
32	people still miss the point. They want it to be magic or a ritual
33	or a ceremony or a snack. But it's not.
34	READER: "That is why you should examine yourself before eating
35	the bread and drinking from the cup" (1 Corinthians 11:28).

1   CAMILLE A: It's all about hope. And freedom. And grace. And
2   deliverance. About the forgiveness that's ours — not when we
3   eat or drink — but when we believe and remember.
4   CAMILLE B: And that's the point. To believe and remember.
5   Until he comes again. *(Freeze and fadeout. Transition into*
6   *worship music and the distribution of the Lord's Supper.)*

The Complaint Department

Summary: In the heavenly complaint department, the receptionist is always hearing from people when things don't go their way. But do they all have a legitimate reason to complain?

Purpose: To show that while we can bring all our problems to God, he is even more interested in hearing us give thanks.

Time: 7–8 minutes

Tone: Humorous and thought-provoking

Cast: Helen — The receptionist for the heavenly complaint department (female)
Caller — A variety of male characters who are complaining to God (male)

Costumes: Helen is wearing professional office clothes; the Caller is dressed in casual, contemporary clothes

Props/Set: A telephone headset, a computer keyboard, desk paraphernalia, a telephone, a fingernail polish kit

Themes: Anger, complaints, frustrations, God's sovereignty, modern life, prayer, priorities, spiritual health, stress, suffering, thanksgiving

Text: "Do not be anxious about anything, but in everything, by prayer and petition, with thanksgiving, present your requests to God" (Philippians 4:6).

Notes: God is always willing to hear our complaints, but he wants us to bring all of our prayers to him with a sense of thanksgiving. Helen is tired of hearing people complain all the time. She speaks in a nasally Brooklyn accent. Have fun making her character a little eccentric. The Caller should take on different mannerisms for each character.

Use two spotlights, one lapel microphone, and one headset microphone for Helen (she could also use a lapel microphone, if no headset microphones are available).

1   *SETTING*: An imaginary complaint department in heaven, where a
2   tired receptionist puts people's prayers through to God. The Caller
3   could be located Off-stage, or on the other side of the stage. If he
4   is On-stage with Helen, then they should both face the audience
5   rather than looking at each other, since they are supposedly
6   talking on the phone.
7
8   SITUATION 1
9
10   HELEN: *(To audience, painting her nails)* **You wouldn't believe how**
11   **many complaints we've had lately. Complain. Complain.**
12   **Complain. But the Boss wants me to answer the phones, so I'll**
13   **answer the phones.** *(CALLER picks up the phone, dials a number*
14   *and, as the phone rings, HELEN answers it.)* **Hello! Heavenly**
15   **Complaint Department. Call to him, and he will answer you**
16   **and tell you great and unsearchable things you do not know.**
17   (See Jeremiah 33:3.) **State the nature of your complaint, please.**
18   JOB: **Yeah, my name is Job.**
19   HELEN: **Hello, Mr. Job, how may I help you?**
20   JOB: **Well, I just lost everything. My workers have been killed by**
21   **terrorists. My kids are all dead, and a tornado destroyed my**
22   **house. My friends and my wife have turned against me, I'm**
23   **suffering from a terrible disease, and all I can do is sit here all**
24   **day in this pile of ashes, scratching my boils with these**
25   **potsherds.** *(1 minute mark)*
26   HELEN: **Potsherds, huh?**
27   JOB: **Yeah. My wife wants me to just curse God and then kill**
28   **myself. This has not been my day.**
29   HELEN: **Apparently not, Mr. Job. And what action would you like**
30   **to take in regards to your complaint? Would you like to send**
31   **God an official "Why is the world ganging up on me?" report**
32   **by certified prayer?**
33   JOB: **No. I just want a fair hearing from him. Why am I suffering**
34   **like this? I need to hear from him. Every time I call, he**
35   **doesn't seem to answer.**

1   HELEN: Hmmm. Let me put you through. *(Pushing some buttons)*
2   I'm sorry, Mr. Job, he says he'll be getting back to you soon.
3   JOB: Yeah. That's what I thought you'd say. *(They both hang up, the*
4   *CALLER redials and, as the phone rings, HELEN answers again.)*
5
6
7   SITUATION 2
8
9   HELEN: Hello! Heavenly Complaint Department. Call upon him
10   in the day of trouble, and he will deliver you. (See Psalm 50:15.)
11   State the nature of your complaint, please. *(2 minute mark)*
12   CAIN: *(Sounding evil)* Yeah, I've got some real problems with God.
13   HELEN: Name, please.
14   CAIN: Cain.
15   HELEN: *(Typing as he answers)* Is that your first name or your last
16   name?
17   CAIN: Both.
18   HELEN: All right Mr. Cain Cain. What is the specific nature of
19   your complaint, please?
20   CAIN: God thinks my brother's offerings are better than mine are.
21   What is that all about? Like I'm not as good as he is or
22   something?!
23   HELEN: And have you tried bringing this up to God directly, Mr.
24   Cain?
25   CAIN: Yeah. And he just told me to do what's right; that I must
26   master the desires within me.
27   HELEN: Uh-huh. And have you done that?
28   CAIN: Look — this is the complaint department, right? So let me
29   complain! I'm not interested in defending myself to you!
30   HELEN: Hmmm ... would you like me to put you through to
31   requests and needs processing? *(3 minute mark)*
32   CAIN: No, that won't be necessary. I've got something else in
33   mind. Good-bye. *(He hangs up.)*
34   HELEN: *(To audience)* Hmmm. That boy is headed for trouble if he
35   doesn't change his attitude. I'll tell you that — *(She hangs up,*

1   *the CALLER redials and, as the phone rings, HELEN answers*
2   *again.)*
3
4
5   SITUATION 3
6
7   HELEN: Hello, Heavenly Complaint Department. You call, he
8   hears, he cares, he answers. State the nature of your
9   complaint, please.
10   LOT: Yeah, it has to do with my wife.
11   HELEN: All right, name please. Last name first, first name last,
12   and middle initial in the middle there someplace —
13   LOT: Ummm, I don't have a last name. Or a middle initial.
14   HELEN: Oh. Why doesn't that surprise me?
15   LOT: The name's Lot.
16   HELEN: Oh, I'll bet you're always getting people giving you a
17   hard time. Like, "Thanks a-lot." "Do you come here a-lot?"
18   "Lot-to," "Lot-ery," "Lot, lot, lot!"
19   LOT: No, actually, um, I don't. *(4 minute mark)*
20   HELEN: Oh. *(Awkward pause)* All right, Mr. Lot. What is your
21   complaint, please? You said it has to do with your wife.
22   LOT: Well, first of all, I'm upset that I had to leave my home, and
23   that God went and destroyed my town with fire and
24   brimstone and burning sulphur from heaven. And then when
25   my wife looked back, she turned into a pillar of salt.
26   HELEN: Really? Once when I was driving to the mall and I looked
27   back, I turned into a telephone pole. Was she hurt in the
28   accident?
29   LOT: She is a pillar of salt!
30   HELEN: Yes, and what seems to be the problem? That she doesn't fit
31   in the shaker? Get it? Fit in the shaker? Oh, I crack myself up.
32   LOT: How can you joke about this? I'd kinda like her back!
33   HELEN: I'm sorry, Mr. Lot. You're right. Would you like to talk to
34   God about your problem directly?
35   LOT: Yeah. That'd be great.

1   HELEN: All right. Please press number two. Thank you for calling.

2   *(After he hangs up, HELEN turns to the audience.)* **That poor**

3   **lady, getting assaulted like that ...** *(5 minute mark. CALLER*

4   *redials and, as the phone rings, HELEN answers again.)*

5

6

7   SITUATION 4

8

9   HELEN: Hello. Heavenly Com —

10   DAVID: Shhh!

11   HELEN: *(Whispering)* Hello. Heavenly Complaint Department.

12   State your name, please.

13   DAVID: *(Whispering)* David.

14   HELEN: David. Right.

15   DAVID: Shhh!

16   HELEN: *(Whispering again)* Let me guess. You don't have a last

17   name.

18   DAVID: How did you know?

19   HELEN: Never mind. How may I help you, Mr. David? And why

20   are we whispering?

21   DAVID: *(Whispering)* They're trying to kill me.

22   HELEN: Who is trying to kill you, sir?

23   DAVID: The king.

24   HELEN: The king is trying to kill you?

25   DAVID: Yeah, and all the king's horses and all the king's men.

26   Also, my best friends have turned on me. I've been on the run

27   for years. Living in caves. Eating grass. I even had to act

28   insane just to stay alive.

29   HELEN: My goodness. You've had quite a time of it, Mr. David. *(6*

30   *minute mark)*

31   DAVID: Yeah, well, I know God is faithful, and he's gonna get me

32   through all this. But it's just, well, tell God I don't get it. I

33   don't understand why he's making me — Wait. I gotta go.

34   Here they come. Bye — *(His line goes dead.)*

35   HELEN: David? Mr. David? *(Sighing)* I hope he remembers to call

1   nine-one-one ... *(She hangs up, the CALLER redials and, as the*
2   *phone rings, HELEN answers again.)*
3
4
5   SITUATION 5
6
7   HELEN: Hello, Heavenly Complaint Department. You call, we
8   answer. State the nature of your complaint, please.
9   AL: Um, yeah. Well, I didn't get a promotion I wanted at work.
10   HELEN: Uh-huh.
11   AL: And I'm kind of upset.
12   HELEN: Yes.
13   AL: And, well, I'd like to place a formal complaint with God.
14   HELEN: Because you didn't get your promotion?
15   AL: Uh-huh.
16   HELEN: You still have a job though, right?
17   AL: Right.
18   HELEN: And your kids are OK?
19   AL: Yeah.
20   HELEN: You still have a house?
21   AL: Uh-huh.
22   HELEN: You're not living in a cave or acting insane, are you?
23   AL: Of course not!
24   HELEN: Are you sitting in ashes and scratching your boils with a
25   potsherd?
26   AL: What?
27   HELEN: What about your wife?
28   AL: She's fine.
29   HELEN: Is she trying to convince you to kill yourself? *(7 minute*
30   *mark)*
31   AL: No.
32   HELEN: Has she been turned into a seasoning, flavoring, or other
33   type of condiment?
34   AL: What are you talking about?
35   HELEN: Is anyone trying to kill you?

1 AL: No!
2 HELEN: Are you jealous that God isn't accepting any of your
3   offerings?
4 AL: Look, I'm just upset about not getting the promotion. That's
5   it!
6   HELEN: Let me get this straight. You're healthy, your family is
7   safe, you have a nice place to live, a steady job, no one is trying
8   to kill you, and you want to complain to God?
9 AL: Yeah, that's right.
10 HELEN: Are you sure you don't want the Thanksgiving
11   Department?
12 AL: No. I can't believe God is letting this happen to me. I want him
13   to hear about this complaint!
14 HELEN: Well, I'll pass this along to him, Mr. —
15 AL: Jones. Al Jones. Be sure he gets the message.
16 HELEN: I will, Mr. Jones. I will. *(Freeze. Fadeout.)*
17
18
19
20
21
22
23
24
25
26
27
28
29
30
31
32
33
34
35

The Trip of a Lifetime

Summary: When Greg is offered the trip of a lifetime, he isn't sure he's ready to sign up.

Purpose: To encourage people to surrender to Christ and choose to follow him.

Time: 4–5 minutes

Tone: Serious and thought-provoking

Cast: Dave — A "travel agent" with an incredible offer (male)
Greg — The man wondering if he wants to sign on for the trip of a lifetime (male)

Costumes: Dave is wearing a Hawaiian shirt; Greg is dressed in contemporary, casual clothes

Props/Set: Posters of Bermuda, Florida, Hawaii, etc., colorful brochures, a small table, two chairs, a pen, and a clipboard

Themes: Calling, choices, church issues, evangelism, faith, following God, forgiveness, missions, service, surrender, witnessing

Text: John 21:15–23

Notes: Don't let Greg's character seem too slick or cheesy. He really *is* interested in what's best for Dave, not just in selling him something. This sketch is an allegory, moving us to a deeper commitment to Christ's call on our lives. Use general stage lighting and two lapel microphones.

1   *SETTING*: Dave's office. As the lights come up, Dave is seated alone
2   at the table with the posters of exotic locations around him. When
3   the lights are up, Greg enters and the scene begins.
4
5   **DAVE: Hello. May I help you?**
6   **GREG: Yeah, I'm Greg Lewison. I called you this morning ...**
7   **DAVE: Oh, yeah! I wasn't sure you'd come by! I'm Dave. I spoke**
8   **with you on the phone. C'mon in.** *(Motioning toward an empty*
9   *chair)* **Have a seat. How can I help you?**
10   **GREG: Well, last week I got some info in the mail from your**
11   **organization about your latest package, and — I've been**
12   **thinking it over. You know, the vacation offer —**
13   **DAVE: Around here we like to say, "It's not just a vacation, it's a**
14   **lifestyle!"**
15   **GREG: Oh, yeah. I read that. Anyway, I have a few questions.**
16   **DAVE: Shoot!**
17   **GREG: Yeah, I guess I've been wondering if there'll be any**
18   **adventure. My last few trips have been, well ... kinda dull.**
19   **DAVE:** *(Confident but not slick)* **If you're looking for adventure, you**
20   **have definitely come to the right place. Take a look at this!**
21   *(Hands him a brochure. 1 minute mark)*
22   **GREG: Whoa. So you actually send people there — into the**
23   **jungles?**
24   **DAVE: On some of our packages, yes. But there's a package to suit**
25   **you, believe me.**
26   **GREG: Impressive.** *(Looking at the posters on the wall)* **It's quite an**
27   **operation you've got here.**
28   **DAVE: It's the doorway to the world. We send people everywhere.**
29   **The tropics. Jungles. Tundra. Mountains. Deserts. We have**
30   **getaway packages for nearly every climate and country in the**
31   **world!**
32   **GREG:** *(Satisfied)* **Wow. OK. Sounds exciting and adventurous.**
33   **But, uh ... is it safe? I mean, these days some countries are a**
34   **little, well, unfriendly. And the more I read about your trips,**
35   **well ... The more I wonder ...**

1   DAVE: *(Sighing)* Is bungee jumping safe? Is parachuting safe? Is
2   scuba diving safe? The question shouldn't be "Is it safe?" but
3   "Are the risks worth taking?" Everything has its risks. Life
4   isn't safe, Greg.
5   GREG: Hmmm. *(2 minute mark)*
6   DAVE: Our trips are exciting, they're rewarding, educational
7   and — in some cases — very challenging ... but I wouldn't
8   use the word "safe" exactly. You see, sometimes we take
9   people to the limit — and even beyond. But no one has ever
10   come back disappointed.
11   GREG: To the limit, huh? I see ... Well, I have to say, I'm
12   impressed by the exotic locations. I mean, sandy beaches,
13   wilderness peaks, Third World countries ... Wow. And I like
14   the idea of challenge and adventure — *(Referring to a*
15   *brochure)* Hmmm ... What about these "urban adventures"?
16   DAVE: Ah, well. You see, Greg, some people aren't trying to get
17   away from it all. They're not looking to escape life, but to face
18   it head on. We designed a package just for them. They
19   actually live and work in the city for a brief time, getting to
20   know the natives firsthand.
21   GREG: Natives? You mean the actual inhabitants of the city?
22   DAVE: Yeah.
23   GREG: Hmmm. I've seen the city. That might not be for me.
24   DAVE: Maybe not. But it's always worth considering ... *(3 minute*
25   *mark)*
26   GREG: *(Thoughtfully)* I do have one more question.
27   DAVE: What's that?
28   GREG: Some of these trips look kinda lengthy. Is packing ever a
29   problem? I mean, do you tell us what we'll need as far as
30   supplies, clothes, visas, passports, stuff like that?
31   DAVE: Actually, we take care of all that for you. You won't need to
32   bring anything except for yourself, your imagination, and
33   your passion for living life to the fullest —
34   GREG: *(Under his breath)* And your wallet.
35   DAVE: Huh?

1   GREG: I said, "And your wallet." I'm gonna need my wallet,
2   right?
3   DAVE: Well —
4   GREG: OK, give me the bottom line. I'm interested in pursuing
5   this, Dave, I really am, but what's a trip like this gonna put me
6   back?
7   DAVE: Put you back?
8   GREG: Yeah, what's it gonna cost me?
9   DAVE: *(Leaning forward)* Everything.
10   GREG: Everything?
11   DAVE: That's right, Greg. But it's the trip of a lifetime. And you
12   won't be disappointed. I guarantee it.
13   GREG: *(Remembering)* It's not just a vacation, it's a lifestyle —
14   *(4 minute mark)*
15   DAVE: That's right. So what do you say? Once you sign up, your
16   life will never be the same again ... *(He hands GREG a pen,*
17   *GREG looks at it, and then freezes as the lights fade.)*
18
19
20
21
22
23
24
25
26
27
28
29
30
31
32
33
34
35

The Conversation

Summary: Billy and Nancy explore what it would be like if talking to God were like calling a radio show, talking to your boss, talking to your mom, or talking to your very best friend.

Purpose: To show that prayer is really a chance to talk to your best friend.

Time: 6–7 minutes

Tone: Humorous and thought-provoking

Cast: Nancy — An actress who can portray a radio hostess, a doting mother, a submissive employee, and a penitent friend (female)
Billy — An actor who can portray a hesitant radio guest, an uncaring boss, a regretful son, and a forgiving friend (male)

Costumes: Casual, contemporary clothes; you may wish to use simple costume pieces to portray the different characters, such as a briefcase for the boss and a scarf and glasses for the mother

Props/Set: A cell phone, a watch, two chairs, a small table or desk, a photo album

Themes: Communication, forgiveness, guilt, Jesus, listening, misconceptions about Christianity, prayer, regrets, repentance, sin, teenagers

Text: "The Lord is compassionate and gracious, slow to anger, abounding in love. He will not always accuse, nor will he harbor his anger forever; he does not treat us as our sins deserve or repay us according to our iniquities" (Psalm 103:8–10).

Notes: Helpful notes for your actors appear at the beginning of each section. Use general stage lighting and two lapel microphones.

1   ***SETTING***: The setting for each scene is different. Billy and Nancy are
2   both On-stage as the lights come up and the scene begins.
3
4   *(Scene 1. BILLY is in his car, calling a radio show, NANCY is the*
5   *announcer in the studio. He wants to talk about his problem; she*
6   *is too quick to give advice without really listening to or addressing*
7   *his real needs. They're both On-stage as the lights come up and*
8   *the scene begins.)*
9   **BILLY:** *(To audience)* **If talking to God were like dialing a call-in**
10 **radio show ...** *(As he finishes announcing the scene, NANCY*
11 *turns to face the audience. Both BILLY and NANCY are*
12 *pretending they can't see each other as he calls her radio show.)*
13 **NANCY: Bill from Chicago. You're live on the air with "Answers**
14 **for Today with Nancy the Answer Lady." What can I do for**
15 **you, Bill?**
16 **BILLY:** *(Sounding distant and high on reverb)* **Hello?**
17 **NANCY: Turn your radio down, Bill.**
18 **BILLY: Hello?!**
19 **NANCY: Turn your radio down!**
20 **BILLY: Oh ... Here ...** *(The reverb is turned down.)* **Hello?**
21 **NANCY: That's better.**
22 **BILLY: OK, well, first of all, thanks for taking my call.**
23 **NANCY: You're welcome, Bill.**
24 **BILLY: I really love your show. I listen to you all the time.**
25 **NANCY: That's great, Bill. How can I help you?**
26 **BILLY: Well, I've been having some problems with guilt.**
27 **NANCY: Guilt?**
28 **BILLY: Yeah.**
29 **NANCY: Guilt?**
30 **BILLY: Right.**
31 **NANCY: Guilt!**
32 **BILLY: Uh-huh.** *(1 minute mark)*
33 **NANCY: Listen to me, Bill. Guilt doesn't help anything. When has**
34 **guilt ever helped you solve a problem?**
35 **BILLY: Well —**

1   NANCY: Do you feel good about yourself, Bill?

2   BILLY: Um, not really. That's why I called —

3   NANCY: There's your problem. You gotta feel good about yourself.

4   Tell yourself you're a nice person. I'm special. Bill, do it right

5   now. Say it: "I'm a nice person."

6   BILLY: You're a nice person.

7   NANCY: No, you're a nice person, Bill. Say, "Bill is a nice person."

8   BILLY: Bill is a nice person.

9   NANCY: Bill is special.

10   BILLY: Bill is special?

11   NANCY: That's right. You're special. I'm special. We're all special,

12   Bill.

13   BILLY: But if everyone is special, what's so special about being

14   special?

15   NANCY: *(Ignoring his question; as she says this, she makes buzzing*

16   *or static sounds)* What's that? We're getting some static here.

17   You're breaking up on me, Bill.

18   BILLY: But some of the stuff I've done is bad ... I shouldn't feel

19   good about that stuff, should I? *(2 minute mark)*

20   NANCY: *(BILLY'S line goes dead.)* Bill, it seems like we've lost you

21   there. Our next caller is ... Jamie from Phoenix. Jamie, what

22   can I do for you? *(They both freeze.)*

23

24   *(Scene 2. BILLY and NANCY are in BILLY'S office. NANCY has*

25   *come to meet with her boss to confess something to him. BILLY*

26   *just doesn't have time for her.)*

27   NANCY: *(To audience)* If talking to God were like talking to your

28   boss ... *(As she finishes announcing the scene, BILLY turns to*

29   *face the audience.)*

30   BILLY: *(Shuffling papers)* Come on in!

31   NANCY: *(Miming walking through a door)* Sir, I've got some things

32   I need to talk to you about.

33   BILLY: Blanderson, is that you?

34   NANCY: Yes, sir. It's me, Nancy Anderson.

35   BILLY: Well, have a seat there, Amberson.

1 NANCY: Anderson, sir.
2 BILLY: Right! I'm always here for my people. You know that.
3 NANCY: Yes, sir. Well, as I was saying —
4 BILLY: Just a minute there, Sanderson. I've gotta take this call. *(As*
5   *he talks, she sits patiently and waits.)* Yes ... McCartt? Yeah, it's
6   me. Wanna hit the links this afternoon? I don't have anything
7   important going on. Just a couple meetings. I'll clear my
8   schedule. No problem. All right, then. *(Mimes hanging up.)* OK,
9   now what did you need there, Landerson?
10 NANCY: It's um, Anderson. Nancy Anderson. *(3 minute mark)*
11 BILLY: Of course, well, what can I do for you? Don't waste my
12   time here. I'm a busy man.
13 NANCY: Well, I've been —
14 BILLY: Lemme guess. You're gonna say you've been working
15   hard. Putting in those extra hours. And you need a little raise.
16   Well, I agree. I'll include it on your next paycheck. Good
17   work. Keep it up. Was there anything else?
18 NANCY: Actually, yes. I didn't come in here for a raise, it's more —
19 BILLY: *(Checking his watch)* Right. Just a minute, looks like I've
20   got an important lunch meeting I gotta get to. But it's been
21   great talking. Let's do it again soon, OK, Flanderson? *(Turns*
22   *his back to NANCY, takes a couple steps, and freezes.)*
23 NANCY: *(To herself)* It's Anderson. Nancy Anderson. *(She freezes.)*
24
25   *(Scene 3. BILLY has just come home to visit his mom. He is a*
26   *grown man, but she still treats him as if he were a little boy. The*
27   *scene takes place in NANCY's living room.)*
28 BILLY: *(To audience)* If talking to God were like talking to your
29   mother ... *(As he finishes announcing the scene, NANCY*
30   *welcomes him into her living room.)*
31 NANCY: Hello? Who's there?
32 BILLY: *(Miming walking through a door)* Hey, Mom?
33 NANCY: Billy! It's you, my little Billy! *(Pinching his cheek)* I am so
34   glad you're here to visit your aging, decrepit mother ...
35   *(4 minute mark)*

1 BILLY: Oh, Mom.

2 NANCY: ... Living all alone in this big cold house. Now that most
3   of my friends have passed away, it's nice to see a familiar face
4   once again.

5 BILLY: Stop it, Mom.

6 NANCY: Have you been brushing your teeth after meals?

7 BILLY: Yeah, Mom.

8 NANCY: And watching those sweets? You always were a little
9   snacker.

10 BILLY: Yeah, Mom, look —

11 NANCY: And wearing your hat outside?

12 BILLY: Mom!

13 NANCY: Oh, Billy, I was looking through these photo albums, and
14   I remember that time when you were two years old and I was
15   having such trouble potty training you —

16 BILLY: Mom —

17 NANCY: Oh, you were so cute running around the house in that
18   little Superman diaper of yours —

19 BILLY: Mom, look, I was hoping we could talk about a few things.

20 NANCY: Of course. Billy, do you remember Lenny Chokowski?

21 BILLY: Was he that kid who always picked on me when I was in
22   first grade?

23 NANCY: No, that was Randy Rimsizki. *(Delivering these lines very*
24   *fast)* Lenny was that nice boy who was in your fifth grade class
25   and his cousin broke his leg playing soccer back when Mr.
26   Brendan was your coach before he got that DWI and had to
27   go into counseling. Anyway, his sister called the other day and
28   — *(5 minute mark)*

29 BILLY: Mom, that's great, but I was really hoping we could talk
30   about some stuff. I did something I'm not too proud of.

31 NANCY: *(Pinching his cheeks)* But I'm so proud of you, Billy.
32   You're such a *nice* boy. You've always been such a good son to
33   me. *(Getting emotional)* Oh, Billy.

34 BILLY: But Mom, I'm serious.

35 NANCY: Oh, just forget about it. Whatever you did, I'm sure it

1. wasn't that bad. I'm sure it really wasn't anything important
2. at all. Now, as I was saying, there is this new family next door.
3. Do you remember when —
4. **BILLY: See you later, Mom.** *(Both freeze.)*
5.
6. *(Scene 4. BILLY and NANCY are best friends. She has just spent*
7. *the last hour asking him to forgive her for something she said the*
8. *other day. He has forgiven her and is just glad to be spending time*
9. *with her, but he's having a hard time convincing her that she really*
10. *is forgiven. Their exchange is quick and friendly and tender.)*
11. **NANCY:** *(To audience)* **If talking to God were like talking to your**
12. **best friend …** *(As she finishes announcing the scene, BILLY*
13. *addresses her.)*
14. **BILLY: Thanks for calling me over here today, Nancy.**
15. **NANCY: Oh boy, look at the time! I can't believe we've just been**
16. **sitting here talking for an hour!**
17. **BILLY: I didn't mind. It was fun.**
18. **NANCY: So anyway, as I was saying, I'm really sorry about those**
19. **things I said the other day —**
20. **BILLY: Nancy?**
21. **NANCY: Yeah.**
22. **BILLY: I told you, I forgive you.** *(6 minute mark)*
23. **NANCY: I know, but it's just —**
24. **BILLY: There's no "but." I'm not angry. OK?**
25. **NANCY: Are you sure?**
26. **BILLY: Of course.**
27. **NANCY: But —**
28. **BILLY: Listen! Drop it. Forget it. I won't ever bring it up again. I**
29. **promise. I forgive you.**
30. **NANCY: Thanks. Thanks for listening.**
31. **BILLY: No problem.**
32. **NANCY: I mean it —**
33. **BILLY: So do I. C'mere.** *(She turns her back to the audience as they*
34. *hug. Fadeout.)*
35.

Part 4
Interpretive and Dramatic Readings

These dramas will work well during a time of reflection, prayer, or worship within your service. Many of them would work well with instrumental backgrounds or interludes.

Take your time and polish these. Since so much depends upon the interchange of lines between the actors in these readings, it's even more important that they not forget their lines or mix up the order of their parts.

Some of these dramas will work as interpretive readings in which the actors could actually have a copy of the script with them. As you read through them, you'll see which ones will work best with your congregation's style of worship.

Stillness

Summary: Two storytellers explore what it means to be still before God.

Purpose: To encourage people to slow down and pursue intimacy with God.

Time: 4–5 minutes

Tone: Worshipful

Cast: Teller #1/God — An actor who portrays both an interpretative storyteller and the personality of God (male)
Teller #2/Bobbie — An actor who portrays both an interpretative storyteller and a man (or woman) who is relieved to finally slow down (male or female)

Costumes: Something simple and stylistic, such as blue jeans and a neutral oxford or turtleneck

Props/Set: Two chairs

Themes: Distractions, faith, following God, Jesus, life, listening, modern life, prayer, rest, spiritual health, stress, work, worship

Text: "Be still, and know that I am God; I will be exalted among the nations, I will be exalted in the earth" (Psalm 46:10).

Notes: Use blocking to contrast our frantic, hurrying lives with the stillness of God. After the actors have finished their interpretive piece, they step into roles as God and Bobbie. Use spotlights at first and then general stage lighting at the switch from storytellers to characters. Use two lapel microphones.

If desired, add audio special effects of a beating heart or peaceful background music. You could also use video images on the screen of busy and frantic, and then peaceful and tranquil settings.

1   *SETTING:* The first part of this drama is interpretive, the second part
2   happens inside Bobbie's heart where he (or she) has finally
3   learned to slow down and listen to God's voice. They're both On-
4   stage as the lights come up and the scene begins.
5
6   TELLER #1: There is only One who does not hurry. Who does not
7   rush about; going here and there.
8   TELLER #2: Wondering — perhaps, if he is being productive
9   enough.
10 TELLER #1: No. The Patient One waits,
11 TELLER #2: And watches,
12 TELLER #1: For just the right moment.
13 TELLER #2: And then he acts in love.
14 TELLER #1: If he wants a world, he tells a story, one day at a time;
15 TELLER #2: A story of life slowly budding at his command;
16   springing forth upon a lonely rock in a sea of stars.
17 TELLER #1: If he wants a tree,
18 TELLER #2: He plants a seed.
19 TELLER #1: If he wants a river,
20 TELLER #2: He trickles a stream down a mountainside, one
21   raindrop at a time.
22 TELLER #1: If he wants a child, He waits with the parents,
23   expectantly, month after month —
24 TELLER #2: Until the moment of birth arrives. *(1 minute mark)*
25 TELLER #1: If he wants a Savior, he waits and waits,
26 TELLER #2: Until the time is right.
27 TELLER #1: And then he sends a Son of his own
28 TELLER #2: Into this hustling, bustling world.
29 TELLER #1: *(After a pause)* Perhaps it is his patience that helps
30   him see past the urgent to the important;
31 TELLER #2: Past the tear-stained present to the radiant future.
32 TELLER #1: Perhaps that is why he speaks in a still small voice,
33   whispering
34 TELLER #2: Rather than shouting,
35 TELLER #1: Inviting

1   TELLER #2: Rather than coercing.

2   TELLER #1: Trying to get our attention as we rush headlong,

3   TELLER #2: Ever onward.

4   TELLER #1: Faster and faster toward an unseen goal, weary and
5   burdened and lonely and confused,

6   TELLER #2: Seeking shelter and peace and rest.

7   TELLER #1: For the only time the Patient One hurries,

8   TELLER #2: Is to greet a wandering child back into his arms,

9   TELLER #1: And then he runs to greet them!

10   TELLER #2: Even now he is calling.

11   TELLER #1: Even now he is running. *(2 minute mark)*

12   TELLER #2: Listen to him,

13   TELLER #1: Turn to him.

14   TELLER #2: He is here

15   TELLER #1: In the depths of your soul.

16   TELLER #2: I urge you,

17   TELLER #1: Be still,

18   TELLER #2: And know the stillness of God. (See Psalm 46:10.)

19   *(As the actors freeze, play the sound effect of a slowly beating*
20   *heart. Then, the actors step out of their storytelling roles into their*
21   *parts. BOBBIE looks around in wonder. GOD is glad they finally*
22   *have the chance to be together. If possible, turn up the reverb on*
23   *their microphones so that it sounds like they are in a large*
24   *cavernous room.)*

25   BOBBIE: *(Looking around)* Wow. It sure is quiet in here.

26   GOD: Yup.

27   BOBBIE: So this is what it's like to be inside a still heart.

28   GOD: Mm-hmmm. *(GOD nods.)*

29   BOBBIE: I've never noticed how calming it can be to just slow
30   down ... Peaceful.

31   GOD: Yeah.

32   BOBBIE: And calm.

33   GOD: Uh-huh.

34   BOBBIE: Kinda spooky.

35   GOD: Why do you say that?

1   BOBBIE: Well, my life is usually the opposite of this. It's full of
2   noise and distractions.

3   GOD: Most people's lives are.

4   BOBBIE: Do this. Do that. Deadlines, traffic jams, phone calls,
5   last-minute meetings. *(Sitting down and sighing)* It seems like
6   I'm always in a hurry. I almost never take the time to just sit
7   and be. Usually I'm so busy making a living that I forget to
8   really live. *(3 minute mark)*

9   GOD: You're not the only one. Nearly everyone I meet these days is
10   so busy that they don't have time to sit and talk. And listen. But
11   they're not only busier than ever before. They're lonelier, too.

12   BOBBIE: I fill up my life with all these activities and new
13   commitments, and then I complain about how busy I am! It
14   doesn't make any sense.

15   GOD: No, it doesn't.

16   BOBBIE: But I never noticed it before now.

17   GOD: It usually takes something pretty traumatic to slow people
18   down. The noise and the busyness get in the way. It's harder
19   to hear me then. 'Cause I prefer not to shout.

20   BOBBIE: Yeah. So how long can I stay in here with you?

21   GOD: As long as you want.

22   BOBBIE: What's your name? *(4 minute mark)*

23   GOD: My name? I am ... I am with you. I am beside you. I am
24   nearby. Call me "The one who is close by. The one who is
25   always present." Is that good enough?

26   BOBBIE: Yeah, it is.

27   GOD: Why don't we get reacquainted, me and you?

28   BOBBIE: Yeah. That sounds good. That sounds really good. *(They*
29   *freeze as the heartbeat fades out with the lights. When the stage is*
30   *finally dark, they exit. Transition to worship or to the message.)*

31
32
33
34
35

Evidence of the Wind

Summary: Two storytellers explore the mystery and wonder of the Holy Spirit's work.

Purpose: To show that the Holy Spirit gives people spiritual birth and new life.

Time: 3 minutes

Tone: Worshipful

Cast: Teller #1 — (female)
Teller #2 — (female)

Costumes: Something simple and stylistic, such as blue jeans and a neutral oxford or turtleneck

Props/Set: None; or you may wish to have the tellers hold up props that relate to specific ideas related to the text of the script

Themes: Conversion, Easter, faith, God's power, God's sovereignty, grace, Holy Spirit, hope, new life, questions, truth

Text: "Just as you can hear the wind but can't tell where it comes from or where it is going, so you can't explain how people are born of the Spirit" (John 3:8, NLT).

Notes: Keep the exchanges quick, so that the drama sounds smooth and conversational, even though it involves two storytellers. Most of the exchanges are addressed to the audience, but there are a few sections where the storytellers address each other. Encourage your actresses to use natural gestures that relate to the text and images of the script.

Use general stage lighting and two lapel microphones. When the storytellers quote Scripture, post it on your screen through a presentation program. Consider having light, airy, worship music play in the background. The entire script could be a done as a voiceover.

1   *SETTING*: The storytellers stand on each side of the stage. You may
2   wish to have a liturgical dancer or movement artist with streamers
3   perform in the middle of the stage. Other than that, the stage is bare.
4
5   **TELLER #1: I do not see the wind. I only sense it. I see its evidence**
6   **around me,**
7   **TELLER #2: Swirling through the forest.**
8   **TELLER #1: — A tree heaving eastward.**
9   **TELLER #2: — A flag snapping briskly**
10   **TELLER #1: — A puddle rippling gently at my feet.**
11   **TELLER #2: — Or the touch of a whisper-cool hand sliding past**
12   **my face,**
13   **TELLER #1: — or teasing my hair.**
14   **TELLER #2: Wind gives birth to wind, and a breeze is born**
15   **beyond the horizon.**
16   **TELLER #2: "Just as you can hear the wind but can't tell where it**
17   **comes from or where it is going,**
18   **TELLER #1: … so you can't explain how people are born of the**
19   **Spirit"** (John 3:8, NLT).
20   **TELLER #2: Spirit gives birth to spirit.**
21   **TELLER #1:** *(Turning to the other STORYTELLER)* **How?**
22   **TELLER #2:** *(To other TELLER)* **We do not know, for we do not see**
23   **it. We see only the results of it.**
24   **TELLER #1:** *(To other TELLER)* **Like the mystery of the wind, we**
25   **see its work, its playground?**
26   **TELLER #2:** *(To other TELLER)* **Yes. We see only the evidence of**
27   **the wind.**
28   **TELLER #1: But like the wind that whistles by,** *(1 minute mark)*
29   **TELLER #2: Laughing at my searching eyes,**
30   **TELLER #1: … So does the Spirit.**
31   **TELLER #2 : For from the beginning,**
32   **TELLER #1: Life and breath and spirit have been a mystery.**
33   **TELLER #2: "And the Lord God formed a man's body from the**
34   **dust of the ground and breathed into it the breath of life.**
35   **TELLER #1: And the man became a living person"** (Genesis 2:7, NLT).

1   TELLER #2:   For flesh by itself cannot enter heaven.

2   TELLER #1:   So Spirit brought life,

3   TELLER #2:   Wind birthing wind.

4   TELLER #1:   Blowing through the cold hearts of the world.

5   TELLER #2:   A mystery.

6   TELLER #1:   And the same wind of the Spirit

7   TELLER #2:   Still breathes life into hearts cold, dead, and hard.

8   TELLER #1:   Hearts of clay,

9   TELLER #2:   Hearts of stone,

10   TELLER #1:   ... Still, today.

11   TELLER #2:   *(After a pause)* Only the Spirit can give life.

12   TELLER #1:   Where? And when? And how?

13   TELLER #2:   *(To the other TELLER)* Faith comes through hearing
14   the message, and the message is heard through the word of
15   Christ (See Romans 10:17), but when and where we do not
16   know. We trust. *(2 minute mark)*

17   TELLER #1:   Spirit gives birth to spirit.

18   TELLER #2:   A mystery.

19   TELLER #1:   The mystery of life that extends beyond the flesh,
20   beyond death.

21   TELLER #2:   A life that reaches into eternity.

22   TELLER #1:   "They were filled with joy when they saw their Lord!

23   TELLER #2:   He spoke to them again and said,

24   TELLER #1:   'Peace be with you. As the Father has sent me, so I
25   send you.'

26   TELLER #2:   Then he breathed on them and said to them,

27   TELLER #1:   'Receive the Holy Spirit'" (John 20:20b–22, NLT).

28   TELLER #2:   Spirit gives birth to Spirit.

29   TELLER #1:   New birth.

30   TELLER #2:   Rebirth.

31   TELLER #1:   New life.

32   TELLER #2:   And only when the last breath is breathed,

33   TELLER #1:   Will the new life,

34   TELLER #2:   In all its fullness —

35   TELLER #1:   — finally arrive. *(The TELLERS bow their heads and*
36   *freeze as the lights fade.)*

Let There Be Light!

Summary: Two storytellers present a dramatic interpretation of scriptural images concerning the Light of the World.

Purpose: To move listeners to reflect on Scripture's images of light and darkness.

Time: 4 minutes

Tone: Worshipful

Cast: Teller #1 — (male or female)
Teller #2 — (male or female)

Costumes: Something simple and stylistic, such as blue jeans and a neutral oxford or turtleneck

Themes: Christmas, conversion, creation, Easter, faith, forgiveness, God's sovereignty, grace, hope, Jesus, new life, worship

Text: "For God, who said, 'Let light shine out of darkness,' made his light shine in our hearts to give us the light of the knowledge of the glory of God in the face of Christ" (2 Corinthians 4:6; see also John 1:4–14).

Notes: This interpretive dramatic piece could be done as Readers Theatre, with the storytellers reading, rather than reciting, their parts. If desired, use lighting changes to reflect the differing moods of the drama. Consider having the storytellers light and then extinguish candles during the piece. If desired, use background music for all or part of this sketch. Use two handheld or lapel microphones.

1   *SETTING*: The stage is bare. Both storytellers are On-stage as the
2   lights come up and the scene begins.
3
4   **TELLER #1:** **In the beginning...**
5   **TELLER #2:** **... In the confusion**
6   **TELLER #1:** **... In the simplicity of creation,**
7   **TELLER #2:** **There was God ...**
8   **TELLER #1:** **... And there was darkness.**
9   **TELLER #2:** *(Pause for a beat)* **But God sought light — eternal**
10   **light.**
11 **TELLER #1:** **And so creation began.**
12 **TELLER #2:** **And as a universe unfolded from his imagination,**
13 **TELLER #1:** **Light became alive, even before —**
14 **TELLER #2:** **... It was bound to the stars,**
15 **TELLER #1:** **... Found in the sun,**
16 **TELLER #2:** **... Reflected by the moon,**
17 **TELLER #1:** **... Captured by the eye.**
18 **TELLER #2:** **God whispered the words, "Let there be light."**
19 **TELLER #1:** **And there was.**
20 **TELLER #2:** **Light in the darkness.**
21 **TELLER #1:** **Separate from the darkness.**
22 **TELLER #2:** **And so life began.**
23 **TELLER #1:** *(After a pause)* **But soon, light from the sun and the**
24   **moon and the stars was not enough,**
25 **TELLER #2:** **Because humans sought darkness ...**
26 **TELLER #1:** **... And darkness sought them,**
27 **TELLER #2:** **... And they embraced it with their hearts.**
28 **TELLER #1:** **Darkness on the inside.** *(1 minute mark)*
29 **TELLER #2:** **And the warmth of outer light could not penetrate so**
30   **deep.**
31 **TELLER #1:** *(After a pause)* **So God spoke a promise, a spark of**
32   **hope —**
33 **TELLER #2:** **... A hint of light,**
34 **TELLER #1:** **... Into the hearts of his children.**
35 **TELLER #2:** **God whispered the words, "Let there be light."**

1   TELLER #1: And there was.

2   TELLER #2: Light in the darkness —

3   TELLER #1: Of their hearts.

4   TELLER #2: And that promise, that Word,

5   TELLER #1: Lived inside to guide their paths and light their

6   journeys.

7   TELLER #2: As long as they remembered the Promise,

8   TELLER #1: ... Light warmed their hearts

9   TELLER #2: ... And gave them the sight

10   TELLER #1: To move through the dark world they had created.

11   TELLER #2: *(After a pause)* Yet, darkness grew and clouded their

12   vision,

13   TELLER #1: Confusing them,

14   TELLER #2: And leading them into the greatest darkness of all —

15   TELLER #1: Death.

16   TELLER #2: And so,

17   TELLER #1: God knew it was time.

18   TELLER #2: He sent the Light that would always shine,

19   TELLER #1: ... The Light that the darkness could not overcome,

20   *(2 minute mark)*

21   TELLER #2: ... That death could not destroy.

22   TELLER #1: He spoke,

23   TELLER #2: And his Promise became a child

24   TELLER #1: ... Born in the night.

25   TELLER #2: And there! A star!

26   TELLER #1: ... A point of light in a distant sea of darkness!

27   TELLER #2: ... And the star sang out his arrival and pointed

28   seekers through the night,

29   TELLER #1: ... To his side.

30   TELLER #2: God whispered the words, "Let there be Light."

31   TELLER #1: And there was.

32   TELLER #2: Light in the darkness.

33   TELLER #1: Light in the world.

34   TELLER #2: *(After a pause)* And the Light lived and walked

35   among us.

1   TELLER #1: The Light shone brighter and brighter ...

2   TELLER #2: ... Drawing darkness out of the world,

3   TELLER #1: ... And out of the hearts of the children of men.

4   TELLER #2: Until one night,

5   TELLER #1: When the time had come,

6   TELLER #2: Light yielded to darkness,

7   TELLER #1: And darkness reigned.

8   TELLER #2: And the Light of the world went out. *(Both TELLERS*

9   *freeze for a moment. Let the words hang in the air.)*

10   TELLER #1: But the Light could not be extinguished.

11   TELLER #2: Not this time. *(3 minute mark)*

12   TELLER #1: Not forever.

13   TELLER #2: And so the Light swallowed the darkness

14   TELLER #1: That lived in the world.

15   TELLER #2: As God whispered the words, "Let there be Light,"

16   TELLER #1: There was:

17   TELLER #2: ... Light in the darkness,

18   TELLER #1: ... Light in the sleeping tomb of the world,

19   TELLER #2: ... Life over death,

20   TELLER #1: ... Light over darkness!

21   TELLER #2: And with the dawning of that new day,

22   TELLER #1: Light shone again!

23   TELLER #2: ... And walked among those still blinded by the dark.

24   TELLER #1: *(After a pause)* And now the Light is waiting for the

25   day it will be released,

26   TELLER #2: *(Picking up the speed of the delivery)* To sweep through

27   the universe and shine forever,

28   TELLER #1: ... Unhindered,

29   TELLER #2: ... Unhampered,

30   TELLER #1: ... Within the hearts of all those who believe,

31   TELLER #2: ... And surrounding all the children who have heard

32   and known the promise.

33   TELLER #1: As God first intended so long ago,

34   TELLER #2: At the beginning of time,

35   TELLER #1: When he spoke into the darkness and said those

1   words
2   **TELLER #2: That forever changed**
3   **TELLER #1: The destiny of man:**
4   **TELLER #2: "Let there be —**
5   **TELLER #1: ... Light!"** *(4 minute mark. Freeze and fadeout or*
6   *immediately transition to worship music.)*
7
8
9
10
11
12
13
14
15
16
17
18
19
20
21
22
23
24
25
26
27
28
29
30
31
32
33
34
35

No Excuse

Summary: Celia and Josh list a variety of common excuses.

Purpose: To show people how easy it is to excuse behavior that God wants us to confess.

Time: 3 minutes

Tone: Thought-provoking

Cast: Celia — A lady who is ready with a lot of different excuses (female)

Josh — A guy with excuses of his own (male)

Costumes: Casual contemporary clothes

Themes: Adultery, excuses, forgiveness, guilt, hiding, repentance, sin, teenagers

Text: "If we claim to be without sin, we deceive ourselves and the truth is not in us. If we confess our sins, he is faithful and just and will forgive us our sins and purify us from all unrighteousness. If we claim we have not sinned, we make him out to be a liar and his word has no place in our lives" (1 John 1:8–10).

Notes: Work on the timing of this piece. To vary the pace, emphasize specific lines. By changing only a few lines that refer to husbands and wives, this sketch could be done with male or female actors. Use two spotlights and two lapel microphones.

1   *SETTING*: Josh and Celia enter simultaneously. Josh stands just right
2   of Center Stage; Celia, just left of center. There is a spotlight on
3   each actor. The rest of the stage is bare.

4

5   **JOSH: Who, me?**

6   **CELIA: You think I did it?**

7   **JOSH and CELIA:** *(Together)* **No way!**

8   **JOSH: It must have been someone else.**

9   **CELIA: After all, I'm a pretty good person,**

10   **JOSH: I follow the rules,**

11   **CELIA: I try my hardest,**

12   **JOSH: I do my best.**

13   **CELIA: What more could anyone ask?**

14   **JOSH: And besides, it's not as bad as what *most* people do.**

15   **CELIA: Compared to those things, it's nothing!**

16   **JOSH: It's no big deal.**

17   **CELIA: Everyone makes mistakes.**

18   **JOSH: No one's perfect.**

19   **CELIA: After all, we're only human.**

20   **JOSH: And I was having a bad day,**

21   **CELIA: I didn't get enough sleep.**

22   **JOSH: I'm not a morning person.**

23   **CELIA: The kids were screaming.**

24   **JOSH: The dog was barking.**

25   **CELIA: The phone was ringing off the hook.**

26   **JOSH and CELIA:** *(Together)* **I was having one of those days!**

27   **JOSH: Besides, it's all my wife's fault.**

28   **CELIA: It's all my husband's fault.**

29   **JOSH: She made me do it.**

30   **CELIA: He made me do it.** *(1 minute mark)*

31   **JOSH:** *(Pointing at CELIA)* **She started it.**

32   **CELIA:** *(Pointing at JOSH)* **He started it.** *(They turn and glare at*
33   *each other.)*

34   **JOSH and CELIA:** *(Together)* **Humph!**

35   **JOSH: So give me a break.**

1   CELIA: Cut me some slack,

2   JOSH: Stop all your nitpicking.

3   CELIA: Quit your complaining.

4   JOSH: Put a cork in it.

5   CELIA: Stop whining.

6   JOSH: And quit judging people all the time.

7   CELIA: I did what anyone would have done.

8   JOSH: I just couldn't help myself.

9   CELIA: I was only defending myself.

10   JOSH: So don't blame me.

11   CELIA: Everyone else was doing it too!

12   JOSH: Other people were involved.

13   CELIA: So don't go pointing your finger over here!

14   JOSH: Besides, the ends justify the means.

15   CELIA: It's better to ask for forgiveness than permission.

16   JOSH: I didn't really mean anything by it, anyway.

17   CELIA: So what's the big deal?

18   JOSH: Everyone makes mistakes.

19   CELIA: I'm a victim of my circumstances.

20   JOSH: A product of a bad home life.

21   CELIA: My dad was an alcoholic. *(2 minute mark)*

22   JOSH: The kids at school made fun of me.

23   CELIA: My uncle abused me.

24   JOSH: My mom never hugged me.

25   CELIA: So it's not my fault.

26   JOSH: I'm suffering from low self-esteem.

27   CELIA: So I just couldn't help it.

28   JOSH: And nobody will miss the money.

29   CELIA: It was only a few miles over the speed limit.

30   JOSH: They overprice this stuff anyway.

31   CELIA: It's the big corporations they're after, not the little guys

32   like us.

33   JOSH: And anyways, it's not wrong unless you get caught.

34   CELIA: And they'll never find out.

35   JOSH: The temptation was just too great.

1   CELIA: I was tired.

2   JOSH: And stressed.

3   CELIA: And overworked.

4   JOSH: And I guess I was just in the wrong place at the wrong time.

5   CELIA: So that's what happened.

6   JOSH: Like I said, it wasn't my fault.

7   CELIA: So don't blame me.

8   JOSH: It must have been someone else.

9   CELIA: After all, I'm a pretty good person.

10   JOSH: I follow the rules,

11   CELIA: I try my hardest,

12   JOSH: I do my best.

13   JOSH and CELIA: *(Together)* **What more could anyone ask?**

14   *(3 minute mark. Freeze. Fadeout.)*

15

16

17

18

19

20

21

22

23

24

25

26

27

28

29

30

31

32

33

34

35

A Tidy Little Religion

Summary: Two storytellers describe the kind of religion they would create if it were up to them.

Purpose: To reveal the unique nature and characteristics of the Christian faith.

Time: 4–5 minutes

Tone: Serious and thought-provoking

Cast: Teller #1 — (male or female)
Teller #2 — (male or female)

Costumes: Something simple and stylistic, such as blue jeans and a neutral oxford or turtleneck; consider having your actors wear the same outfits

Props/Set: None; or, you may wish to have the tellers hold up props that relate to specific ideas related in the text of the script

Themes: Christmas, church issues, conversion, distractions, Easter, faith, following God, forgiveness, grace, misconceptions about Christianity, modern life, relativism, sin, worship

Text: "See to it that no one takes you captive through hollow and deceptive philosophy, which depends on human tradition and the basic principles of this world rather than on Christ" (Colossians 2:8) and, "And if by grace, then it is no longer by works; if it were, grace would no longer be grace" (Romans 11:6).

Notes: Keep the exchanges quick, so that the drama sounds smooth and conversational, even though it involves two storytellers. Consider staging this drama with the actors standing back to back.

Since this drama ends with a reference to grace, but doesn't explain all the facets of what it involves, be sure that your pastor or speaker addresses the reality and extent of God's grace. Use general stage lighting and two lapel microphones.

1   *SETTING*: The stage is bare. The actors address the audience rather
2   than each other. Both storytellers are On-stage as the lights come
3   up and the scene begins.
4
5   TELLER #1: If I were going to invent a religion, it wouldn't have
6   that little thing called "grace."
7   TELLER #2: Because I like earning my way in this world.
8   TELLER #1: I like earning a living and earning respect and
9   earning a good reputation.
10 TELLER #2: And that's why grace is so hard for me to accept.
11 TELLER #1: Because grace means something isn't earned;
12 TELLER #2: And that means I wouldn't get any credit for it.
13 TELLER #1: But I like getting credit for it.
14 TELLER #2: So if I were creating my own religion, it would have
15   hard work and equal rewards and fair play.
16 TELLER #1: It would be a "do-it-yourself" religion
17 TELLER #2: With lots of good advice,
18 TELLER #1: And a list of rules with helpful guidelines for living a
19   practical and productive life.
20 TELLER #2: And yeah, I'd include ceremony and ritual and
21   traditions that would comfort people and give them a sense of
22   security.
23 TELLER #1: And there would be a hierarchy — *(1 minute mark)*
24 TELLER #2: — A chain of command —
25 TELLER #1: Of religious mentors and spiritual advisors,
26 TELLER #2: With different levels of enlightenment, because those
27   who put in their time deserve to be rewarded for it
28 TELLER #1: And in my religion, what you *do* would make all the
29   difference in the world.
30 TELLER #2: Not what you believe.
31 TELLER #1: My religion wouldn't have a bloody cross or a dying
32   Savior.
33 TELLER #2: Those things are offensive to people.
34 TELLER #1: No, the religion I'd make up wouldn't offend anyone.
35 TELLER #2: Instead, it would make them feel welcomed and

1   **affirmed.**

2   **TELLER #1:** No matter what they believe.

3   **TELLER #2:** Of course, there wouldn't be only one way to God,

4   but many ways;

5   **TELLER #1:** So that no one's feelings would get hurt.

6   **TELLER #2:** Nearly everyone would get to heaven in my religion.

7   The road to God would be wide, not narrow.

8   **TELLER #1:** And heaven wouldn't be given away for free. It

9   would be earned the old-fashioned way,

10   **TELLER #2:** Through hard work

11   **TELLER #1:** — And good deeds

12   **TELLER #2:** — And right living

13   **TELLER #1:** — And wise choices. *(2 minute mark)*

14   **TELLER #2:** There wouldn't be a hell in my religion.

15   **TELLER #1:** Just a place where you keep getting second chances

16   until you finally get it right

17   **TELLER #2:** And reach perfection.

18   **TELLER #1:** Truth would depend on what you perceive reality

19   to be —

20   **TELLER #2:** Not on what someone else tells you is real.

21   **TELLER #1:** I guess you could say it would all be a matter of

22   opinion.

23   **TELLER #2:** If I were making up a religion, it would be inclusive.

24   **TELLER #1:** I would draw from all the major religions in the

25   world and take what was best from each of them and create

26   my own unique set of beliefs.

27   **TELLER #2:** No one would tell me what to believe,

28   **TELLER #1:** And I would never tell people that things like "sexual

29   sins, theft, murder or evil thoughts" come from within, or

30   from their own hearts. (See Mark 7:21.)

31   **TELLER #2:** Because people are basically good

32   **TELLER #1:** And they only learn negative choices from their

33   environments.

34   **TELLER #2:** So instead, I would tell them that they must follow

35   their hearts and be true to themselves. *(3 minute mark)*

1   **TELLER #1: I wouldn't tell people that, "The man who loves his**
2   **life will lose it, while the man who hates his life in this world**
3   **will keep it forever"** (John 12:25, author's paraphrase).
4   **TELLER #2: Instead, I'd tell them to feel good about themselves,**
5   **and value all their accomplishments.**
6   **TELLER #1: I would tell people to find themselves,**
7   **TELLER #2: Not lose themselves.**
8   **TELLER #1: To love themselves,**
9   **TELLER #2: Not hate themselves.**
10   **TELLER #1: I would never tell people to, "deny themselves."** (See
11   Matthew 16:24.)
12   **TELLER #2: Or to "take up a cross."** (See Matthew 16:24.)
13   **TELLER #1: I'd tell them, "Don't deny yourself any of life's little**
14   **pleasures!"**
15   **TELLER #2: "Do whatever you want!"**
16   **TELLER #1: "Grab all the gusto you can."**
17   **TELLER #2: "After all, you only go around once."**
18   **TELLER #1: "And you deserve a break today."**
19   **TELLER #2: My religion would be easy to understand.**
20   **TELLER #1: It would be rational and sensible and logical.**
21   **TELLER #2: It wouldn't break out of the box,**
22   **TELLER #1: Explode your worldview,**
23   **TELLER #2: Or stun you into silence.**
24   **TELLER #1: It wouldn't be filled with paradoxes,**
25   **TELLER #2: Mystery,**
26   **TELLER #1: Wonder,**
27   **TELLER #2: Or awe.**
28   **TELLER #1: You could sum up my new religion in two words, "Be**
29   **nice."** *(4 minute mark)*
30   **TELLER #2: Yeah, that's the kind of religion I'd invent. Where**
31   **you earn your way,**
32   **TELLER #1: And you make up the rules.**
33   **TELLER #2: And everything depends on how nice you are to**
34   **others.**
35   **TELLER #1: That's the kind of religion I'd invent.** *(Optional*

1   *ending point. As you direct this drama and work to make it mesh*

2   *with the message in your service, consider ending here.)*

3   **TELLER #2:** *(After a pause)* **But it's not the kind of religion I need.**

4   **TELLER #1: No,**

5   **TELLER #2: I need grace.**

6   **TELLER #1: Because grace means something isn't earned.**

7   **TELLER #2: As hard as it is to admit.**

8   **TELLER #1: As tough as it is to accept.**

9   **TELLER #2: I need grace**

10   **TELLER #1: More than I need religion.**

11   **TELLER #2: More than I need anything else in the world.** *(Freeze.*

12   *Fadeout.)*

13

14

15

16

17

18

19

20

21

22

23

24

25

26

27

28

29

30

31

32

33

34

35

Those People

Summary: During this series of mini-monologs, the audience is exposed to a variety of different prejudices.

Purpose: To reveal common prejudices and motivate people to change their attitudes and accept others, just as God does.

Time: 5–6 minutes

Tone: Serious and thought-provoking

Cast: Tad — An actor who can portray different characters and prejudices (male)
Chondra — An actress who can portray different characters and prejudices (female)

Costumes: Simple costume pieces such as glasses, a jacket, a hat, a scarf

Themes: Appearances, assumptions, community, complaints, following God, frustrations, homosexuality, love, prejudice, stereotypes, witnessing

Text: "Accept one another, then, just as Christ accepted you, in order to bring praise to God" (Romans 15:7).

Notes: This drama will probably end up offending just about everyone! At least it should touch a raw nerve with most of the people in your congregation. Even though we don't like to admit it, we all tend to look down on people for a variety of reasons.

Because this sketch touches on such sensitive issues, be sure your pastor or teacher brings closure and healing to people who may have been affected by this drama or wounded in the past by the prejudices of others. Use spotlights at first and then general stage lighting at the switch from characters to storytellers.

1   **SETTING**: To begin this drama, Tad and Chondra enter, take their
2   places Stage Right and Stage Left, and sit on musician's stools.
3   Then, after the mini-monologs, they stand and deliver the lines for
4   the second half of the drama, while moving step by step toward
5   Center Stage. As they say the last lines, they are standing side by
6   side. As soon as they have delivered the last lines, they turn their
7   backs to the audience and exit together. Bring the spotlights up on
8   each actor in turn, first onto Chondra.
9

10   **CHONDRA**: *(Wearing a scarf and glasses)* **I never felt prejudice —**
11   **real prejudice — until I started home-schooling my kids. I**
12   **hate to say it, but people judge you. They look down on you or**
13   **act like you're a weirdo or a disgrace. Or a threat. It hurts**
14   **when people judge you simply based on where you send your**
15   **kids to school.** *(She turns and freezes.)*
16   **TAD**: *(Wearing a jacket and no glasses)* **For a long time I didn't**
17   **invite Ben to our church. I knew what people would say if they**
18   **ever found out the truth. But I guess one day a couple months**
19   **ago, I decided to give it a shot. I asked Ben to come to one of**
20   **the services, and pretty soon word leaked out that he was gay.**
21   **I had no idea people would react so bitterly. I thought the**
22   **people at my church would be different. But they weren't.**
23   **Needless to say, Ben hasn't been back.** *(He turns and freezes.*
24   *1 minute mark)*
25   **CHONDRA**: *(Wearing no scarf and no glasses)* **I ain't that smart. I**
26   **never went to no college or nothin'. I didn't get none of them**
27   **degrees. Didn't even finish up high school. But I ain't stupid**
28   **either. And I hear the things people say. I know it's just 'cause**
29   **I don't talk like them. They think I'm dumb or something.**
30   **Well, I might not be that smart, but I got feelings, ya know. I**
31   **got feelings too.**
32   **TAD**: *(Wearing a jacket and glasses)* **I was passed over for the**
33   **graduate assistantship at the university I'd applied to. Why?**
34   **Because a woman applied with me. A woman who happens to**
35   **belong to an ethnic minority. Now, don't get me wrong, it**

1   wouldn't have been right for her to be discriminated against
2   in any way, but I was more experienced and better qualified.
3   They have policies, though. And I'm a guy ... who just
4   happens to be white. *(2 minute mark)*
5   CHONDRA: *(Wearing no scarf and glasses)* I usually don't tell
6   people I'm a stay-at-home mom. They give me that look —
7   "Oh, so you're one of them." As if there was something
8   repulsive about raising your own children. About making the
9   choice to give up a career and give your time to your family.
10   Sometimes I feel like a second-class citizen just because I don't
11   work outside the home.
12   TAD: *(Wearing no jacket and no glasses and a backward baseball cap)*
13   I served time for what I did. Six years. I'm still on probation.
14   But I don't usually tell people. They act like I'm some kind of
15   a monster when they find out what it is I did. They treat me
16   fine, just like everyone else, 'til they find out I'm a convicted
17   sexual offender. That's all they need to hear. That's all they
18   hear. That's all it takes. *(3 minute mark. They freeze, then stand*
19   *and address the audience.)*
20   CHONDRA: I'm just glad I don't have any prejudices —
21   TAD: Like those people do ...
22   CHONDRA: One of them went to school with me.
23   TAD: One of them used to work with me.
24   CHONDRA: One of them used to live in my apartment complex.
25   TAD: One of them used to date my sister.
26   CHONDRA: Those men Randy's father hangs out with are all the
27   same.
28   TAD: You see 'em coming into the club sometimes. You'd think
29   they could keep people like that out.
30   CHONDRA: You can always tell which kids come from broken
31   homes.
32   TAD: Women drivers!
33   CHONDRA: Skateboarders!
34   TAD: Drug dealers.
35   CHONDRA: Drunks.

1   TAD: Divorced people.

2   CHONDRA: Those people!

3   TAD: They're always demanding equal treatment. What they
4   really want is special treatment.

5   CHONDRA: People who go to that church aren't really believers.

6   TAD: Oh, she's from the South. She probably lives in a trailer and
7   watches wrestling.

8   CHONDRA: Why doesn't he get a haircut? *(4 minute mark)*

9   TAD: The way she dresses, what does she expect people to think?
10   She's practically advertising her services.

11   CHONDRA: All college students do is drink and party.

12   TAD: Teenagers are rude, irresponsible, and disrespectful.

13   CHONDRA: Kids are always in the way.

14   TAD: Old people are a burden on us all.

15   CHONDRA: He works and she stays at home. Why doesn't she
16   enter this century? Why doesn't she make herself useful?

17   TAD: She works and he stays at home. What is he — lazy or
18   something?

19   CHONDRA: They both work. Don't they care anything about
20   their kids?

21   TAD: Neither of 'em work? Are they living on some kind of
22   inheritance or something?

23   CHONDRA: Those people!

24   TAD: She's blonde. That explains everything.

25   CHONDRA: He's still single. That explains everything.

26   TAD: *(Picking up the pace of the presentation)* They talk funny.

27   CHONDRA: They look funny.

28   TAD: They're different.

29   CHONDRA: They're dangerous.

30   TAD: They all look the same.

31   CHONDRA: Those blacks.

32   TAD: Whites.

33   CHONDRA: Hispanics.

34   TAD: Fat people.

35   CHONDRA: Skinny people.

1 TAD: Rich people.
2 CHONDRA: Poor people.
3 TAD: Catholics.
4 CHONDRA: Protestants.
5 TAD: Baptists.
6 CHONDRA: Buddhists.
7 TAD: The "liberal elite." *(5 minute mark)*
8 CHONDRA: The right-wing fundamentalists.
9 TAD: Those bleeding-heart Democrats.
10 CHONDRA: Those big-business Republicans.
11 TAD: They always have an agenda.
12 CHONDRA: You just can't trust *those* people.
13 TAD: Yeah, I'm just glad I don't have any prejudices —
14 CHONDRA: Like those people do ... *(They both turn their backs to*
15 *the audience and exit. Fadeout.)*
16
17
18
19
20
21
22
23
24
25
26
27
28
29
30
31
32
33
34
35

The Real Me

Summary: Brendan and Kiera reveal some of their many masks to the audience, but they aren't willing to reveal their true selves to each other.

Purpose: To motivate people to remove their masks and be real before God and each other.

Time: 4 minutes

Tone: Serious and thought-provoking

Cast: Brendan — A normal guy with lots of masks (male)
Kiera — His fiancée who has plenty of masks of her own (female)

Costumes: Casual, contemporary clothes

Themes: Addictions, appearances, authenticity, communication, divorce, excuses, hiding, honesty, integrity, married life, running away, secrets, stereotypes, truth

Text: "Yes, what joy for those whose record the Lord has cleared of sin, whose lives are lived in complete honesty!" (Psalm 32:2, NLT).

Notes: The sketch is stylistic and interpretative. The actors address the audience rather than each other until the very last scene. Use two spotlights at the beginning and fade in some additional general stage lighting as they greet each other at the end of the sketch. Use two lapel microphones.

1 *SETTING*: Both Kiera and Brendan are facing the audience. One is
2 standing Stage Right, the other is standing Stage Left. Both are
3 On-stage as the lights come up and the scene begins.
4
5 BRENDAN: Sometimes I find it's safer to keep my feelings private.
6 KIERA: It's not that I'm trying to be dishonest or anything. It's
7 just that it makes life easier if I wear certain masks.
8 BRENDAN: I guess you could say I hide behind a number of
9 different masks.
10 KIERA: I have one for each area of my life.
11 BRENDAN: I have one mask that I wear in front of my boss at
12 work. It's called: "The Happy Worker Who's Here to Serve
13 You in Every Possible Way" mask. I only wear it when my
14 boss is looking.
15 KIERA: I have one that I wear when I'm talking to people at
16 parties and get-togethers and things like that. It's the: "Oh,
17 I'm Having Such a Pleasant Time Talking with You and
18 You're Just the Most Engaging Conversationalist I've Ever
19 Met" mask.
20 BRENDAN: *(Addressing an imaginary boss)* Oh yes, sir. I'd be glad
21 to get that proposal to you right away, Mr. Lehman! By the
22 way, nice tie! *(1 minute mark)*
23 KIERA: *(Addressing an imaginary man at a social function)* Oh, that
24 is so interesting! I never knew that Wrigley Field didn't have
25 lights until 1988! What a fascinating memory you have!
26 BRENDAN: In front of the guys at the fitness center I always wear
27 my, "I'm Still in as Good of Shape as I Was in High Sschool"
28 mask. Sometimes it seems like everyone else is aging but me.
29 KIERA: I wear another mask to church. It's called the "Nice Little
30 Christian Girl Who Never Breaks Any Rules" mask. I almost
31 took it off one Sunday, right in the middle of the sermon, but
32 I caught myself just in time.
33 BRENDAN: *(Addressing an imaginary buddy at the club)* Hey guys,
34 wanna go another round of hoops? Or are you starting to feel
35 it?! Me? Of course! I've got another couple games in me!

1   KIERA: *(Cheerily addressing an imaginary church member)* **Wasn't**
2   **that a *nice* message? Me? Oh, I'm doing good. Yeah!**
3   **Everything is great! See ya!**
4   **BRENDAN: I have another mask that I wear in front of the people**
5   **I pass on the street. It's the "Get Out of My Way. I Have More**
6   **Important Things to Do Than Look You in the Eye Mask." It**
7   **saves me a lot of time.** *(2 minute mark)*
8   **KIERA: And then there's the mask I wear in front of my friends.**
9   **It's the "I Can Work Full-Time, Take Care of My Kids and**
10   **My Home, Honor My Husband, and Still Look Like I'm**
11   **Holding It All Together" mask. I used to wear it all the**
12   **time ... before my divorce.**
13   **BRENDAN:** *(Addressing an imaginary homeless person)***Sorry,**
14   **buddy. Get a job. Earn some money of your own."**
15   KIERA: *(Talking to an imaginary friend)* **Oh, everything's great at**
16   **home. Yeah, the kids are at a soccer game, and Alan is out of**
17   **town for the weekend. I got promoted last month, so that's**
18   **keeping me busy. Yeah! I'm hoping to be vice president by this**
19   **time next year.**
20   **BRENDAN: I even have a mask that I wear in front of my fiancée,**
21   *(Gesturing toward KIERA)* **Kiera and her kids. She doesn't**
22   **even know I have it. Her kids have never seen me without it.**
23   **It's called the "Cool Single Guy Who's in Control of**
24   **Everything and Never Gets Phased" mask. Yeah, I've got a lot**
25   **of masks. They really help me manage my life.** *(3 minute mark)*
26   **KIERA: Oh, yes.** *(Gesturing toward BRENDAN)* **I even have a mask**
27   **that I wear in front of my fiancé, Brendan. It's called the "I'm**
28   **Completely Over My Divorce" mask. He doesn't even know I**
29   **have it.**
30   **BRENDAN:** *(Picking up the pace of the presentation)* **I mean, what**
31   **would people think?**
32   **KIERA: I can't imagine what it would be like ...**
33   **BRENDAN: If I took off all my masks ...**
34   **KIERA: If I took off all my masks ...**
35   **BRENDAN: And let people know**

1 KIERA: And let people see
2 BRENDAN: The real me.
3 KIERA: What I'm really like.
4 BRENDAN: Deep down, inside. *(Pausing and then turning to face*
5   *KIERA, while wearing his COOL GUY mask)* Hey, how are ya,
6   Kiera?
7 KIERA: *(Turning to face him and wearing her OVER MY DIVORCE*
8   *mask)* Oh, I'm good, Brendan.
9 BRENDAN: Your boys?
10 KIERA: Great!
11 BRENDAN: Wanna grab some dinner? I know this great Italian
12   place down on Lancaster Avenue.
13 KIERA: Sounds nice. *(4 minute mark.)*
14   *(They approach each other and first KIERA, then BRENDAN,*
15   *turn to the audience and say "See? Just like I told you." She takes*
16   *his arm and they turn with their backs to the audience and walk*
17   *Upstage, where they freeze. Fadeout.).*
18
19
20
21
22
23
24
25
26
27
28
29
30
31
32
33
34
35

Part 5
Youth Ministry Dramas

Teens of today have grown up in a media-rich, image-saturated culture. They don't think in text, but in story. Use the dramas in this section to explore issues teens are wondering about — meaning, hope, identity, belonging, and acceptance. You'll find sketches that address these questions and more:

- Does God really exist?
- What do I do when I struggle with temptation?
- How can I follow Jesus and still be popular with my friends?
- What do I really want out of life?
- What does it really mean to be forgiven?
- Is the Bible reliable? Can I really trust it?

These scripts were all written with teen performers in mind.

Who Is My Neighbor?

Summary: When Joey is attacked on his way home, he is offered help, but his prejudices get in the way.

Purpose: To help teens think about prejudice and compassion.

Time: 4–5 minutes

Tone: Serious

Cast: Joey — A teenage guy who has been injured and ignored in his time of need (male)
An actor who plays the parts of a gangster, a high school basketball coach, a doctor, and a neo-Nazi skinhead (male)

Costumes/Props: A bandanna (for the gangster character); a basketball and a Windbreaker (for the coach); a stethoscope (for the doctor); a jacket with a Nazi insignia (for the skinhead)

Themes: Choices, compassion, consequences, love, prejudice, stereotypes

Text: The story of "The Good Samaritan" (Luke 10:29–37)

Notes: Use general stage lighting and two lapel microphones.

1   *SETTING*: The stage is bare. Joey and the other actor enter
2   simultaneously. Joey stands Stage Right, the other actor Stage Left.
3   There is a spotlight on each actor. The rest of the stage is black.
4
5   **JOEY: OK, so I'm walking down the road. Yeah, I know I shouldn't**
6   **have been in that part of town by myself. I've heard the stories.**
7   **But my mom had to show a house to some couple from out of**
8   **town, and she just couldn't pick me up after track practice. So**
9   **I had to walk home, and that was the shortest route.**
10   **GANGSTER: We knew right away he was from Washington Valley**
11   **High** *(Or another local rival school.)* **His letter jacket gave him**
12   **away … You don't flash colors like that around here and just**
13   **expect to walk by without any trouble. He was taunting us. So**
14   **we did what anyone would have done.**
15   **JOEY: There were at least three or four of 'em. I don't know how**
16   **many. They jumped me as I rounded the corner onto**
17   **Montgomery Avenue.**
18   **GANGSTER: We pounded him pretty good. Took everything he**
19   **had. His wallet. His jacket. And then, just before we were**
20   **ready to go, Jimmy knifed him. Cut him bad. After all, we**
21   **didn't want him identifying any of us in a lineup.** *(Turns his*
22   *back and freezes. 1 minute mark)*
23   **JOEY: It was weird. There wasn't a lot of pain. I couldn't move**
24   **much. But I could feel the blood soaking through my shirt. I**
25   **started praying that somebody, anybody would come by.**
26   **COACH:** *(Before turning to face the audience, the COACH slips on a*
27   *Windbreaker and grabs a basketball off the table.)* **I was coming**
28   **home from scouting some of the players at Lincoln High** *(Or*
29   *another local high school)* **when I saw him. At first I thought**
30   **maybe he was dead. And then I realized he was alive — and**
31   **that it was Joey.**
32   **JOEY: I couldn't believe who it was! Coach Sims, the basketball**
33   **coach at my high school! We'd known each other for, like, four**
34   **years. I knew he'd help me.**
35   **COACH: I don't know why I left him there. Maybe I was scared. I**

1   mean, what if his muggers were still close by? And besides,
2   I've got a wife and two kids to take care of. I couldn't risk
3   getting hurt. I couldn't risk stopping to help. *(Turns his back*
4   *and freezes. 2 minute mark)*
5   JOEY: He saw me. I know he saw me. And I just laid there in shock
6   as he walked away. I was calling out, "Coach! Coach! Where
7   are you going?" But he didn't turn around. He just left me
8   there to die ...
9   DOCTOR: *(Turning to face the audience, the ACTOR has hung a*
10   *stethoscope around his neck and taken on a new identity as a*
11   *DOCTOR.)* It'd been a long day. I'd been volunteering at the
12   downtown clinic since five a.m. without a break. Treating a lot
13   of nasty cases. And then I'm coming home and I hear this
14   groaning sound from a nearby alley.
15   JOEY: It was getting harder to breathe. I knew I'd lost a lot of
16   blood.
17   DOCTOR: I didn't want to get involved. Whoever it was, was
18   probably too far gone to make it anyway. I just walked on by.
19   Headed home to get some well-deserved rest. *(Turns his back*
20   *and freezes.)*
21   JOEY: I just lay there on the sidewalk, staring up at the sky — at
22   the stars blinking above me through the night ... I knew I
23   wasn't gonna make it. I knew my time was up. I was gonna
24   bleed to death on the sidewalk. I was gonna die. *(3 minute*
25   *mark)*
26   SKINHEAD: *(Turning to face the audience, the ACTOR has taken on*
27   *a new identity as a SKINHEAD.)* I had a meeting with some of
28   the other guys in my group. We liked this side of town. It was
29   a good place to recruit new kids.
30   JOEY: I couldn't tell who it was at first.
31   SKINHEAD: And then I saw him. I just leaned over and said. "I'm
32   here to help you, man. Don't struggle — you'll only make it
33   worse."
34   JOEY: Then I saw the swastika on his jacket, and I knew who it
35   was. One of "them."

1   SKINHEAD: I did my best. I tried.

2   JOEY: There's a bunch of 'em at my high school. Neo-Nazis.

3   Skinheads. We keep our distance. After all, everyone knows

4   what they're like. I told him to leave me alone. "Get away

5   from me you racist pig! Don't touch me!" I knew someone else

6   would come along.

7   SKINHEAD: But when he refused to let me help him ... what was I

8   supposed to do? What could I do? I called an ambulance on my

9   cell phone. But who knows how long it'll take them to get there.

10   They don't come to this part of town much. Then I just headed

11   to my meeting. *(Turns his back and freezes. 4 minute mark)*

12   JOEY: It took me awhile to convince him, but he finally left me

13   alone. Just like I wanted. And I waited. Surely someone else

14   would come by. Surely someone would stop. I just lay there,

15   staring up at the sky as the stars slowly faded to black. *(Freeze.*

16   *Fadeout.)*

17

18

19

20

21

22

23

24

25

26

27

28

29

30

31

32

33

34

35

Forgiven

Summary: Derek is trying to pay Troy back for knocking over his drink, but Troy says he has forgiven him and that Derek doesn't owe him anything.

Purpose: To show that forgiveness erases a debt.

Time: 4–6 minutes (depending on your staging and how much time they spend eating)

Tone: Humorous

Cast: Derek — A guy who wants to pay back his friend (male)
Troy — His friend who just wants to forgive Derek and move on (male)

Costumes: Casual contemporary teen clothes

Props/Set: A table, two chairs, fast-food burgers and fries, three soft drinks, two school backpacks

Themes: Easter, forgiveness, grace, guilt, pride, purity, regrets, repentance, second chances, sin

Text: "Get rid of all bitterness, rage and anger, brawling and slander, along with every form of malice. Be kind and compassionate to one another, forgiving each other, just as in Christ God forgave you" (Ephesians 4:31–32).

Notes: When the scene begins, one of the sodas is Off-stage. The two guys carry everything else On-stage with them. The opening comments (when they first enter) could be changed to something more local or relevant to your group. The idea is to show that the guys are good friends carrying on an informal conversation. Use general stage lighting and two lapel microphones.

1   *SETTING*: Benny's Burger Joint. It's suppertime, and Derek and Troy
2   have just purchased their meals and are now looking for a place to
3   sit down. Both are Off-stage when the lights come up. Then they
4   enter, carrying their backpacks and the food.
5

6   **DEREK:** *(They are talking informally as they look for a place to sit.)*
7   **Man, I can't believe you had 'em put all those pickles on your**
8   **cheeseburger. I can't stand pickles.**
9   **TROY: Pickles are cool.**
10   **DEREK: Pickles are gross. I bet you eat mushrooms on your pizza,**
11   **too.**
12   **TROY: Mushrooms and anchovies.**
13   **DEREK: Oh, man. That's nasty.** *(They sit down and pull out their*
14   *food when they realize they don't have any ketchup.)* **Hey, you**
15   **want some ketchup for your fries?**
16   **TROY: Oh, yeah. Great.**
17   **DEREK: I'll be right back.** *(As DEREK stands up, he bumps a*
18   *backpack sending TROY's drink sailing onto the floor.)* **Oh, sorry,**
19   **man!**
20   **TROY: Oh, it's all right. I forgive you.**
21   **DEREK: Oh, you forgive me. Huh?**
22   **TROY: Yeah.**
23   **DEREK: All right, I'll go buy you another one.**
24   **TROY: No thanks.**
25   **DEREK: Really, it's OK, really. I bumped it over. I'll get you**
26   **another one.**
27   **TROY: I don't need it.** *(1 minute mark)*
28   **DEREK: Oh … so you're really not that thirsty, huh?**
29   **TROY: No, actually I am thirsty. Real thirsty. That's why I bought**
30   **it in the first place. I was really looking forward to drinking it,**
31   **too.**
32   **DEREK: Hey, what are you trying to do? Make me feel guilty?! I**
33   **told you I'd buy you another one!**
34   **TROY: Dude, I said I forgive you.**
35   **DEREK: Yeah, but then you're talking about how much you**

1   wanted to drink it!

2   TROY: You're the one who asked me if I was thirsty.

3   DEREK: But I thought you were gonna say something like, "Oh,

4   it's no big deal" or "Just forget about it" or "Oh, I wasn't

5   thirsty anyhow" or something.

6   TROY: It is a big deal. I am thirsty. And I love having an ice cold

7   root beer with my cheeseburger and pickles.

8   DEREK: All right, that's it. I'm getting you a drink.

9   TROY: No, it's all right.

10   DEREK: I'll get you a root beer.

11   TROY: No thanks.

12   DEREK: Now you're making me feel bad!

13   TROY: How could I make you feel bad when I've already forgiven

14   you?

15   DEREK: Look, let me buy you another drink.

16   TROY: I don't want you to.

17   DEREK: I want to.

18   TROY: Why? *(2 minute mark)*

19   DEREK: I've got a bunch of extra money saved up that I've been

20   wanting to spend.

21   TROY: Really?

22   DEREK: No, because I knocked over your drink!

23   TROY: So you feel guilty and think if you buy me another drink

24   you can undo what you've done? Even out the scales? Make

25   up for it? Maybe make yourself feel better?

26   DEREK: Look, man. I knocked over your drink. It's only fair I get

27   you another one.

28   TROY: But I *forgave* you. So we're even.

29   DEREK: What do you mean, even? I knocked it over — how could

30   we be even?

31   TROY: I forgave you.

32   DEREK: *(After a pause)* OK ... so you don't want another drink?

33   TROY: No.

34   DEREK: You're sure?

35   TROY: Yeah.

1   DEREK: Positive?

2   TROY: Uh-huh.

3   DEREK: OK. And you're not, like, mad at me or anything?

4   TROY: Uh-uh.

5   DEREK: OK, then I'm gonna get the ketchup.

6   TROY: Great. *(DEREK exits and TROY quietly eats his food. A*

7   *moment later, DEREK reappears with the ketchup and a drink..*

8   *3 minute mark)*

9   DEREK: Here.

10   TROY: What's that?

11   DEREK: I thought you might want it.

12   TROY: I told you not to buy me one!

13   DEREK: Yeah, well, you said you were thirsty a minute ago. And I

14   know how much you like an ice cold root beer with your

15   cheeseburger and pickles.

16   TROY: Why did you get this for me?

17   DEREK: It was on sale.

18   TROY: No it wasn't! I'm not drinking that! Listen, I forgave you.

19   Why is it so hard for you to accept that?

20   DEREK: OK, I accept it.

21   TROY: You sure?

22   DEREK: Yeah.

23   TROY: Good.

24   DEREK: All right.

25   TROY: Great. Let's eat.

26   DEREK: OK. *(They begin to eat. After a pause)* Wanna borrow my

27   car?

28   TROY: No.

29   DEREK: *(After a pause)* Wanna date my sister? I can set you guys

30   up.

31   TROY: No!

32   DEREK: *(After a pause)* You can have my comic book collection

33   when I die.

34   TROY: Would you drop it already?!

35   DEREK: Look, I just want to pay you back.

1   TROY: You can't pay someone back when you don't owe 'em
2   anything!
3   DEREK: But I owe you a drink.
4   TROY: Haven't you been listening? I said I forgive you. That
5   means you don't owe me anything. Not now. Not ever.
6   Nothing! OK? Get it? It's over! Done! *(4 minute mark)*
7   DEREK: I'll do your laundry for you next semester.
8   TROY: *(Grabbing his stuff)* That's it. I'm outta here.
9   DEREK: But I wanna do something for you!
10   TROY: Why?
11   DEREK: So ... I can feel like I don't owe you anything.
12   TROY: Look, I'm going home.
13   DEREK: Wait! *(He knocks his own drink over.)* There! Now we're
14   even!
15   TROY: You knocked your own drink over so we could be even?!
16   DEREK: Yup. Now I don't owe you nothing.
17   TROY: Now you owe yourself one!
18   DEREK: Oh. Yeah ... *(As they exit)* Unless I forgive myself, right?
19   OK, I forgive myself. There! Now I'm really even.
20   TROY: You need professional help, you know that?
21   DEREK: Let me carry that backpack for you.
22   TROY: Leave me alone. *(As they exit, DEREK comes back to the*
23   *table, grabs the extra drink he bought for TROY, takes a sip, and*
24   *then exits. Fadeout.)*
25
26
27
28
29
30
31
32
33
34
35

Persevering

Summary: Jessie is reflecting on how following Jesus didn't turn out to be as easy as she thought it would be.

Purpose: To encourage teens to stick with Christ, even when it's not easy.

Time: 2 minutes

Tone: Serious

Cast: Jessie — A teenage believer who has faced ridicule for her faith and wonders if it's worth it to follow Christ (female)
Reader — A person who is reading (or reciting) verses from Hebrews (male or female)

Costumes: Jessie is dressed in typical teen attire; the Reader is dressed in something unobtrusive and neutral

Themes: Appearances, calling, following God, integrity, misconceptions about Christianity, suffering, teenagers

Text: Hebrews 10:32–36 (New Living Translation text is included in the script)

Notes: This brief drama will help set up a message on perseverance. These verses were written to encourage early believers to hold onto their faith when they faced persecution. The struggle that modern-day believers in North America face is more an issue of popularity than of physical persecution, but the struggle is still real. Consider having the Scripture verses flash on a screen up front whenever they are read / recited. Use two spotlights and two lapel microphones.

1   *SETTING*: Jessie is addressing the audience. The Reader could be Off-
2   stage or off to the side. He or she could either read the text or
3   recite it. Keep a spotlight on Jessie the whole time.
4
5   READER: "Don't ever forget those early days when you first
6   learned about Christ" (Hebrews 10:32a).
7   JESSIE: When I first became a Christian, I thought life would be
8   easy. That all my troubles would just go away ...
9   READER: "Remember how you remained faithful even though it
10   meant terrible suffering" (Hebrews 10:32b).
11   JESSIE: But that's not what it's been like. Not at all. A lot of my
12   friends started saying things behind my back. It's not what I
13   expected. I don't always know what to do now. It's like life has
14   gotten harder instead of easier.
15   READER: "Sometimes you were exposed to public ridicule and
16   were beaten, and sometimes you helped others who were
17   suffering the same things" (Hebrews 10:33).
18   JESSIE: I didn't really fit in with my old friends, and when I tried
19   to explain that I didn't look down on 'em or anything, they
20   just shook their heads and walked away. It's not just me,
21   either. It's all the kids at my high school who are Christians.
22   We're all pretty much treated the same. *(1 minute mark)*
23   READER: "You suffered along with those who were thrown into
24   jail. When all you owned was taken from you, you accepted it
25   with joy. You knew you had better things waiting for you in
26   eternity" (Hebrews 10:34).
27   JESSIE: Once, I overheard some of the things they were saying
28   about me. And, to tell you the truth, it really hurt. I wonder if
29   anyone else has ever felt this way, too?
30   READER: "Do not throw away this confident trust in the Lord, no
31   matter what happens. Remember the great reward it brings
32   you!" (Hebrews 10:35).
33   JESSIE: Sometimes I wonder if it's all worth it. Sometimes I'm not
34   really sure I made the right decision when I chose to follow
35   Christ.

1　READER: "Patient endurance is what you need now, so you will
2　continue to do God's will. Then you will receive all that he has
3　promised" (Hebrews 10:36).
4　JESSIE: I guess if it were up to me, I'd give up. I'd drop out of the
5　race, 'cause I can't make it on my own ... *(After a pause)* I'm
6　just glad it's not up to me ... I'm just glad I'm not on my
7　own ... *(Freeze. Fadeout.)*
8
9
10
11
12
13
14
15
16
17
18
19
20
21
22
23
24
25
26
27
28
29
30
31
32
33
34
35

Get a Life

Summary: Austin is tired of his life and is searching for a new one. But he isn't really sure what he wants, and every new life he "tries on" turns out to be disappointing.

Purpose: To explore the reality and uniqueness of the Christian life.

Time: 7–8 minutes

Tone: Humorous and thought-provoking

Cast: Austin — A teenage guy who is tired of his life and is looking for a change (male)
Mr. Jones — The salesman who is trying to get Austin to make a purchase (male)

Costumes: Austin is dressed like a normal teenager; Mr. Jones is dressed in a suit with a nametag (if desired, use a letter jacket, a sport coat, and a lab coat to represent he different "lives" that Austin tries out)

Themes: Ambition, appearances, boredom, choices, complaints, conversion, distractions, following God, frustrations, life, meaning, misconceptions about Christianity, new life, priorities, purpose, second chances, suffering, surrender

Text: "In the same way, any of you who does not give up everything he has cannot be my disciple" (Luke 14:33; see also Luke 14:25–35).

Notes: As you're blocking and planning the movements of your actors, imagine that they are in a department store. You may wish to use real props, but for simplicity and to retain the illusion that Austin is trying on alternative "lives," you can have your actors mime their use of props. The more distinctively different Austin can act with each new life, the better. Use general stage lighting and two lapel microphones.

1   *SETTING*: The scene takes place in "Lives-R-Us," a place where
2   anyone can go to buy a new life. Mr. Jones is straightening the
3   shelves and racks of "lives" (which are imaginary coats and shirts)
4   when the lights come up. Austin enters and the scene begins.
5
6   MR. JONES: Hello, may I help you?
7   AUSTIN: Um, yeah. I'm here to get a new life.
8   MR. JONES: Hmmm. A new life, huh?
9   AUSTIN: Yeah, I'm tired of this one. I thought I'd try out
10   something a little different. Something fresh and exciting. A
11   new start.
12   MR. JONES: Bigger, better, faster, stronger …
13   AUSTIN: Yeah.
14   MR. JONES: New and improved!
15   AUSTIN: Yeah! That's it!
16   MR. JONES: Well, you've come to the right place. Here at Lives-
17   R-Us we specialize in giving people a fresh start. I'm sure we
18   can find you just the right model.
19   AUSTIN: OK. I'd really like a life where I'm popular and, you
20   know, cool. I want people to like me.
21   MR. JONES: *(Searching)* Ah! Here's a nice model! Slip that one on for
22   size … *(AUSTIN mimes pulling on a shirt.)* How does that feel?
23   AUSTIN: *(Acting, standing, and talking cool)* Kinda nice.
24   MR. JONES: It is nice! It's a very popular model. Try it out a little.
25   Walk around and see how it fits. *(AUSTIN walks around a little,*
26   *acting cool. 1 minute mark)*
27   AUSTIN: It feels cool.
28   MR. JONES: It is cool! With this brand you'll get lots of new
29   friends, the girls will be all over you, and the teachers will
30   always be on your side.
31   AUSTIN: Awesome.
32   MR. JONES: Of course, you'll notice a few things are missing from
33   your old life.
34   AUSTIN: Like what?
35   MR. JONES: Well, you don't get as many convictions or principles

1   with this model. You always have to give up some of the things

2   you believe in to be popular. Otherwise, you'd offend too many

3   people. Part of being popular is trying to please everyone.

4   AUSTIN: OK, I can live with that.

5   MR. JONES: However, you'll also make some enemies.

6   AUSTIN: But why?

7   MR. JONES: The more popular and powerful you get, the more

8   some people will resent it. Mostly your old friends. But don't

9   worry, you'll have plenty of new friends now — *(2 minute*

10   *mark)*

11   AUSTIN: *(Slipping off the pretend shirt and talking normally again)*

12   Maybe that's not exactly what I was looking for. Do you have

13   any other models?

14   MR. JONES: Let's see ... OK, here you go! This one should work

15   out fine for you. This is the life of a football star. Quarterback.

16   You won't have to worry about being cool or keeping up your

17   image. People will like you just because you're good at sports!

18   AUSTIN: *(Slipping it on and acting, standing, and talking like an*

19   *athlete)* Yo! I like this one! I feel —

20   MR. JONES: Bigger, better, faster, stronger?

21   AUSTIN: Yeah. And better reflexes. *(Doing karate moves)* A lot

22   more athletic than I used to be.

23   MR. JONES: You are! You're an athlete now!

24   AUSTIN: Yo!

25   MR. JONES: Let me see something ... *(Looking at the tag on the*

26   *back of the imaginary shirt)* Oh, yeah. This is nice.

27   AUSTIN: What does it say?

28   MR. JONES: It says you're gonna get a college scholarship.

29   AUSTIN: All right! Where?

30   MR. JONES: Florida. *(3 minute mark)*

31   AUSTIN: Couldn't it be Tennessee?

32   MR. JONES: You a Vols fan?

33   AUSTIN: Yo!

34   MR. JONES: OK, I think I could arrange that ... I'll throw it in

35   for free. How about that?

1   AUSTIN: Yo! I won't have to pay for college?

2   MR. JONES: Nope.

3   AUSTIN: This is perfect! I'll take it!

4   MR. JONES: Super. Let's see the price on that ... um ... oh boy ...

5   OK, let me ring it up for you.

6   AUSTIN: What do you mean by "um"? Why did you say, "oh boy"?

7   MR. JONES: Oh, it's ... it's nothing. *(Pretending to ring up a*

8   *purchase at a cash register)* Now let me add the discount in

9   there from your trade-in life, and ...

10   AUSTIN: Wait. Why did you say "oh boy"?!

11   MR. JONES: Really, it's nothing to worry about.

12   AUSTIN: What is it?

13   MR. JONES: Oh, just a little injury.

14   AUSTIN: Injury? What kind of injury?

15   MR. JONES: *(Sighing)* Broken neck. Your freshman year. During

16   homecoming. But it's OK, really. You'll survive. You'll still

17   have forty years of life in front of you. *(4 minute mark)*

18   AUSTIN: Broken neck? *(Miming taking the shirt off)* No way! Forget

19   it. No thanks. I don't want that life. Give me something where

20   I'm rich. And smart. How about that?

21   MR. JONES: *(Starting to get a little exasperated)* Rich and smart.

22   All right. *(Choosing another life)* Here. Try this one on.

23   AUSTIN: *(Mimes putting the shirt on.)* Hmmm. Wanna know the

24   national rainfall level in Guatemala?

25   MR. JONES: Not really.

26   AUSTIN: Forty-two inches.

27   MR. JONES: How nice.

28   AUSTIN: $E=mc^2$.

29   MR. JONES: So I've heard. Look, do you want this life?

30   AUSTIN: Am I gonna be famous?

31   MR. JONES: Yup. Rich and famous.

32   AUSTIN: Popular? Will people like me?

33   MR. JONES: They'll love you.

34   AUSTIN: Any broken necks?

35   MR. JONES: No broken necks. No injuries. No illnesses. You live a

1   perfectly healthy life.
2   AUSTIN: Really?
3   MR. JONES: Yup.
4   AUSTIN: Hmmm ... It sounds almost too good to be true. If I live
5   such a happy life, how do I die? *(5 minute mark)*
6   MR. JONES: Let's see ... *(Looking at the tag)* Suicide.
7   AUSTIN: What?! Why on earth would I kill myself when I have
8   everything going for me?
9   MR. JONES: This is the American Dream model: fame, fortune,
10   glory, and all the cash you need. Everything money can buy,
11   but nothing it can't. I guess you never learn to be happy or
12   content. And one day, I guess you just decide to end it all.
13   AUSTIN: *(Miming taking the shirt off)* No way!
14   MR. JONES: What exactly are you looking for? First you tell me
15   you want to be popular, then athletic, then rich and smart.
16   What do you really want out of life?
17   AUSTIN: *(Thoughtfully)* I don't really know.
18   MR. JONES: Well then, that's the problem, isn't it? I've got lives
19   of all different shapes and sizes here. And each one, well, it's
20   got its ups and downs. It's got its good points and its bad ones.
21   *(6 minute mark)*
22   AUSTIN: *(Looking on the racks)* What about this one?
23   MR. JONES: That one?
24   AUSTIN: Yeah.
25   MR. JONES: Oh, you wouldn't want that one.
26   AUSTIN: Why not?
27   MR. JONES: Well, look at the tag.
28   AUSTIN: Suffering. Getting made fun of. Losing a bunch of your
29   friends. Learning to follow rather than lead. Giving up fame
30   and fortune. Trusting in what you can't prove. What kind of
31   life is this, anyway?
32   MR. JONES: That's the Christian life.
33   AUSTIN: Oh ... But I always thought that it was supposed to be
34   about acting happy and going to church and living a good life.
35   MR. JONES: That's what most people think. But it's really a life

1   full of pain and joy and hope and mystery.

2   AUSTIN: Huh. So what does a life like this go for, anyhow?

3   MR. JONES: It costs everything.

4   AUSTIN: *(Putting it back)* Why would anyone want a model like

5   that? *(7 minute mark)*

6   MR. JONES: Not many people do. I can tell you that. Not many

7   people at all. So what do you say? Are you gonna get a new life

8   today, or not? *(Freeze. Fadeout.)*

9

10

11

12

13

14

15

16

17

18

19

20

21

22

23

24

25

26

27

28

29

30

31

32

33

34

35

The Tempt-Detector

Summary: Garrick thinks he can handle Jose's Tempt-Detector, but he's in for a little surprise.

Purpose: To show that we need to be careful with temptations of all shapes and sizes.

Time: 5–6 minutes

Tone: Humorous

Cast: Garrick — A guy who thinks he can handle any temptation that comes his way (male)
Jose — His friend, who is ready to put him to the test (male)

Costumes: Casual, contemporary teen clothes

Props/Set: The tempt-detector (a blood pressure kit, a laptop computer, jumper cables, and other odd paraphernalia, all connected together), a chair, a packet of exam papers, a sports magazine's swimsuit issue, beeping and siren sound effects, an instruction manual (for the tempt-detector)

Themes: Adultery, following God, lust, obedience, pride, purity, self-control, sin, spiritual health, teenagers

Text: "Don't let anyone look down on you because you are young, but set an example for the believers in speech, in life, in love, in faith and in purity" (1 Timothy 4:12) and "So, if you think you are standing firm, be careful that you don't fall! No temptation has seized you except what is common to man. And God is faithful; he will not let you be tempted beyond what you can bear" (1 Corinthians 10:12–13a).

Notes: This drama ends abruptly when Garrick finally falls into the temptation of pride. Be sure your speaker addresses the difference between temptation and sin. Temptations are inevitable, and there's nothing wrong with being tempted — it's how we deal with temptation that matters. Even Jesus was tempted, but he never gave in to sin. Use general stage lighting and two lapel microphones.

1   *SETTING*: Jose's garage. Jose is On-stage tinkering with his new
2   "tempt-detector" when the lights come up. Then Garrick enters
3   and the scene begins.
4
5   GARRICK: Hey, Jose. What's that thing?! It looks like an old-
6   fashioned lie detector!
7   JOSE: Well, it's a tempt-detector.
8   GARRICK: A what?
9   JOSE: A tempt-detector. I got it off the Internet. It just arrived last
10   week.
11   GARRICK: What on earth is a tempt-detector?
12   JOSE: Well, a lie detector tells you how much someone's lying,
13   right?
14   GARRICK: Yeah.
15   JOSE: A tempt-detector tells you how much someone's being
16   tempted!
17   GARRICK: For real?
18   JOSE: Yeah.
19   GARRICK: Let me try it.
20   JOSE: I don't know.
21   GARRICK: C'mon! You gotta let me try it!
22   JOSE: Well, OK. But I should warn you, it's pretty sensitive.
23   GARRICK: Oh, no problem, man. I'm good at dealing with
24   temptation.
25   JOSE: You sure about this?
26   GARRICK: Trust me. Strap me in, buddy.
27   JOSE: All right, here goes …
28   GARRICK: OK, what do I do? *(1 minute mark)*
29   JOSE: Well, you just sit there, and then I throw temptations at you.
30   And this monitor over here *(Gesturing to the laptop computer)*
31   registers your level of temptation.
32   GARRICK: So how do you know if you beat the machine?
33   JOSE: Well, it makes a beeping sound when you're tempted. And
34   if you give into the temptation, this siren goes off.
35   GARRICK: This is gonna be no problem, man. *(GARRICK sits in*

1 *the chair. JOSE puts the blood pressure kit on his arm, pumps it a*
2 *little [not tightly!], and connects the jumper cables up to him and*
3 *to the machine. They talk informally as all this occurs.)*
4 JOSE: *(Mumbling, fumbling with the instruction manual)* **The**
5   **flabulator is adjusted to sixteen googa-joules — check — the**
6   **neural responsive pathway indicator is set to zero — check —**
7   **and the unit is turned on — check. OK! I think we're all set.**
8 GARRICK: **Fire away. I'm ready. Tempt me, baby. Tempt me.**
9 JOSE: *(Slyly, holding up some papers)* **Hey Garrick, I've got the**
10   **answers to tomorrow's algebra exam right here. Wanna take**
11   **a peek?** *(2 minute mark)*
12 GARRICK: **No thanks, Jose. I don't cheat. It's against my morals**
13   **and my better judgment.**
14 JOSE: **Hmmm. Sure. OK, how about this? Hey Garrick, did you**
15   **hear about Shannon and Joe? Tracy told me she saw them —**
16 GARRICK: *(Putting his hand up)* **Stop right there, my good friend.**
17   **I can see through your shallow masquerade. You're trying to**
18   **tempt me to gossip about my friends, and I won't do it. I**
19   **won't even listen to a word of it.**
20 JOSE: **Man, you're good.**
21 GARRICK: **Told you.**
22 JOSE: **Say, I saw a wallet on the ground with a thousand bucks**
23   **cash in it. Wanna keep it?**
24 GARRICK: **Nope, let's turn that in to the police right away.**
25 JOSE: **I heard that movie *Killer Blonde Zombies From Outer Space***
26   **is playing in town. Wanna sneak into it?**
27 GARRICK: **Sneaking into movies isn't honest, Garrick. And**
28   **besides, it's rated "R" and I'm only sixteen.** *(3 minute mark)*
29 JOSE: **You are amazing!**
30 GARRICK: **Thanks.**
31 JOSE: **OK, how about this? I know these guys who can hook us up**
32   **with some ecstasy. No one will know. No one will ever find out.**
33 GARRICK: **Hmmm.**
34 JOSE: **It's a real trip. I'm tellin' ya —**
35 GARRICK: **Hmmm …**

1 JOSE: I'm gonna get ya!

2 GARRICK: Nope. No thanks. I don't do drugs. When I'm offered

3   drugs, I just say no.

4 JOSE: Whew. OK, that's it — time for the heavy artillery. How

5   about this? *(Pulling out a sports magazine's swimsuit issue)* Last

6   year's hottest swimsuit issue.

7 GARRICK: Hey, I heard about those ... What are you doing with

8   a copy of that?!

9 JOSE: Um ... It's research ... for the tempt-detector ... *(He hands*

10   *GARRICK the magazine.)* Here, check this out ...

11 GARRICK: *(Paging through the magazine)* Hmmm. Look at the

12   fabric on this suit! Isn't that a nice shade of blue? And the

13   shoreline is attractive, too. They really chose a great location

14   for this year's photo shoot, don't you think? *(4 minute mark)*

15 JOSE: Aren't you tempted?! At least a little?!

16 GARRICK: Self-control, buddy. Self-control.

17 JOSE: But take a look at that ... At her ... *(Staring at the magazine)*

18   She's ... Oh boy ... we better put that away.

19 GARRICK: Good idea.

20 JOSE: *(Hopefully)* Why, were you getting tempted?

21 GARRICK: No, you were drooling.

22 JOSE: Oh. Hey, that reminds me. I heard about this website you

23   can get into with a whole library of pictures. Girls doing stuff

24   you've never even —

25 GARRICK: It's not gonna work, man. I'm not buying it. I'm not

26   giving in.

27 JOSE: Man, you are unbelievable!

28 GARRICK: Thanks.

29 JOSE: I could take you on the road and make you famous. People

30   would pay lots of money just to watch you get tempted and

31   resist. Your name would be in lights! They'd write books

32   about you! They'd make movies —

33 GARRICK: It's not gonna work, Jose. You're trying to tempt me

34   with fame and fortune. But I'm not interested in being

35   famous. *(5 minute mark)*

1 JOSE: I don't know how you do it. You've made it further than
2   anyone else has so far.
3 GARRICK: Really?
4 JOSE: Yeah. If they didn't fall for the drugs, the swimsuit issue got
5   'em every time.
6 GARRICK: Huh.
7 JOSE: Yeah, that or the *Blonde Zombies From Outer Space.*
8   You're pretty amazing at standing up against temptation, I'll
9   give you that.
10 GARRICK: Yeah, I guess I am. *(The machine starts beeping softly.)*
11 JOSE: Whew, you could say that again.
12 GARRICK: Well, I told you this machine was no match for me. I
13   told you I could — *(Before he can finish his sentence, the*
14   *machine starts blaring out a siren sound. The actors freeze.*
15   *Blackout.)*
16
17
18
19
20
21
22
23
24
25
26
27
28
29
30
31
32
33
34
35

What Tomorrow Will Bring

Summary: Kelly gives Reanne a hard time about trusting her horoscope until Reanne turns the tables on her.

Purpose: To explore the reliability of the Bible versus other means of predicting the future.

Time: 5–6 minutes

Tone: Humorous and thought-provoking

Cast: Reanne — A girl who believes in horoscopes (female)
Kelly — Her friend who thinks horoscopes are ridiculous (female)

Costumes: Casual, contemporary teen clothes

Props/Set: The horoscope section of the newspaper

Themes: Bible study, faith, horoscopes, prophecy fulfillment, truth

Text: "Above all, you must understand that no prophecy of Scripture came about by the prophet's own interpretation. For prophecy never had its origin in the will of man, but men spoke from God as they were carried along by the Holy Spirit" (2 Peter 1:20–21).

Notes: Kelly and Reanne are good friends. Even though they disagree throughout the sketch, they do so good-naturedly. Use general stage lighting and two lapel microphones.

1   *SETTING*: Kelly and Reanne are at the mall after school. Reanne is
2   reading through the newspaper, looking at her horoscope. The
3   lights come up, Kelly enters, and the scene begins.
4
5   **KELLY: Hey, girl, whatcha reading?**
6   **REANNE: Hey, Kelly! I'm just checking out my horoscope!**
7   **KELLY: What?**
8   **REANNE: You know, seeing what the stars have lined up for me**
9   **today.**
10   **KELLY: Your horoscope!**
11   **REANNE: Well, yeah.**
12   **KELLY: Horoscopes?**
13   **REANNE: Sure!**
14   **KELLY: You don't really believe in that stuff, do you?**
15   **REANNE: Well, I mean, I don't know. I —**
16   **KELLY: Reanne! I cannot believe you!**
17   **REANNE: I mean, they're pretty accurate sometimes —**
18   **KELLY: You're kidding me!**
19   **REANNE: No, I read my 'scope every day.**
20   **KELLY: Lemme see that thing... "You will meet someone important**
21   **today. It could be a once-in-a-lifetime opportunity."**
22   **REANNE: See? I'm applying for this job at Rizzo's Pizzeria this**
23   **afternoon. That might be my once-in-a-lifetime opportunity!**
24   **KELLY: You think working at Rizzo's is a once-in-a-lifetime**
25   **opportunity?**
26   **REANNE: Maybe. Who knows? This could be my big break. Go**
27   **on, read the rest of it.** *(1 minute mark)*
28   **KELLY: "Be cautious about new projects, but never fear what**
29   **your heart tells you. Think carefully before making any major**
30   **decisions."**
31   **REANNE: See? I've been thinking about which college to apply to.**
32   **And this horoscope talks about major decisions. That thing is**
33   **right on the nose!**
34   **KELLY: Oh, come on. That could be written for anyone! Reanne,**
35   **it's so vague!**

1   REANNE: It's all about me!
2   KELLY: Listen to me, Reanne. These things are a bunch of
3   garbage! Someone just sits around making this stuff up all
4   day. I can't believe you even read these things.
5   REANNE: Oh yeah? Look at yours. See how accurate it is.
6   KELLY: OK, sure. No problem ... Let's see ... "You'll talk to
7   someone today who is *(Making this part up as she reads)* acting
8   like a total airhead and won't listen to what you have to say."
9   REANNE: Does it really say that?
10 KELLY: Close enough ... "When you're tempted to lose your
11   patience, hold your tongue. It'll protect you from future
12   harm."
13 REANNE: Well?
14 KELLY: Yeah? *(2 minute mark)*
15 REANNE: Have you met a total airhead today who won't listen to
16   anything you're saying?
17 KELLY: *(Rolling her eyes)* Yikes.
18 REANNE: Well?
19 KELLY: Reanne, this could be written for anyone! Yours could be
20   written for anyone! Any of 'em could be written for anyone!
21 REANNE: So if you don't scope your 'scope, how do you deal with
22   life? Or plan for the future?
23 KELLY: That's easy.
24 REANNE: What?
25 KELLY: The Weather Channel, girl.
26 REANNE: I'm serious.
27 KELLY: Me too. They do pretty good ... and that new guy they
28   have ... Oh! Can he name the hurricanes!
29 REANNE: C'mon. The Weather Channel?! That's the best you
30   can do?!
31 KELLY: No, sometimes I toss my dirty laundry in a pile and if the
32   socks and T-shirts land on top, I know I'm gonna have a good
33   day. And if I can't see any jeans, I can be sure I'll have an
34   argument with my mom that night.
35 REANNE: Wow! I've heard of stuff just like that! *(3 minute mark)*

1 KELLY: Yeah, or I dump out all my cosmetics, and if the lipstick
2 lands next to the eye shadow, I know my boyfriend will try
3 kissing me on our next date.
4 REANNE: You know, my psychic told me about that technique!
5 Cool!
6 KELLY: Or I just toss dice or flip a coin or —
7 REANNE: Wow! See, this stuff really works!
8 KELLY: Yeah, and sometimes I slaughter small farm animals and
9 then toss their intestines across the floor and predict the
10 future based on the configuration of their entrails and the
11 color of their stomach bile!
12 REANNE: Really? That's what the ancient Babylonians used to
13 do!
14 KELLY: Reanne! Hello! I was *kidding*!
15 REANNE: Oh. But what about the lipstick thing and your
16 boyfriend?
17 KELLY: When doesn't he try kissing me?!
18 REANNE: Oh.
19 KELLY: Listen, do you remember when the President had those
20 three alien babies that all looked like Elvis?
21 REANNE: No.
22 KELLY: Neither do I. But I'll bet some psychic predicted he would ...
23 REANNE: Maybe ... *(4 minute mark)*
24 KELLY: C'mon, Reanne. Psychics? Horoscopes? A roll of the dice?
25 Dirty laundry? Stomach acids? Do you really buy all this
26 stuff?
27 REANNE: I don't know ...
28 KELLY: There's gotta be a better way to deal with life. Look —
29 what about the Bible?
30 REANNE: The Bible?
31 KELLY: Yeah, it's got all kinds of predictions. Why don't you base
32 your life on that?
33 REANNE: But they're even more vague than the horoscopes,
34 Kelly!
35 KELLY: What are you talking about?

1   REANNE: When Jesus said the end of the world was coming, he

2   was like, "There'll be wars and rumors of wars." Now there's

3   a safe prediction! I mean when *haven't* there been wars or

4   rumors of wars?

5   KELLY: I don't know.

6   REANNE: "And famines and earthquakes." (See Matthew 24) I

7   mean, Jesus was pretty safe with that one, too.

8   KELLY: Um —

9   REANNE: And "many will turn away from the faith." How about

10   that? It's no better than my horoscope!

11   KELLY: Well—

12   REANNE: You can look in the Bible if you want to, Kelly, but I'm

13   gonna stick to my horoscopes. At least they're relevant today.

14   Look, I'll see you around. Oh Kel, wish me luck at Rizzo's!

15   *(She exits. 5 minute mark)*

16   KELLY: *(To herself, facing the audience)* But the Bible really is

17   accurate. I mean ... Isn't it? *(Freeze. Fadeout.)*

18

19

20

21

22

23

24

25

26

27

28

29

30

31

32

33

34

35

How Big Is Your God?

Summary: All the "gods" in Josie's research project fit easily into her box. But has she really captured the essence of all the world's religions?

Purpose: To get people thinking about what Christianity really means.

Time: 4–6 minutes (depending on how much time they spend interacting with the props)

Tone: Humorous and thought-provoking

Cast: Josie — A girl who wants to find out which God she left out of her project (female)
Xavier — Her curious friend who keeps asking her to explain her ideas to him (male)

Costumes: Casual, contemporary teen clothes

Props/Set: A large cardboard box with a rock, a penny, a baseball glove, a bikini, a report card, and a yo-yo

Themes: Christmas, Easter, God's power, Jesus, misconceptions about Christianity, truth, worship

Text: "For what I received I passed on to you as of first importance: that Christ died for our sins according to the Scriptures, that he was buried, that he was raised on the third day according to the Scriptures … " (1 Corinthians 15:3–4).

Notes: You may wish to encourage your speaker to follow the drama by asking the audience, "What do you think Josie used to represent Christianity? What *should* be in the box? A rule book? A cross? A candle? Is there one symbol that sums up the Christian life and message? If so, what is it?" Perhaps you could have a group discussion before continuing. Use general stage lighting and two lapel microphones.

1   *SETTING*: Josie's house. She is On-stage looking through the items in
2   her box when the lights come up. Her friend Xavier enters and the
3   scene begins.
4
5   **XAVIER: Hey, Josie. Whatcha got in the box?**
6   **JOSIE: Um ... I'm just finishing up this project for school. It's**
7   **supposed to be examples of all the world's major religions for**
8   **my humanities class.**
9   **XAVIER: Oh, cool.**
10   **JOSIE: But I just can't tell which one I left out ...**
11   **XAVIER: Well, let's see what you've got ...** *(He reaches in the box*
12   *and pulls out a rock.)* **What's this for, your science project?**
13   **JOSIE: No, that's the first religion.**
14   **XAVIER: Rock worship? Who worships rocks?**
15   **JOSIE: No, it's for nature. Like, all throughout history people have**
16   **worshiped the sun and the stars and mountains and stuff. In a**
17   **lot of countries, people still pray to the moon and the clouds**
18   **and the rain.**
19   **XAVIER: But what's with the rock?**
20   **JOSIE: It represents all the people who worship nature.**
21   **XAVIER: Oh, I get ya.**
22   **JOSIE: Yeah.** *(1 minute mark)*
23   **XAVIER: So what other gods do you have in here?** *(Pulling out a*
24   *penny)* **A penny? What?! Is this for people who worship**
25   **Abraham Lincoln? Oh, wait — "In God we trust," right?**
26   **JOSIE: No, that's for *money*. You know, for all the people who**
27   **think money will bring them happiness.**
28   **XAVIER: But they don't worship money, do they?**
29   **JOSIE: Well, they build their lives around it, and whatever's most**
30   **important to you — that's your god. Everyone who builds**
31   **their life around getting money, saving money, spending**
32   **money, or buying stuff is really just worshiping —**
33   **XAVIER: A penny.**
34   **JOSIE: Yeah.**
35   **XAVIER: Worshiping a penny. Huh. Pretty depressing.**

1   JOSIE: Yeah.

2   XAVIER: OK, what about this? *(Pulling out a clothes hanger)* **Wait,**

3   **let me guess — all those who pray to St. Levi, the great clothes**

4   **god?** *(2 minute mark)*

5   JOSIE: Something like that. That stands for your image. You

6   know, your looks, your clothes, stuff like that. Most people are

7   more worried about how they look in front of their friends

8   than how they look to God.

9   XAVIER: Yeah, no kidding. *(Pulling out a baseball mitt)* **What's**

10   **this? Baseball? America's favorite pastime?**

11 JOSIE: You mean America's favorite religion.

12 XAVIER: Religion? Baseball's a sport! How do you figure? How

13   could a sport be a religion?

14 JOSIE: Well, do people get more excited about going to a ball game

15   or church? And how many people do you know who would

16   spend forty dollars to go to church?

17 XAVIER: Not too many.

18 JOSIE: Right. And do people know more about their sports heroes

19   or the saints of the church? Who gets bigger salaries,

20   preachers or pitchers?

21 XAVIER: Good point. But baseball doesn't, like, answer the big

22   questions, like, "Why am I here?" or "What's the meaning of

23   life?" or anything.

24 JOSIE: Neither does a rock or a penny.

25 XAVIER: Hmmm. I guess you're right.

26 JOSIE: Not too impressive as gods, are they? *(3 minute mark)*

27 XAVIER: Nope. OK, so there's nature, money, clothes, and sports.

28   What else do people worship? *(Looking in the box)* **Is that what**

29   **I think it is?** *(JOSIE nods.)*

30 XAVIER: You gotta be kidding me. *(He picks up a bikini.)*

31 JOSIE: Think about it. Besides money and sports, what do most

32   guys think about all the time?

33 XAVIER: Oh.

34 JOSIE: Yup.

35 XAVIER: Oh boy.

1   JOSIE: Mm-hmmm.

2   XAVIER: Yeah.

3   JOSIE: Right.

4   XAVIER: I get it. OK, I can see why you put that in there after

5   all ... *(Pulling out a report card)* **A report card?**

6   JOSIE: Yeah. Knowledge. Grades. Success.

7   XAVIER: *(Pulling out a yo-yo)* **A yo-yo?**

8   JOSIE: Hinduism. Good karma, bad karma. Up and down, back

9   and forth, yin and yang.

10 XAVIER: *(Looking in the box)* **Man, you sure got a lot of stuff in**

11   **here. It's kinda sad that people really do spend their whole**

12   **lives worshiping stuff like rocks and pennies and report cards**

13   **and yo-yos.** *(4 minute mark)*

14 JOSIE: Yeah, I've got stuff in there for all the major religions —

15   Muslims and Mormons and Buddhists and Jews. You name it.

16   But I can't help but think I might have forgotten one ...

17 XAVIER: *(Pointing to something in the box)* **What religion is that**

18   **for?**

19 JOSIE: Oh, that's for Christianity.

20 XAVIER: Is that really what Christianity is all about?

21 JOSIE: I'm not sure. I've always thought so.

22 XAVIER: You're kidding me!

23 JOSIE: No, that's what I heard at church once.

24 XAVIER: Wow. Really? So that's what it's all about, huh?

25 JOSIE: Yeah. At least I think so ...

26 XAVIER: Well, then it looks to me like you've got 'em all covered,

27   Josie. Well, gotta go. See ya later! *(He exits.)*

28 JOSIE: OK, see ya. *(To herself)* **Well, if that's what Christianity is**

29   really all about, then I guess I do have all the world's major

30   religions in this one little box after all. *(She closes up the box,*

31   *picks it up, and exits. As she exits, fadeout. The audience never*

32   *sees what else is in the box.)*

33

34

35

The Chess Match

Summary: When Andy tells his friend Danielle that he doesn't believe God exists because there isn't enough proof, she tries to show him that evidence and proof are two different things.

Purpose: To show that there really is evidence for God's existence, but believing in him is a matter of faith, not logic.

Time: 8–9 minutes

Tone: Thought-provoking

Cast: Andy — A guy who doesn't believe in God because he hasn't found enough proof (male)
Danielle — His friend who tries to show him that there really is enough evidence for God's existence to have faith in him (female)

Costumes: Casual contemporary teen clothes

Props/Set: A wooden chess set, a table, two chairs

Themes: Apologetics, conversion, evangelism, faith, God's existence, Jesus, questions, truth

Text: "Now faith is being sure of what we hope for and certain of what we do not see. This is what the ancients were commended for. By faith we understand that the universe was formed at God's command, so that what is seen was not made out of what was visible" (Hebrews 11:1–3; see also 1 Peter 3:15).

Notes: Be careful that this drama doesn't get too "heavy-handed." While this sketch delves into evidence for God's existence, it shouldn't be presented in a preachy tone. Keep the references to God lighthearted and inviting. You may choose to leave short sections of Danielle's arguments out of the piece, as long as it doesn't affect the outcome of the discussion. Depending on your audience, you could make the sketch a little more lighthearted and allegorical by talking about "Bob" instead of "God."

As Andy and Danielle talk, they move their chess pieces at various times during the sketch. Suggested places to move the chess pieces have been included, but use your discretion and encourage your actors to add informal dialog that reflects what is happening in the game of chess. Use general stage lighting and two lapel microphones.

1 *SETTING*: Danielle's house after school. Andy and Danielle are
2   playing a game of chess. They're both On-stage as the lights come
3 .   up and the scene begins.
4

5 **ANDY:** Danielle, I've decided something.
6 **DANIELLE:** What's that, Andy?
7 **ANDY:** There is no such thing as God. *(He moves a piece.)*
8 **DANIELLE:** No God? *(She moves a piece.)*
9 **ANDY:** Nope.
10 **DANIELLE:** Are you sure?
11 **ANDY:** Absolutely.
12 **DANIELLE:** But how do you know there's no God?
13 **ANDY:** I haven't met him. *(He moves a piece.)*
14 **DANIELLE:** What if I told you I have? That he talks to me —
15 **ANDY:** I'd say you're nuts, because there is no such thing as God.
16 **DANIELLE:** Oh, so you know everything.
17 **ANDY:** Of course not!
18 **DANIELLE:** Well then, in all the things that you *don't* know, isn't
19   it possible there could be proof of God?
20 **ANDY:** Huh?
21 **DANIELLE:** You know, proof. But you just haven't discovered it
22   yet. *(She moves a piece.)*
23 **ANDY:** I guess.
24 **DANIELLE:** So it's possible?
25 **ANDY:** OK, it's possible. But I still say I need more proof before
26   I'm gonna believe in God. *(He moves a piece.)*
27 **DANIELLE:** Why is that? *(1 minute mark)*
28 **ANDY:** I don't believe in anything I can't prove!
29 **DANIELLE:** Prove it. *(She moves a piece.)*
30 **ANDY:** Prove what?
31 **DANIELLE:** Prove what you just said. That you don't believe in
32   anything you can't prove.
33 **ANDY:** Um, OK. I just don't believe in that stuff. *(He moves a
34   piece.)*
35 **DANIELLE:** That's not proof.

1   ANDY: How am I supposed to prove it?!

2   DANIELLE: I don't know. How am I supposed to prove there's a

3   God?

4   ANDY: Physical evidence, Danielle! Like, I can't see God or smell

5   him or hear him or taste or touch him. Therefore, there's no

6   proof, and I don't believe he exists!

7   DANIELLE: You have a brain, right Andy?

8   ANDY: Of course!

9   DANIELLE: And there are thoughts in your brain, I assume? *(She*

10   *moves a piece.)*

11   ANDY: Last time I checked, yeah.

12   DANIELLE: Are you sure they're real?

13   ANDY: What do you mean? *(He moves a piece.)*

14   DANIELLE: Can you touch 'em?

15   ANDY: No.

16   DANIELLE: See 'em?

17   ANDY: Uh-uh.

18   DANIELLE: Smell your thoughts, hear 'em, or taste 'em?

19   ANDY: Of course not!

20   DANIELLE: Then there's no physical evidence that your thoughts

21   really exist, is there? *(2 minute mark)*

22   ANDY: Um, hang on a minute —

23   DANIELLE: I mean, even if we cut your brain open, we wouldn't

24   find any thoughts floating around in there. *(She moves a piece.)*

25   ANDY: Hey, what are you insinuating?

26   DANIELLE: Nothing. My point is, thoughts are invisible, and

27   there's no physical proof that they exist. But we all believe

28   they do!

29   ANDY: Wait, you can track brain activity!

30   DANIELLE: Yeah, but that's just electrical impulses, not thoughts.

31   It's evidence, but it's not proof.

32   ANDY: *(He moves a piece.)* What's the difference?

33   DANIELLE: Does Melanie like you? *(She moves a piece.)*

34   ANDY: Sure. Of course. She's my girlfriend.

35   DANIELLE: How do you *know* she likes you?

1   ANDY: Well, she does stuff for me. Hangs out with me. And,
2   *(Suggestively)* well ... let's just say I can tell. *(He moves a*
3   *piece.)*
4   DANIELLE: OK, well, all that stuff is evidence, it's not proof. You
5   weigh the evidence and reach a conclusion.
6   ANDY: Hmmm. *(3 minute mark)*
7   DANIELLE: And there's evidence of God too. Like things are
8   designed for a purpose — eyes are designed to see, ears to
9   hear, wings to fly. *(She moves a piece.)*
10   ANDY: Yeah, so?
11   DANIELLE: So who designed 'em if there's no God?
12   ANDY: Well, maybe they just happened.
13   DANIELLE: How could a wing just happen? Or an eye? That
14   would be like a lumberyard exploding and these chess pieces
15   just carving themselves. It couldn't happen.
16   ANDY: I still say I want proof. I only believe in things that can be
17   proven true or false. *(He moves a piece.)*
18   DANIELLE: Is your car in my driveway?
19   ANDY: Of course.
20   DANIELLE: Do you *know* that it is, or *believe* that it is?
21   ANDY: I know it is ... Um ... Wait ... I think I see where you're
22   going with this. Someone might have stolen it, right?
23   DANIELLE: Maybe. I mean, for all you know it's there. You can
24   reason that it's probably there, but it's not guaranteed. And
25   from where we're sitting here in the living room, you can't
26   prove it. We can't see out the window. Our view is limited. But
27   you trust it's still there. *(4 minute mark)*
28   ANDY: Are you saying it's the same with God?
29   DANIELLE: Kind of. There's evidence he exists, even though we
30   can't see him right now. Even though, from our limited point
31   of view, we may not be able to prove it. But we can believe he's
32   there, out of sight ... *(She moves a piece)* just like your car is.
33   ANDY: Hmmm ... Hang on a minute. I think there's another way
34   to prove something exists.
35   DANIELLE: How's that?

1   **ANDY:** By thinking it out. Like, I can reason that all living people
2   have thoughts, and I'm a living person, so I must have
3   thoughts. Therefore my thoughts exist! *(He moves a piece.)*
4   **DANIELLE:** So you're using logic to prove your point?
5   **ANDY:** Yeah. Logic.
6   **DANIELLE:** Well, how about this then? "If something is
7   intelligently designed, it must have a designer. All living
8   creatures are intelligently designed, so therefore they must all
9   have a designer."
10   **ANDY:** Um, OK. And you're saying God is the designer? *(5 minute*
11   *mark)*
12   **DANIELLE:** Yeah.
13   **ANDY:** Then who designed God?
14   **DANIELLE:** No one, Andy!
15   **ANDY:** Ah-ha! I got ya!
16   **DANIELLE:** Andy, something must exist beyond this world simply
17   because this world exists.
18   **ANDY:** Why?
19   **DANIELLE:** To get things started! Look at this chess set. I reach
20   down and pick up a piece and move it. *(She moves a piece.)* But
21   I'm beyond the chess set. Outside of it. I reach down and cause
22   the piece to move.
23   **ANDY:** It doesn't move by itself …
24   **DANIELLE:** Right. Without a beginning move to get it started,
25   nothing else could have happened. Nothing would be here at
26   all. So just that there *is* world is evidence for a creator who is
27   outside of the picture — beyond it.
28   **ANDY:** So you're saying if astronauts found a computer chip on the
29   moon, they'd know someone left it there. It couldn't have just
30   happened naturally. Design proves that there is a designer …
31   **DANIELLE:** Right.
32   **ANDY:** Hmmm. I still think I need more proof. I'm not gonna
33   believe in anything I can't prove. *(6 minute mark)*
34   **DANIELLE:** Oh really?
35   **ANDY:** Yeah. *(He moves a piece.)*

1   DANIELLE: Do you believe your thoughts are your own and no
2   one else's?
3   ANDY: Of course.
4   DANIELLE: Prove it.
5   ANDY: Prove what?
6   DANIELLE: That no one else in the world is thinking the same
7   thing you are right now.
8   ANDY: Um ... *(After a pause)* I can't.
9

10   *(Optional section)*
11   DANIELLE: OK, try this. Some people believe the world was
12   created, others think there was a big bang, right?
13   ANDY: Yeah. So?
14   DANIELLE: Well, prove that the world wasn't just created one
15   second ago with all our memories intact. *(She moves a piece.)*
16   ANDY: There's no way to prove or disprove it either way!
17   DANIELLE: Well, do you believe it was?
18   ANDY: Of course not. *(End of optional section)*
19

20   DANIELLE: So then, you believe some things and don't believe
21   other things, even though you don't have any proof?
22   ANDY: I guess so. *(He moves a piece.)*
23   DANIELLE: Well, do you set an alarm clock?
24   ANDY: Huh?
25   DANIELLE: Your alarm clock. Do you set it each night? *(She*
26   *moves a piece. 7 minute mark, with optional section included)*
27   ANDY: Well, sure. At least when I gotta get up in the morning.
28   DANIELLE: Then you have faith.
29   ANDY: What are you talking about? *(He moves a piece.)*
30   DANIELLE: There's no proof that tomorrow will come, or that the
31   electricity will be working in the morning, or that you'll even
32   survive the night. But you set your clock because you believe
33   you'll be getting up in the morning and that life will pretty
34   much go on as usual. *(She moves a piece.)*
35   ANDY: So you're saying that since I set my alarm clock, I know

1 what faith is?!

2 DANIELLE: Would you set it if you knew you were gonna die

3 tonight?

4 ANDY: Good point.

5 DANIELLE: We set alarm clocks for one reason — we have faith.

6 We have faith that tomorrow will come. You can't prove you'll

7 wake up, but you still set your clock. That's faith in action.

8 ANDY: So you're saying I can't help but live with faith? *(He moves*

9 *a piece.)*

10 DANIELLE: Right.

11 ANDY: Even in little things like setting an alarm clock? *(8 minute*

12 *mark)*

13 DANIELLE: Yeah. You use faith every day. You take your keys to

14 the car because you have faith it'll start, you keep your money

15 in the bank because you trust it'll be there when you need it.

16 You sit down in a chair because you believe it'll hold your

17 weight! You couldn't survive in our world without faith in

18 things you can't prove logically! *(She moves a piece.)*

19 ANDY: Hmmm ... So can you logically prove there's a God?

20 DANIELLE: I can give you evidence. Then you gotta weigh the

21 evidence, just like a jury would, and decide for yourself. But

22 I've got something even better I'd like to do.

23 ANDY: What's that?

24 DANIELLE: Introduce you to him personally.

25 ANDY: I don't know... If there is a God, why isn't he more visible?

26 *(He moves a piece.)*

27 DANIELLE: Because he wants us to have faith — not just

28 knowledge. *(She moves a piece.)*

29 ANDY: I'm not quite ready to say there is a God yet. But I'll think

30 about it.

31 DANIELLE: OK, then. *(Leaning back)* It's your move. *(Freeze.*

32 *Fadeout.)*

33

34

35

Part 6
Scripts for Children's Services or Puppet Plays

Children love Bible stories, especially when they're told with a little dose of humor and silliness. These scripts will work great for VBS programs, children's church, family programs, or elementary-aged Sunday school classes. Most of the them will even work well as scripts for puppet plays.

Although written for children to listen to, these scripts are not written for children to memorize or perform. They were written with adult performers in mind.

The Delivery Boy

Summary: Two storytellers retell the story of the "Feeding of the 5000," but one of them keeps getting things mixed up.

Purpose: To show children that God can use them, even if they don't feel like they have much to offer.

Time: 4 minutes

Tone: Humorous

Cast: Morgan — A storyteller who is trying to tell the children the story of the "Feeding of the 5000" (male or female)
Gene — His friend, who keeps mixing things up and making silly comments (male or female)

Costumes: None; or you may wish to have Gene dressed in a little bit of a goofy outfit, and Morgan dressed more conservatively

Props/Set: None; although you may wish for Gene to pull out some silly props such as suntan lotion, a lunchbox, etc.

Themes: Calling, compassion, God's power, Jesus, purpose, service

Text: "When Jesus looked up and saw a great crowd coming toward him, he said to Philip, 'Where shall we buy bread for these people to eat?' He asked this only to test him, for he already had in mind what he was going to do" (John 6:5–6; see also John 6:1–15).

Notes: Morgan plays the "straight" person who is trying to tell the story accurately, while Gene keeps mixing things up. I gave the actors male names, but either actors or actresses could be used. Be sure that as they address each other, they keep their bodies open to the audience so that all the children can see them. This story could also be read as a Readers Theatre piece or used as a puppet script. Use general stage lighting and two lapel microphones.

1   *SETTING*: The stage is bare. Both storytellers are On-stage as the
2   lights come up and the scene begins.
3
4   **MORGAN: Once upon a time, Jesus and his followers were on the**
5   **side of a mountain near a beach —**
6   **GENE: Sunbathing.**
7   **MORGAN: Not sunbathing.**
8   **GENE:** *(Talking like a California surfer)* **Surfing. Dude.**
9   **MORGAN: They weren't surfing, either. Jesus was on the side of**
10   **the mountain teaching the people about —**
11   **GENE: The dangers of ultraviolet radiation and the importance of**
12   **using an FDA-approved suntan lotion —**
13   **MORGAN: What on earth are you talking about? Look, he was**
14   **teaching them about God, and they were so impressed that**
15   **they stayed for three days listening to Jesus tell stories. And as**
16   **the third day was passing, they were hungry —**
17   **GENE: So they had a barbeque.**
18   **MORGAN: They didn't have a barbecue! That's not how the story**
19   **goes. Instead, Jesus said,**
20   **GENE: "Somebody order a pizza! I'm starving!"**
21   **MORGAN: Would you stop?! You're getting everything mixed up!**
22   **Jesus told his friends to give some food to the people. And do**
23   **you know how many people were there that day?**
24   **GENE: At least five or six.**
25   **MORGAN: More than that.**
26   **GENE: Eight?**
27   **MORGAN: Higher.**
28   **GENE: Fifty?** *(1 minute mark)*
29   **MORGAN: There were over five thousand men plus their families!**
30   **There might have been ten or fifteen thousand people there**
31   **that day!**
32   **GENE: That's a lot of pizzas.**
33   **MORGAN: The disciples said, "We don't have enough money to**
34   **buy food for all these people."**
35   **GENE: "And besides, Domino's doesn't deliver out here."**

1   MORGAN: So do you know what happened next?
2   GENE: Yes, I do.
3   MORGAN: Are you sure?
4   GENE: Absolutely.
5   MORGAN: What happened?
6   GENE: I have no idea.
7   MORGAN: The disciples went looking for food. One of them, a
8   man named Philip, began looking through the crowd.
9   GENE: Philip went to fill 'em up. Go and fill 'em up, Philip!
10 MORGAN: Until he finally said, "Hey, here's a kid with — "
11 GENE: "A cell phone, so we can finally order some pizzas!"
12 MORGAN: He didn't have a cell phone. He had five small loaves
13   of bread and two fish —
14 GENE: In his lunchbox.
15 MORGAN: He didn't have a lunchbox! Andrew brought him to
16   Jesus, and Jesus said,
17 GENE: "Cool lunchbox!" *(2 minute mark)*
18 MORGAN: *(Frustrated)* Argghh! There was *no* lunchbox!
19 GENE: Oh.
20 MORGAN: Or pizzas!
21 GENE: OK.
22 MORGAN: Or barbecues!
23 GENE: Right.
24 MORGAN: Or surfboards!
25 GENE: Gotcha.
26 MORGAN: Good! There were just a bunch of people on the side of
27   a mountain near a beach —
28 GENE: Sunbathing.
29 MORGAN: *(Getting exasperated)* Not sunbathing. And Jesus said,
30   "We'll use this fish and bread to feed the people." So he
31   prayed over the meal and then he broke the bread in half and
32   handed it to some people.
33 GENE: And the people he handed it to broke some and took some
34   and ate some and handed it around.
35 MORGAN: That's right.

1 GENE: And they broke some and took some and ate some and
2   handed it around.
3 MORGAN: Uh-huh.
4 GENE: And they broke some and took some and ate some and
5   handed it around.
6 MORGAN: Um, let's not get carried away here.
7 GENE: And they broke some and took some and ate some and
8   handed it around.
9 MORGAN: OK, I think they get the picture
10 GENE: And they broke some and took some and ate some and
11   handed it around.
12 MORGAN: All right, already! That's enough! *(GENE mouths the*
13   *words "And they broke some and took some and ate some and*
14   *handed it around" and acts them out, really getting into it.)* **Until**
15   **thousands and thousands of them,**
16 GENE: Had eaten their fill. *(3 minute mark)*
17 MORGAN: Ah!
18 GENE: What a meal!
19 MORGAN: And they all said,
20 GENE: "We like it! We love it! We want more of it! We like it! We
21   love it! We want more of it!"
22 MORGAN: Until there was nothing but crumbs left.
23 GENE: It must have been really crummy bread.
24 MORGAN: And they gathered up twelve baskets full of bread.
25 GENE: *(Surprised)* What?! There was more at the end than at the
26   beginning?
27 MORGAN: Yup.
28 GENE: Jesus had changed everything around?
29 MORGAN: Yeah. That's what he specializes in. Taking the little
30   that we bring —
31 GENE: And turning it into crumbs.
32 MORGAN: No! Turning it into more than we could ever imagine.
33 GENE: Jesus can take whatever we have to offer and change it,
34 MORGAN: From leftovers to the main course.
35 GENE: From small to big.

1   **MORGAN:** From nothing special into a meal for a thousand
2   people ...
3   **GENE:** *(After a pause)* **From a lunch box into suntan lotion.**
4   **MORGAN: Oh brother.** *(They begin to exit.)*
5   **GENE: Hey, wanna catch a wave?**
6   **MORGAN: Why do I put up with this?** *(Fadeout.)*
7
8
9
10
11
12
13
14
15
16
17
18
19
20
21
22
23
24
25
26
27
28
29
30
31
32
33
34
35

Laz and the Man from Naz

Summary: Stella Reporta is interviewing Lazarus about his "near-death experience." But when she finds out about Jesus, she uncovers the real story!

Purpose: To show that Jesus is the Son of God and has power to give new life to those he loves.

Time: 4–5 minutes

Tone: Humorous

Cast: Lazarus — A man who has just been raised back to life (male)
Stella — The lady interviewing him for the six o'clock news (female)

Costumes: Stella is dressed like a TV anchorwoman. Lazarus is dressed in typical informal clothes (blue jeans and a T-shirt) and has toilet paper wrapped around him.

Props/Set: A live microphone that Stella can use to interview Lazarus

Themes: Compassion, death, evangelism, faith, God's power, hope, Jesus, new life, witnessing

Text: "When he had said this, Jesus called in a loud voice, 'Lazarus, come out!' The dead man came out, his hands and feet wrapped with strips of linen, and a cloth around his face. Jesus said to them, 'Take off the grave clothes and let him go.' Therefore many of the Jews who had come to visit Mary, and had seen what Jesus did, put their faith in him" (John 11:43–45; see also John 11:1–45).

Notes: Have fun with the exchange between Lazarus and Stella. The crazier their characters are, the better. Use general stage lighting and one hand-held microphone that they share during the interview.

1	***SETTING***: Stella is on the scene reporting live from the grave where
2	Lazarus has just been raised from the dead. They're both On-stage
3	as the lights come up and the scene begins.
4	
5	STELLA: *(To the audience)* **This is Stella Reporta reporting live**
6	**from the graveyard where a man has just now had a**
7	**remarkable near-death experience!**
8	**LAZARUS: Um, it wasn't a near-death experience. It was a total-**
9	**death experience. I was totally dead.**
10	**STELLA: Totally?**
11	**LAZARUS: Totally.**
12	**STELLA: Totally?!**
13	**LAZARUS: Totally!**
14	**STELLA: Whatever. And here he is himself — Lazarus, otherwise**
15	**known as "The Laz."**
16	**LAZARUS: Um, that's Lazarus.**
17	**STELLA: So, Laz, that's an interesting outfit you've got on there —**
18	**LAZARUS: These are my grave clothes, Stella. I've been buried**
19	**for four days.**
20	**STELLA: It almost looks like toilet paper wrapped around you.**
21	**LAZARUS: Uh, it is toilet paper.**
22	**STELLA: Oh.**
23	**LAZARUS: Yeah, well, we're working with a small budget here.**
24	**STELLA: Oh. And when was the last time you had a shower there,**
25	**Laz?**
26	**LAZARUS: Showers haven't been invented yet, Stella.**
27	**STELLA: Oh, what about deodorant?**
28	**LAZARUS: That hasn't been invented either.** *(1 minute mark)*
29	**STELLA: Oh.**
30	**LAZARUS: And neither have microphones, but who cares? What**
31	**other questions do you have?**
32	**STELLA: So tell us, is it true that you were really dead for four**
33	**days and now you're alive again?**
34	**LAZARUS: Dead as a doorknob.**
35	**STELLA: And is it true you're now alive?**

1   LAZARUS: Um, I'm talking to you, Stella.

2   STELLA: Right, but are you really alive?

3   LAZARUS: How could I be talking to you if I were dead?!

4   STELLA: *(She reaches over and takes his pulse.)* OK. I believe you.

5   You're alive.

6   LAZARUS: Of course I'm alive! How else could I be giving a live

7   interview?!

8   STELLA: Good point.

9   LAZARUS: Thank you.

10 STELLA: So, what were you thinking when you were dead?

11 LAZARUS: Um, I was dead. I wasn't thinking anything.

12 STELLA: So you were actually brain dead?

13 LAZARUS: I was all dead! Totally dead!

14 STELLA: Totally?

15 LAZARUS: Totally.

16 STELLA: Totally?!

17 LAZARUS: Totally!

18 STELLA: Oh. And what was it like?

19 LAZARUS: I don't know.

20 STELLA: Why not?

21 LAZARUS: I was dead!

22 STELLA: Totally?

23 LAZARUS: Oh boy ... Totally.

24 STELLA: Totally?!

25 LAZARUS: Totally! *(2 minute mark)*

26 STELLA: Oh. No longer the life of the party then, huh? Get it? Life

27   of the party!

28 LAZARUS: Very funny, Stella.

29 STELLA: So really, Laz, can I call you Laz?

30 LAZARUS: Um, I prefer Lazarus.

31 STELLA: OK, Laz. So really, what was it like being dead? Did you

32   see a bright light at the end of the tunnel?

33 LAZARUS: No, but I saw a bright light at the end of the cave.

34 STELLA: You did?! Unbelievable! A classic near-death experience!

35 LAZARUS: It wasn't a near-death experience, Stella. It was a

1   total-death experience. I was totally dead! *(He says all of them*

2   *by himself, imitating Stella.)* Totally? Totally. Totally?! Totally.

3   Totally!

4 STELLA: Then what about the light at the end of the cave? How

5   do you explain that Mr. I-Was-Totally-Dead?

6 LAZARUS: I was brought back to life, Stella. I was buried in a

7   cave. And when I opened my eyes, I could see light coming

8   into the cave!

9 STELLA: Oh. So what was the name of the doctor who brought

10   you back from beyond?

11 LAZARUS: Jesus. And he wasn't a doctor.

12 STELLA: He wasn't? He was practicing medicine without a

13   license? *(3 minute mark)*

14 LAZARUS: He wasn't practicing medicine! He was a healer. It was

15   Jesus, a man from Nazareth.

16 STELLA: Lazarus and the Man from Nazarus!

17 LAZARUS: No, Nazareth.

18 STELLA: Lazareth and the Man from Nazareth!

19 LAZARUS: No, Lazarus and the Man from Nazareth.

20 STELLA: Laz and the Man from Naz! That's a-maz-ing!

21 LAZARUS: Look, the point is, I was dead and I'm alive again.

22   Jesus brought me back to life. No one can do that but God. It

23   proves Jesus really is who he claimed to be!

24 STELLA: The Man from Naz?

25 LAZARUS: No, the Son of God!

26 STELLA: The Son of God! Are you serious?

27 LAZARUS: Yes.

28 STELLA: Then that's the *real* story! Anyone who can bring the

29   dead to life is worth getting to know! What am I doing wasting

30   my time talking to you? Where is this guy Jesus? I gotta get

31   an interview with *him*!

32 LAZARUS: Well, come on. I'll introduce you to him. I'm sure he'd

33   be glad to meet you.

34 STELLA: OK! *(To audience)* This is Stella Reporta, signing off. *(To*

35   *LAZARUS)* Let's go! I can't wait to meet this man who can

1   **bring dead people back to life. Lead on, Laz!**

2 **LAZARUS: That's Lazarus.** *(4 minute mark)*

3 **STELLA: Oh yeah.** *(They begin to exit.)* **Maybe we can get you some**

4   **real clothes on the way. That toilet paper has got to go. Right,**

5   **Laz?**

6 **LAZARUS: Lazarus.**

7 **STELLA: Oh yeah, right.** *(As they exit, fadeout.)*

8

9

10

11

12

13

14

15

16

17

18

19

20

21

22

23

24

25

26

27

28

29

30

31

32

33

34

35

The World's Most Famous Ghost Story

Summary: Peter and a narrator tell the story of the night when Peter and Jesus walked on the water.

Purpose: To show that when we reach out to Jesus, he will rescue us.

Time: 4–5 minutes

Tone: Serious

Cast: Peter — A man who is struggling with wholeheartedly believing Jesus is really the Son of God (male)
Narrator — A storyteller who also plays the part of Jesus for role of the story (male)

Costumes: You may wish to have the characters dressed either in biblical period attire, or in casual, contemporary clothes

Themes: Distractions, doubt, faith, fear, forgiveness, God's power, hope, Jesus, second chances

Text: "Let us fix our eyes on Jesus, the author and perfecter of our faith, who for the joy set before him endured the cross, scorning its shame, and sat down at the right hand of the throne of God" (Hebrews 12:2; see also Matthew 14:22–33).

Notes: At times the two actors address the audience, and at some points they carry on a dialog between themselves. As you rehearse, practice the transitions to and from these sections so that they occur naturally when the sketch is performed. You could also use four characters for this drama: two female narrators, and two males to play Peter and Jesus. Use general stage lighting and two lapel microphones.

1   *SETTING*: The stage is bare. Both actors are On-stage as the lights
2   come up and the scene begins.
3
4   **TELLER:** *(To audience)* **Once long ago, a large crowd of people**
5   **followed Jesus and listened to him, and he ended up feeding**
6   **thousands and thousands of them with a few fish and pieces**
7   **of bread.**
8   **PETER: Jesus had just finished feeding all those people with that**
9   **little boy's lunch when he told us to get into a boat.**
10   **TELLER:** *(This dialog is between the two actors.)* **"Go on, I'll meet**
11   **up with you guys later."**
12   **PETER: "But Jesus, where will we meet you?"**
13   **TELLER: "Across the lake."**
14   **PETER: "But how are you gonna get across the lake if we take the**
15   **boat?"**
16   **TELLER: "Don't worry about me. Just get going now. It's**
17   **important. Now go!"**
18   **PETER: So we got onto the boat. We could hear him as he told all**
19   **those people to head back to their homes. And as we sailed out**
20   **into deeper water, we could see the clouds rolling in.** *(1 minute*
21   *mark)*
22   **TELLER: After dismissing the crowds, Jesus went up on the side**
23   **of the mountain, by himself, to pray. He'd meant to quietly**
24   **pray with his disciples, but the crowds had shown up and he'd**
25   **stopped to help and heal and teach the people.**
26   **PETER: As it started getting dark, we were talking about Jesus.**
27   **We still didn't have any idea how he planned to get to the**
28   **other side of the lake.**
29   **TELLER: As the night wore on, the winds picked up. And the**
30   **disciples stopped worrying about Jesus, and started thinking**
31   **about themselves.**
32   **PETER: "Tie that rope down, John! Hurry, James! Watch out!**
33   **Here comes another wave. Everybody, quick — grab onto**
34   **something so you don't slip overboard!"**
35   **TELLER: By three o'clock in the morning, the disciples were**

1   afraid for their lives. Then they saw something that looked

2   like it was hovering above the waters.

3   PETER: "What is that? What's that white form out there? Do you

4   think it could be a ... a ... no ... it couldn't be ... there's no

5   such thing. It's coming this way!" *(2 minute mark)*

6   TELLER: It was just like one of those scary stories when the storm

7   blows in and then you start to see things that just aren't

8   supposed to be there.

9   PETER: We'd been though some tough storms before. I wouldn't

10   say we were superstitious or anything, but we believed in

11   spirits. Angels and demons. And yeah, we believed in ghosts.

12   TELLER: The creature got closer and closer.

13   PETER: "It's coming for us! It's a ... a ghost! What else could

14   walk across the water?"

15   TELLER: "It's OK! It's just me. Don't be scared."

16   PETER: "Huh? Jesus?"

17   TELLER: "It's me!"

18   PETER: I looked at the other guys on the boat. None of us believed

19   it could really be Jesus. I didn't know what to do, but I had to

20   know the truth. I had to know for sure. "OK! If it's really you,

21   tell me to come out there with you!"

22   TELLER: "Come on in, Peter. The water's fine! It's really me."

23   PETER: I peered over the edge of the boat. All I could see were the

24   swirling waves churning in the night. But that thing I saw had

25   claimed to be Jesus. And I was willing to trust his voice with

26   my life. *(3 minute mark)*

27   TELLER: Peter leaned over the edge and jumped down. As he

28   landed on the water, it wasn't like water at all. It was solid. It

29   held his weight as if he were walking across dry ground!

30   PETER: It was unbelievable! We were both walking on the water!

31   It was like surfing without a surfboard! Totally cool!

32   TELLER: At first, Peter kept his eyes on Jesus. But the closer he

33   came to Jesus, the more he began to doubt.

34   PETER: I was walking across a lake in the middle of a hurricane!

35   The waters were splashing up against my legs; the wind was

1   biting into my face. And then, as I started to get more and
2   more afraid, I began to sink. Little by little. When I took my
3   eyes off Jesus and looked at the storm all around me, I lost my
4   cool. The more I doubted, the more I sank, until I was sure I
5   would drown, out there in the storm.
6   TELLER: Jesus was only a few feet away.
7   PETER: "Lord! Save me!" I screamed for all I was worth. And
8   then he reached out his hand. *(4 minute mark)*
9   TELLER: "Your faith is so small, Peter. Why did you doubt?"
10   PETER: *(JESUS grabs PETER's hand and pulls him up.)* I leaned on
11   him the whole way back to the boat. I wouldn't let go. This
12   was no ghost. A ghost doesn't grab your arm. A ghost doesn't
13   pull you up out of the waves.
14   TELLER: When they got back to the boat and climbed inside, the
15   winds calmed down, the waves became still, the storm
16   disappeared.
17   PETER: There was nothing left to do but bow down and worship
18   Jesus. He wasn't a ghost after all.
19   TELLER: Jesus is really the Son of God.
20   PETER: And when you realize that, you can't help but worship
21   him. Alone. *(Freeze. Fadeout.)*
22
23
24
25
26
27
28
29
30
31
32
33
34
35

Something Fishy Going On

Summary: Two storytellers relate the tale of Jonah and the big fish. The only problem is, one of them thinks he already knows the story and keeps mixing things up.

Purpose: To reveal that God's grace is universal and extends to people everywhere.

Time: 7–8 minutes

Tone: Humorous

Cast: Teller #1 — A storyteller who is trying to tell the story of Jonah and the big fish (male or female)
Teller #2 — A storyteller who keeps mixing things up and making silly comments (male or female)

Props/Set: None; although you may wish for Teller #2 to pull out some silly props such as a plastic whale, a driver's license, etc.

Themes: Boredom, compassion, complaints, excuses, forgiveness, frustrations, God's power, grace, love, missions, obedience, prejudice, regrets, running away, second chances, stereotypes, witnessing

Text: "The word of the Lord came to Jonah son of Amittai: 'Go to the great city of Nineveh and preach against it, because its wickedness has come up before me.' But Jonah ran away from the Lord and headed for Tarshish" (Jonah 1:1–3a; see also the rest of the book of Jonah).

Notes: Have fun with the interaction between the two storytellers. Work on the timing so that the exchanges are natural-sounding. Be sure that as they address each other, they keep their bodies open to the audience so that all the children can see them. This story could also be read as a Readers Theatre piece or used as a puppet script. Use general stage lighting and two lapel microphones.

1   *SETTING*: The stage is bare. Both storytellers are On-stage as the
2   lights come up and the scene begins.
3
4   **TELLER #1: So what's the Bible story for today?**
5   **TELLER #2: Today's story is about a man named Jonah!**
6   **TELLER #1: Oh, no.**
7   **TELLER #2: What do you mean, "oh, no"?**
8   **TELLER #1: Not this story again.**
9   **TELLER #2: What are you talking about?**
10   **TELLER #1: I've heard the story of Jonah and the whale like a**
11   **thousand times.**
12   **TELLER #2: It wasn't a whale.**
13   **TELLER #1: What do you mean?**
14   **TELLER #2: The Bible says it was a fish. It doesn't say anything**
15   **about a whale. It was probably a shark.**
16   **TELLER #1: Really?**
17   **TELLER #2: Yeah, maybe a basking shark. They don't have a lot**
18   **of teeth, and they have a throat large enough to actually**
19   **swallow a man.**
20   **TELLER #1: A shark, huh? Jonah was eaten by a shark?**
21   **TELLER #2: Well, probably. We don't know for sure.**
22   **TELLER #1: I always thought it was a whale.**
23   **TELLER #2: I know. Most people do. Most people don't really take**
24   **the time to look closely enough at the story to see what it's**
25   **really about. I'll bet if you listen carefully, you'll find there's**
26   **more to this story than meets the eye.** *(1 minute mark)*
27   **TELLER #1: OK, go ahead.**
28   **TELLER #2: So, there was this guy named Jonah.**
29   **TELLER #1: What was his last name?**
30   **TELLER #2: I don't know if he had one.**
31   **TELLER #1: Just Jonah? That's it?**
32   **TELLER #2: Well, that's all we're told. We know his dad's name**
33   **was Amittai —**
34   **TELLER #1: How did he get a driver's license without a last name?**
35   **TELLER #2: They didn't have driver's licenses back then.**

1   TELLER #1: People drove without a license?
2   TELLER #2: Listen, they didn't have cars! Now one day God
3   spoke to him and said —
4   TELLER #1: "Jonah! Why don't you invent some cars so people
5   can get to work faster?"
6   TELLER #2: That's not what he said. God said,
7   TELLER #1: "Go to Nineveh!"
8   TELLER #2: Right.
9   TELLER #1: "It's near Chicago!"
10 TELLER #2: What?
11 TELLER #1: Just kidding. "Preach to the people!"
12 TELLER #2: Uh-huh.
13 TELLER #1: "And get swallowed by a shark who doesn't have a
14   driver's license!"
15 TELLER #2: No! Just preach to the people in Nineveh.
16 TELLER #1: So Jonah was a preacher?
17 TELLER #2: Right.
18 TELLER #1: So why don't we call him Pastor Jonah?
19 TELLER #2: I guess you can.
20 TELLER #1: Cool.
21 TELLER #2: But Pastor Jonah didn't want to obey God. *(2 minute
22 mark)*
23 TELLER #1: Why not?
24 TELLER #2: Huh?
25 TELLER #1: Why didn't he want to obey God?
26 TELLER #2: Well, he didn't like the people of Nineveh.
27 TELLER #1: Why not? 'Cause they had cooler cars?
28 TELLER #2: Nobody had cars! The people who lived there were
29   cruel. Mean! They'd attacked the Jews. And Jonah was a Jew.
30   And he hated 'em so much he refused to tell 'em about God.
31 TELLER #1: Whoa.
32 TELLER #2: Yeah, so instead, Jonah went and hopped on a boat
33   headed in the opposite direction.
34 TELLER #1: Toward Miami.
35 TELLER #2: Huh?

1   **TELLER #1: Oh, nothing. But why didn't he just stay there?**

2   **TELLER #2: He wanted to get as far away from Nineveh as he**

3   **could. So while they were there in the boat, a storm blew in.**

4   **TELLER #1:** *(Making storm sounds)* **Whoosh! Whoosh!**

5   **TELLER #2: Right. It was a bad storm!** *(3 minute mark)*

6   **TELLER #1:** *(Making even louder storm sounds)* **Whoosh! Whoosh!**

7   **TELLER #2: It was a terribly bad storm!**

8   **TELLER #1:** *(Making even louder storm sounds, then stopping to*

9   *address the audience)* **Whoosh! Whoosh! It was so bad they had**

10   **to cancel the shuffleboard tournament on the aft deck.**

11   **TELLER #2: What did you say?**

12   **TELLER #1: Never mind.**

13   **TELLER #2: But Jonah —**

14   **TELLER #1: Pastor Jonah —**

15   **TELLER #2: Was asleep. They woke him up and told him to pray**

16   **to his God so the ship wouldn't be destroyed. They'd already**

17   **tried praying to their gods, but it didn't help.**

18   **TELLER #1: Did he pray?**

19   **TELLER #2: No.**

20   **TELLER #1: Why not?**

21   **TELLER #2: Well, he knew that God might answer his prayer and**

22   **might end up sending him to the people of Nineveh after all.**

23   **And he didn't want that.**

24   **TELLER #1: He really hated 'em, didn't he?**

25   **TELLER #2: Yeah. So he told the sailors to —**

26   **TELLER #1: Swab the deck, Matey. Here's a Q-tip!**

27   **TELLER #2: What?**

28   **TELLER #1: Swab the deck. Q-tip. Get it?**

29   **TELLER #2: I get it. I get it. But he didn't say that. He told the**

30   **sailors to throw him overboard —**

31   **TELLER #1: What?!**

32   **TELLER #2: Because he would rather die than tell the people of**

33   **Nineveh about God. And once he was dead, he figured God**

34   **would save the rest of the men on the boat.** *(4 minute mark)*

35   **TELLER #1: Man, this guy had some issues.**

1 TELLER #2: Yeah, Jonah said, "It's all my fault. God is angry
2   with me because I didn't obey him." And then …
3 TELLER #1: *(Making the scary music sound from the movie* Jaws*)*
4   Dum, dum.
5 TELLER #2: They grabbed him.
6 TELLER #1: Dum, dum. Dum, dum.
7 TELLER #2: And threw him overboard!
8 TELLER #1: Dum, dum. Dum, dum. Dum, dum. Dum, dum!
9 TELLER #2: And a giant shark swam up!
10 TELLER #1: Dum, dum. Dum, dum. Dum, dum. Dum, dum! Ah!!!
11   *(Gagging, pretending to be attacked by a shark. Falling on the floor)*
12 TELLER #2: Would you stop?! The shark didn't chew him up into
13   little pieces. It just swallowed him whole.
14 TELLER #1: Oh. *(Standing up again)* Gulp. Ah!
15 TELLER #2: And the people on the boat said,
16 TELLER #1: "Here fishy, fishy, fishy! Spit up the nice little
17   preacher man!"
18 TELLER #2: No, they praised God because the storm stopped.
19   Now Jonah was — *(5 minute mark)*
20 TELLER #1: Being digested by all those stomach acids! Ah! Help
21   me! I'm dissolving. Ah! *(Getting carried away again until finally*
22   *TELLER #2 just stares down at him. Then, in an embarrassed*
23   *tone responds.)* Hi.
24 TELLER #2: He prayed to God from inside the fish. And the fish
25   spit him out on the beach.
26 TELLER #1: *(Sounding bored)* Oh yeah. He preached to the people.
27   They turned to God. The end.
28 TELLER #2: Well, that's not quite the end.
29 TELLER #1: Why not?
30 TELLER #2: Well, Jonah still hadn't gotten over his hatred for
31   the people.
32 TELLER #1: Even after preaching to 'em?
33 TELLER #2: Nope. He told God, "See? I knew if they heard your
34   Word they'd turn to you. Now they're all believers. That's
35   why I ran from you in the first place! It's all your fault!"

1   TELLER #1: Wow!

2   TELLER #2: Then he pouted and complained when a vine that had

3   been giving him shade withered and died.

4   TELLER #1: I don't get it. Why would he be sad and upset because

5   the people believed in God? And why would the vine bug him

6   more than the fact that these people had been far from God?

7   *(6 minute mark)*

8   TELLER #2: That was God's point! Jonah didn't want 'em to

9   know God. He was more concerned for himself than for those

10   people. But God is concerned about people everywhere. And

11   he wants them all to hear about his grace.

12   TELLER #1: Huh. There really is more to this story than I thought.

13   I always thought it was just about the whale and preaching to

14   the people.

15   TELLER #2: The real story is about his attitude toward others.

16   And we never find out if that changed or not.

17   TELLER #1: Huh?

18   TELLER #2: The book ends before we discover if there was a

19   change in Jonah's heart.

20   TELLER #1: But I thought he repented in the belly of the shark.

21   TELLER #2: Well, he changed his mind about obeying God, but

22   not his attitude about the people of Nineveh.

23   TELLER #1: Really?

24   TELLER #2: Yeah. Even at the end of the book, he still hated 'em.

25   TELLER #1: Yikes!

26   TELLER #2: This book is the only one in the Bible to end with a

27   question. God asks him, "Should I not be concerned about

28   that great city?" (Jonah 4:11).

29   TELLER #1: Huh. So God is concerned about people everywhere,

30   TELLER #2: Yeah.

31   TELLER #1: Even the people we might not like. *(7 minute mark)*

32   TELLER #2: You got it! And he's concerned with how we act as

33   well as our attitudes toward others.

34   TELLER #1: And if we get a driver's license.

35   TELLER #2: Oh brother.

36   TELLER #1 and #2: *(Together)* **The end.** *(Fadeout.)*

God's Fan Club

Summary: Tyler and Allie are each starting fan clubs. But as they get talking, they wonder which one they should join.

Purpose: To help children understand that we're made to worship God alone.

Time: 4–5 minutes

Tone: Humorous

Cast: Tyler — A guy who is starting a fan club for God (male)
Allie — A girl who wants to start a fan club for herself (female)

Costumes: Two T-shirts: one that says "GFC" and another that reads "MFC"

Props/Set: Magazines, a pile of black-and-white glossy photographs, (optional) "GFC" stickers and paraphernalia

Themes: Christmas, church issues, conversion, distractions, Easter, evangelism, God's power, Jesus, missions, prayer, pride, priorities, spiritual health, witnessing, worship

Text: "Therefore God exalted him to the highest place and gave him the name that is above every name, that at the name of Jesus every knee should bow, in heaven and on earth and under the earth" (Philippians 2:9–10).

Notes: Consider giving each child in the audience a sticker with "GFC" printed on it. This drama will work well with puppets. Use two lapel microphones and general stage lighting.

1 *SETTING*: Tyler's house. Allie and Tyler are both On-stage as the
2   lights come up.
3
4 ALLIE: Hey Tyler, guess what I'm starting?
5 TYLER: I don't know.
6 ALLIE: My own fan club!
7 TYLER: Really? That's amazing! So am I!
8 ALLIE: No, I mean, *my own* fan club. A fan club about *me*!
9 TYLER: A fan club about you?
10 ALLIE: *(Beaming)* Yeah! Little old me.
11 TYLER: Who would want to join that?
12 ALLIE: Everybody!
13 TYLER: Oh brother.
14 ALLIE: Look. *(Holds up a T-shirt that says "MFC")*
15 TYLER: MFC ... What does that stand for? My Fried Chicken?
16 ALLIE: No.
17 TYLER: Monkeys Feel Chunky?
18 ALLIE: No! My Fan Club.
19 TYLER: Oh.
20 ALLIE: MFC. My Fan Club. Get it?
21 TYLER: I get it.
22 ALLIE: And when you join, you get a picture of me *(She holds up*
23   *one of the eight-by-ten glossy photographs)*, a magazine, my
24   personal e-mail address, and lots of other stuff — including a
25   chance to appear with me in my latest movie!
26 TYLER: You're gonna be in a movie?
27 ALLIE: Well, not yet. But anyone with a fan club oughtta have at
28   least one movie! Right? *(1 minute mark)*
29 TYLER: Wow!
30 ALLIE: Cool, huh?
31 TYLER: Yeah, it sounds almost as good as the fan club I'm
32   starting.
33 ALLIE: Oh yeah? Who's your fan club about? *(TYLER holds up a*
34   *T-shirt that says "GFC.")* GFC ... Golden Fried Chicken?
35 TYLER: Nope.

1   ALLIE: Giant Flying Chihuahuas?

2   TYLER: Nope!

3   ALLIE: Gerbils from China?

4   TYLER: No. God's Fan Club! GFC!

5   ALLIE: God's Fan Club? You're starting a fan club for God?!

6   TYLER: Why not?

7   ALLIE: A fan club for God?!

8   TYLER: Sure! Who deserves a fan club more than God?

9   ALLIE: No one, I guess. But what happens in your fan club?

10 TYLER: Well, it's just like any fan club. You get a magazine — I

11   write it — and you get discounts on all the Jesus stuff and

12   God products.

13 ALLIE: Jesus stuff and God products?

14 TYLER: Yeah, bracelets, bumper stickers, hats, shirts, jewelry,

15   toys.

16 ALLIE: God toys? *(2 minute mark)*

17 TYLER: Why not? And even Jesus-brand footwear. I'm working

18   with this idea of inflatable sandals that help you walk on

19   water. You know, like this. *(Pretends to walk on water.)*

20 ALLIE: This is nuts. Where does all the money go?

21 TYLER: Well, I need a small salary to keep things going. But, of

22   course, I'll donate ten percent to charity.

23 ALLIE: What's a charity?

24 TYLER: You know, a group that does things to help people.

25 ALLIE: Oh. What charity are you gonna give the money to?

26 TYLER: God's Fan Club!

27 ALLIE: Oh.

28 TYLER: Great, huh?

29 ALLIE: Something doesn't seem right about all this.

30 TYLER: And you get everything for the low monthly rate of only

31   nineteen dollars and ninety-five cents.

32 ALLIE: You gotta pay to be in God's Fan Club?

33 TYLER: Of course! You gotta pay to be in any fan club. I even take

34   credit cards. But if you sign up today, you also get an

35   autographed, life-sized poster of God himself! *(3 minute mark)*

1   ALLIE: Where did you get a life-sized poster of God?!

2   TYLER: I'm still working on that.

3   ALLIE: Look, I don't think this is ever gonna catch on. God

4   doesn't need a fan club.

5   TYLER: What do you mean? He deserves one, doesn't he?

6   ALLIE: Of course! But isn't that what worship is all about? And

7   going to church or Sunday school?

8   TYLER: *(Thoughtfully)* Yeah, I guess so.

9   ALLIE: And you don't need all that other stuff to be in God's fan

10   club. All you gotta do to join is believe in him, love him, and

11   worship him.

12 TYLER: Believe, love, and worship ...

13 ALLIE: Right.

14 TYLER: Well, then I guess I don't need these GFC signs anymore.

15 ALLIE: Well, you could still give them away when you tell people

16   all about God. We can *still* be fans of God!

17 TYLER: *(Realizing the truth)* But just without the magazine and

18   poster and monthly fee and all that other stuff?

19 ALLIE: Right.

20 TYLER: So what about your fan club?

21 ALLIE: Come to think of it, I'd rather be in God's fan club than

22   mine any day ... You know anybody that might want an MFC

23   shirt? *(4 minute mark)*

24 TYLER: How 'bout Marvin Frankenheimer Calabalabinski?

25 ALLIE: Who?

26 TYLER I don't know, I just made him up ...

27 ALLIE: Oh. *(They begin to exit.)*

28 TYLER: I still like that inflatable sandals idea ...

29 ALLIE: Oh brother. *(As they exit, fadeout.)*

30

31

32

33

34

35

The Bush Man!

Summary: Two storytellers retell the story of "Moses and the Burning Bush," but one of them keeps getting things mixed up.

Purpose: To show children that when we stop making excuses and say "yes" to God, he can do amazing things through us to help other people.

Time: 6–7 minutes

Tone: Humorous

Cast: Marvin — A storyteller who is trying to tell the children the story of "Moses and the Burning Bush" (male or female)
Gary — His friend, who keeps mixing things up and making silly comments (male or female)

Costumes: None; or you may wish to have Gary dressed in a goofy outfit and Marvin dressed more conservatively

Props/Set: A broom handle to serve as Moses' shepherd's staff and a white glove. Before the drama begins, set the broom handle on the floor and slip the white glove inside Gary's pocket.

Themes: Calling, choices, complaints, excuses, fear, giftedness, ministry, obedience, purpose

Text: Exodus 3–4:17; Hebrews 11:24–28

Notes: In the script, the storytellers have masculine names, but they could be either men or women. Be sure that as they address each other, they keep their bodies open to the audience so that all the children can see them. This story could also be read as a Readers Theatre piece or used as a puppet script. Use general stage lighting and two lapel microphones.

1   **SETTING**: The stage is bare. Both storytellers are On-stage as the
2   lights come up and the scene begins.

3

4   **MARVIN: One day Moses was watching over his sheep in the**
5   **wilderness near Sinai Mountain.**
6   **GARY: Suddenly, an angel of the Lord appeared to him in a**
7   **burning bush.**
8   **MARVIN:** *(Seriously, pretending to be the bush)* **Snap. Sizzle.**
9   **Crackle. Pop ... Snap. Sizzle. Crackle. Pop ...**
10   **GARY: It sounded a little like a bowl of breakfast cereal —**
11   **MARVIN: Hey.**
12   **GARY: Sorry.**
13   **MARVIN:** *(Seriously again)* **Snap. Sizzle. Crackle. Pop ... Snap.**
14   **Sizzle. Crackle. Pop ... And Moses was amazed! How could**
15   **that bush appear to burn but not be consumed?**
16   **GARY: "It must be special effects," he thought. "Maybe I'm on a**
17   **movie set."**
18   **MARVIN: I'm gonna go and check this out!**
19   **GARY: Maybe Steven Spielberg is around here somewhere.**
20   **MARVIN: But Steven Spielberg wasn't there. Instead, it was**
21   **someone much more famous and important.**
22   **GARY: Alfred Hitchcock.**
23   **MARVIN: No! It was God speaking to Moses through the burning**
24   **bush.**
25   **GARY: That is the weirdest microphone I've ever heard of.**
26   *(1 minute mark)*
27   **MARVIN: It wasn't a microphone. So Moses carefully approached**
28   **the bush. And, when he saw that indeed it was burning and not**
29   **being consumed, he knew there was only one thing to do —**
30   **GARY: Get a roasting stick and some marshmallows.**
31   **MARVIN: What?**
32   **GARY: Nothing.**
33   **MARVIN: But then the Lord himself spoke to Moses through the**
34   **bush!**
35   **GARY: And he told him a campfire story.**

1   MARVIN: Are you done?

2   GARY: Yeah.

3   MARVIN: So God said —

4   GARY: *(Pretending to be God)* "Moses! Moses!"

5   MARVIN: Right!

6   GARY: *(Pretending to be God again)* "Go get a roasting stick and
7   some marshmallows!"

8   MARVIN: *(Clearing his throat)* That's not what God said.

9   GARY: Oh.

10 MARVIN: God said, "Take off your sandals, for you are — "

11 GARY: Stepping on my foot!

12 MARVIN: All right, look. You're mixing everything up.

13 GARY: Sorry.

14 MARVIN: Are you ready to take this seriously?

15 GARY: *(Nodding his head "yes")* Yes.

16 MARVIN: Are you sure?

17 GARY: *(Nodding his head "yes")* No.

18 MARVIN: Look, God told Moses he was standing on holy ground.

19 GARY: Holy cow! *(2 minute mark)*

20 MARVIN: No, holy ground. And then God said, "I am the God of
21   your great-great-great-great-grandpappy!"

22 GARY: Did he really say "grandpappy"?

23 MARVIN: Well, close enough. Then Moses hid from the bush,
24   because he knew it was really God speaking to him.

25 GARY: Cool.

26 MARVIN: And God told him, "I'm going to deliver my people
27   from Egypt and lead them into the land of the Canaanites,
28   Hittites, Amorites, Perizzites, Hivites and Jebusites!"

29 GARY: And stalactites!

30 MARVIN: No. "And I'm sending you to lead my people!" And
31   Moses said,

32 GARY: Who, me?

33 MARVIN: Yeah, you!

34 GARY: Couldn't be.

35 MARVIN: Then who?

1   GARY: I have no idea. But I know it ain't gonna be me.

2   MARVIN: "But I'll be with you, Moses!" Snap. Sizzle. Crackle.

3   Pop ... Snap. Sizzle. Crackle. Pop ...

4   GARY: They won't believe that you really sent me. They'll say,

5   "OK, Moses, who really sent you here?" What name should I

6   tell them?

7   MARVIN: "I AM THE ONE WHO ALWAYS IS!" Tell them "I

8   AM" sent you to them.

9   GARY: Tell 'em I am sent me?

10   MARVIN: Sent you.

11   GARY: Right, me. I am sent me. *(3 minute mark)*

12   MARVIN: Right. That's who I am.

13   GARY: I am?

14   MARVIN: I am.

15   GARY: You know what I am?

16   MARVIN: Yes. Confused.

17   GARY: Right. How'd you know that?

18   MARVIN: Because I know everything.

19   GARY: Oh. So then, you know I don't really want to go and deliver

20   your people from the Canaanites, Hittites, Dynamites, Flying

21   kites, Parasites, and Overbites.

22   MARVIN: That's Canaanites, Hittites, Amorites, Perizzites,

23   Hivites, and Jebusites.

24   GARY: Right. But I'm just not the right man for the job. No one

25   will believe me.

26   MARVIN: What's that you're holding there? *(Clearing his throat*

27   *and motioning toward the walking stick laying on the floor*

28   *nearby)* I said, "What's that you're holding there?"

29   GARY: Oh. *(Picks up the stick and then says)* My shepherd's staff!

30   Which looks an awful lot like a broom handle.

31   MARVIN: Throw it down!

32   GARY: But I just picked it up —

33   MARVIN: Throw it down! *(GARY throws down the broom handle.*

34   *MARVIN narrates.)* And Moses threw down the broom handle —

35   uh, the shepherd's staff. And it turned into a deadly snake!

1   **GARY:** *(Yells.)* **Ah!** *(If your MARVIN is big and strong enough, jump*
2   *into his arms after yelling.)*
3   **MARVIN:** *(Grunting)* **Um ... Moses. Go and pick up the snake by**
4   **its tail.** *(4 minute mark)*
5   **GARY: Will it bite?**
6   **MARVIN: No, of course not. Tails don't bite.**
7   **GARY: I mean its mouth!**
8   **MARVIN: No. Go on.** *(GARY climbs down and picks up the broom*
9   *handle by the tip.)* **So Moses went over and picked up the snake**
10   **and it turned back into —**
11   **GARY: A broom handle.**
12   **MARVIN: A shepherd's staff!**
13   **GARY: Oh ... Huh. I wasn't scared for a minute.**
14   **MARVIN: Yeah, right ... So do that to prove who sent you!**
15   **GARY:** *(Meekly)* **OK.**
16   **MARVIN: And try this: Stick your hand into your robe.**
17   **GARY: I don't have a robe.**
18   **MARVIN: Use your jeans pocket instead.** *(GARY sticks his hand into*
19   *his pocket. As he does, he slides the white glove on over his hand.)*
20   **Now pull it out!**
21   **GARY:** *(Pulls it out.)* **Ah! My hand is covered with leprosy, an**
22   **incurable, dreaded, and deadly skin disease of the ancient**
23   **world!**
24   **MARVIN: Now put your hand in there again.**
25   **GARY:** *(Puts his hand in. This time, he slips off the glove before*
26   *removing his hand.)* **Whew! I wasn't scared for a minute.**
27   **MARVIN: Yeah, right ... So if the snake doesn't do the trick,**
28   **they'll believe you when you do the whole hand-in-the-robe**
29   **routine. I'll also help you turn water into blood.**
30   **GARY: Ew!**
31   **MARVIN: Along with the plagues, I'll convince 'em to let my**
32   **people go. Then they'll know I'm serious and they'll give you**
33   **what you ask for. OK, now go!** *(5 minute mark)*
34   **GARY: Um ... I'm not really very good at speaking in front of**
35   **large groups. I get all tongue-fried.**

1 MARVIN: You mean tongue-tied.
2 GARY: Right. See?
3 MARVIN: Who makes mouths, Moses?
4 GARY: Um ... you do?
5 MARVIN: Right. Now, go! Snap. Sizzle. Crackle. Pop ... Snap.
6   Sizzle. Crackle. Pop...
7 GARY: Um ... Couldn't you just send someone else?
8 MARVIN: *(Narrating)* Now when Moses said that, God got angry.
9   *(As God)* All right, that's it, Mr. Whiny Guy! You're going, and
10   I don't want to hear another word about it! You can bring your
11   brother Aaron along to do the speaking for you. But you're the
12   man I've called. Now put on your sandals and get going!
13 GARY: OK. I wanted to go anyway.
14 MARVIN: Yeah, right.
15 GARY: So Moses left to do what God commanded him to do —
16 MARVIN: And he became one of the greatest heroes of faith in the
17   whole Bible —
18 GARY: All because he finally said "yes" when God called him that
19   day at the burning bush.
20 MARVIN: Snap. Sizzle. Crackle. Pop ... Snap. Sizzle. Crackle.
21   Pop ...
22 GARY: The end. *(Offhandedly)* Anybody got some milk? I'm
23   getting hungry. *(6 minute mark)*
24 MARVIN: *(Exiting)* I can't believe you kept getting those names
25   mixed up.
26 GARY: Which names?
27 MARVIN: The Canaanites, Hittites, Amorites, Perizzites, Hivites,
28   and Jebusites.
29 GARY: You mean the Canaanites, Hittites, Amorites, Perizzites,
30   Hivites, and Jebusites?
31 MARVIN: *(Impressed)* Right!
32 GARY: Street fights, starry nights, and historical sites?
33 MARVIN: Oh, brother. *(As they exit, fadeout.)*
34
35

Theme Index

260

Verse Index

Cast Index

One Man, One Woman

Two Men

Two Women

Either Men or Women

© 2002 The Light Photography

About the Author

Steven James is an award-winning writer, professional storyteller, and popular conference speaker. He appears weekly at conferences, churches, and special events around the country, sharing his unique blend of storytelling, drama, and comedy. He has published hundreds of articles and stories and is a frequent contributor to *Writer's Digest, YouthWalk, Guideposts for Teens*, and *With: The Magazine for Radical Christian Youth*. He also writes a monthly column for *The Journal of Christian Camping*. This is his fifth book.

Steven's passion lies in creatively communicating the gospel to the next generation, and equipping others to do so as well. Each year he trains thousands of educators nationwide on creative communication and ministry techniques.

When he's not speaking or writing, he enjoys watching science fiction movies, eating chips and homemade salsa, and going hiking in the Appalachian Mountains. He lives with his wife and three daughters in Tennessee.

For more information on his seminars, workshops, speaking schedule, or other books, surf to *www.stevenjames.net.*

Order Form

Meriwether Publishing Ltd.
PO Box 7710
Colorado Springs, CO 80933-7710
Phone: 800-937-5297 Fax: 719-594-9916
Website: www.meriwether.com

Please send me the following books:

_____ **More Worship Sketches 2 Perform #BK-B258** $14.95
by Steven James
A collection of scripts for two actors

_____ **Worship Sketches 2 Perform #BK-B242** $14.95
by Steven James
A collection of scripts for two actors

_____ **Service with a Smile #BK-B225** $14.95
by Daniel Wray
52 humorous sketches for Sunday worship

_____ **Isaac Air Freight: The Works 2 #BK-B243** $16.95
by Dan Rupple and Dave Toole
More sketches from the premier Christian comedy group

_____ **Isaac Air Freight: The Works #BK-B215** $16.95
by Dan Rupple and Dave Toole
Sketches from the premier Christian comedy group

_____ **Divine Comedies #BK-B190** $12.95
by T. M. Williams
A collection of plays for church drama groups

_____ **Sermons Alive! #BK-B132** $14.95
by Paul Neale Lessard
52 dramatic sketches for worship services

These and other fine Meriwether Publishing books are available at
your local bookstore or direct from the publisher. Prices subject to
change without notice. Check our website or call for current prices.

Name: _____

Organization name: _____

Address: _____

City: _____ State: _____

Zip: _____ Phone: _____

❑ **Check enclosed**

❑ **Visa / MasterCard / Discover #** _____

Expiration
Signature: _____ *date:* _____
     (required for credit card orders)

Colorado residents: Please add 3% sales tax.
Shipping: Include $4.95 for the first book and 75¢ for each additional book ordered.

❑ *Please send me a copy of your complete catalog of books and plays.*

Order Form

Meriwether Publishing Ltd.
PO Box 7710
Colorado Springs, CO 80933-7710
Phone: 800-937-5297   Fax: 719-594-9916
Website: www.meriwether.com

Please send me the following books:

_____ **More Worship Sketches 2 Perform #BK-B258 $14.95**
by Steven James
A collection of scripts for two actors

_____ **Worship Sketches 2 Perform #BK-B242 $14.95**
by Steven James
A collection of scripts for two actors

_____ **Service with a Smile #BK-B225 $14.95**
by Daniel Wray
52 humorous sketches for Sunday worship

_____ **Isaac Air Freight: The Works 2 #BK-B243 $16.95**
by Dan Rupple and Dave Toole
More sketches from the premier Christian comedy group

_____ **Isaac Air Freight: The Works #BK-B215 $16.95**
by Dan Rupple and Dave Toole
Sketches from the premier Christian comedy group

_____ **Divine Comedies #BK-B190 $12.95**
by T. M. Williams
A collection of plays for church drama groups

_____ **Sermons Alive! #BK-B132 $14.95**
by Paul Neale Lessard
52 dramatic sketches for worship services

These and other fine Meriwether Publishing books are available at your local bookstore or direct from the publisher. Prices subject to change without notice. Check our website or call for current prices.

Name: _____

Organization name: _____

Address: _____

City: _____ State: _____

Zip: _____ Phone: _____

❑ **Check enclosed**

❑ **Visa / MasterCard / Discover #** _____

Signature: _____ *Expiration date:* _____
      (required for credit card orders)

Colorado residents: Please add 3% sales tax.
Shipping: Include $4.95 for the first book and 75¢ for each additional book ordered.

❑ *Please send me a copy of your complete catalog of books and plays.*

Order Form

Meriwether Publishing Ltd.
PO Box 7710
Colorado Springs, CO 80933-7710
Phone: 800-937-5297 Fax: 719-594-9916
TM Website: www.meriwether.com

Please send me the following books:

_____ **More Worship Sketches 2 Perform #BK-B258** $14.95
by Steven James
A collection of scripts for two actors

_____ **Worship Sketches 2 Perform #BK-B242** $14.95
by Steven James
A collection of scripts for two actors

_____ **Service with a Smile #BK-B225** $14.95
by Daniel Wray
52 humorous sketches for Sunday worship

_____ **Isaac Air Freight: The Works 2 #BK-B243** $16.95
by Dan Rupple and Dave Toole
More sketches from the premier Christian comedy group

_____ **Isaac Air Freight: The Works #BK-B215** $16.95
by Dan Rupple and Dave Toole
Sketches from the premier Christian comedy group

_____ **Divine Comedies #BK-B190** $12.95
by T. M. Williams
A collection of plays for church drama groups

_____ **Sermons Alive! #BK-B132** $14.95
by Paul Neale Lessard
52 dramatic sketches for worship services

These and other fine Meriwether Publishing books are available at your local bookstore or direct from the publisher. Prices subject to change without notice. Check our website or call for current prices.

Name: _____

Organization name: _____

Address: _____

City: _____ State: _____

Zip: _____ Phone: _____

❑ **Check enclosed**
❑ **Visa / MasterCard / Discover #** _____
                                                    Expiration
Signature: _____ *date:* _____
             (required for credit card orders)

Colorado residents: Please add 3% sales tax.
Shipping: Include $4.95 for the first book and 75¢ for each additional book ordered.

❑ *Please send me a copy of your complete catalog of books and plays.*